Beiträge zum Islamischen Recht XII

Leipziger Beiträge zur Orientforschung

Herausgegeben von Hans-Georg Ebert
Begründet von Günter Barthel

Band 36

PETER LANG

Silvia Tellenbach / Thoralf Hanstein

Beiträge zum Islamischen Recht XII

PETER LANG

Bibliografische Information der Deutschen Nationalbibliothek
Die Deutsche Nationalbibliothek verzeichnet diese Publikation in der Deutschen Nationalbibliografie; detaillierte bibliografische Daten sind im Internet über http://dnb.d-nb.de abrufbar.

ISSN 0942-2323
ISBN 978-3-631-74385-0 (Print)
E-ISBN 978-3-631-74806-0 (E-PDF)
E-ISBN 978-3-631-74807-7 (EPUB)
E-ISBN 978-3-631-74808-4 (MOBI)
DOI 10.3726/b13437

Peter Lang – Frankfurt am Main · Bern · Bruxelles · New York · Oxford · Warszawa · Wien

Diese Publikation wurde begutachtet.

www.peterlang.com

Silvia Tellenbach / Thoralf Hanstein

Beiträge zum Islamischen Recht XII

PETER LANG

Bibliografische Information der Deutschen Nationalbibliothek
Die Deutsche Nationalbibliothek verzeichnet diese Publikation in der Deutschen Nationalbibliografie; detaillierte bibliografische Daten sind im Internet über http://dnb.d-nb.de abrufbar.

ISSN 0942-2323
ISBN 978-3-631-74385-0 (Print)
E-ISBN 978-3-631-74806-0 (E-PDF)
E-ISBN 978-3-631-74807-7 (EPUB)
E-ISBN 978-3-631-74808-4 (MOBI)
DOI 10.3726/b13437

Peter Lang – Frankfurt am Main · Bern · Bruxelles · New York · Oxford · Warszawa · Wien

Diese Publikation wurde begutachtet.

www.peterlang.com

VORWORT DER HERAUSGEBER

Zum ersten Mal seit 13 Jahren[1] befasste sich die Jahrestagung der Gesellschaft für Arabisches und Islamisches Recht (GAIR) e. V. wieder mit Strafrecht. In den weitaus meisten muslimischen Ländern ist heute ein Strafrecht europäischer, meist französischer Provenienz in Kraft. Es gibt jedoch einige Länder, in denen islamisches Strafrecht gilt, von Afghanistan und Pakistan im Osten über Saudi-Arabien, die VAE, Jemen, Sudan, Libyen bis Mauretanien und Nigeria im Westen. Der Stand der Kodifizierung des islamischen Strafrechts ist in diesen Ländern sehr unterschiedlich. Während es z. B. in Iran weitgehend in Gesetzesform gefasst ist, verweisen Afghanistan und die VAE am Anfang ihrer Strafgesetzbücher in einer Generalklausel darauf, dass *ḥadd, qiṣāṣ* und *diya,* also das islamische Kernstrafrecht, nach islamischem Strafrecht zu verhängen ist – Afghanistan präzisiert sogar: nach der hanefitischen Schule – und sich das Strafgesetzbuch nur auf die Straftaten beschränkt, die mit *ta'zīr*-Strafen zu bestrafen sind. Saudi-Arabien hat bis heute noch kein kodifiziertes Strafgesetzbuch; es gibt zwar einige als *niẓām (Pl. anẓima)* bezeichnete staatliche Normen mit nebenstrafrechtlichen Bestimmungen, in weiten Bereichen hat der Richter jedoch sein Urteil aus den Schriften und Fatwas hanbalitischer Rechtsgelehrter zu erarbeiten. Weitere Staaten haben die Bestimmungen zum islamischen Strafrecht in ein Strafgesetzbuch eingefügt, das im Großen und Ganzen dem Aufbau europäischer Gesetze folgt (z. B. Mauretanien) oder besondere Gesetze neben dem Strafgesetzbuch geschaffen hat (z. B. Libyen) oder beides (z. B. Pakistan). Auch die Möglichkeiten, Material zur Arbeit über diese Rechte zu bekommen, sind höchst unterschiedlich. Während sie etwa in Iran vergleichsweise günstig sind, herrscht in anderen Ländern mit islamischem Strafrecht ein blutiger Krieg…

Auch dieser Band kann nur Streiflichter zum heutigen islamischen Strafrecht bieten, und es ist kein Zufall, dass sich die überwiegende Zahl der Beiträge mit Iran befasst, dem Land, in dem wohl heute die breiteste Forschung und die größte Fülle an Publikationen zum islamischen Strafrecht existiert.

Der vorliegende Band enthält vier zu Aufsätzen ausgearbeitete Vorträge, die auf der Jahrestagung der Gesellschaft für Arabisches und Islamisches Recht e. V. gehalten wurden, die am 21./22. Oktober 2016 in Freiburg im Max-Planck-Institut für ausländisches und internationales Strafrecht stattgefunden hat. Eine Referentin zog es vor, nicht ihren Freiburger Vortrag, sondern einen anderen

---

[1] Siehe dazu Tellenbach/Hanstein, Beiträge zum Islamischen Recht IV, Frankfurt u.a. 2004.

Aufsatz für diesen Band beizusteuern. Schließlich entspricht es alter Tradition der GAIR e. V., in den Tagungsbänden auch noch etwaigen weiteren Arbeiten Raum zu geben, die besonders gut zu dem Thema der Tagung passen. So wurde hier ein Beitrag einer iranischen Rechtsanwältin mit aufgenommen.

Rudolph Peters skizziert anhand von Kriegsrecht, Minderheitenrecht und Strafrecht, wie der Islamische Staat (IS) diejenigen archaischen, längst nicht mehr praktizierten Auslegungen der Schari'a ausgewählt hat, die die brutalste und grausamste Herrschaft zulassen und wie er gleichzeitig die Anwendung der Schari'a als seine *raison d'être* darstellt.

Firouz Mahmoudi Janaki behandelt die Strafzwecke im islamischen Strafrecht und ihre Widerspiegelung im iranischen Strafrecht, neben Vergeltung sowie General- und Spezialprävention auch Reue, Vergebung, Buße und jenseitige Strafen, die in das System der möglichen Folgen einer Straftat mit einzubeziehen sind. Er stellt fest, dass bei den als unabänderlich geltenden Strafen philosophische Perspektiven und sozialer Wandel keine durchgreifenden Wirkungen auf die Kriminaltheorie haben können, wenn nicht ein neuer Ansatz gefunden wird, der sie veränderlich macht. Dagegen lassen die Sanktionen für Delikte der *ta'zīr*-Kategorie den Weg zu neuen und veränderlichen Kriminaltheorien offen. Abschließend stellt er fest, dass das heutige iranische Strafrechtssystem überwiegend formelle Aspekte des religiösen Rechts berücksichtigt hat, und daher nicht angemessen auf die individuellen und gesellschaftlichen Erfordernisse reagieren kann, die für das Erreichen seiner eigentlichen Strafzwecke nötig wären.

Benedikt Naarmann und Seyed Emadeddin Tabatabaei haben Aspekte des Religionsstrafrechts in Pakistan und Iran behandelt. Nach einer einführenden Skizze zu den historischen und verfassungsrechtlichen Grundlagen der Islamischen Republik Pakistan und seiner Rechtsordnung behandelt Benedikt Naarmann die Prophetenlästerung gem. Art. 295-C pak.StGB und skizziert das Sonderstrafrecht gegen die Ahmadis anhand von Art. 298-C pak.StGB. Er beschreibt die religionsrechtlichen Grundlagen, aber auch die moderne Kritik und die Rechtfertigungsargumente für diese Tatbestände. Schließlich berichtet er über die Rechtspraxis in diesen Fällen, wobei er das Eskalationspotential und die Mängel der Verfahren eindrucksvoll herausarbeitet. S. Emadeddin Tabatabaei beschreibt die Art. 513 *ta'zīrāt*-Gesetz von 1996, Art. 26 Pressegesetz und Art. 262 ir.StGB v. 2013, in denen die Lästerung bzw. Schmähung von *muqaddasāt* – also als geheiligt geltenden Personen oder Gegenständen – unter Strafe gestellt wird und schildert auch hier Fälle aus der Praxis. In beiden Ländern zeigt sich, wie die Unbestimmtheit der Tatbestände und der Hang, sie zu politischer Unterdrückung zu nutzen, sei es durch den

Staat, sei es durch einzelne gesellschaftliche Gruppen, eine große Gefahr darstellen.

Afrooz Maghzi Najafabadi befasst sich mit dem Sexualstrafrecht im weiteren Sinn in der Islamischen Republik Iran; dabei stellt sie die Entwicklung seit der Islamischen Revolution, die Diskussionen insbesondere in der Zeit unter Präsident Khatami und schließlich die Regelungen in dem neuen Strafgesetzbuch von 2013 dar. Sie kommt zu dem Schluss, dass es trotz vieler Punkte, die sich nicht geändert haben, einige vorsichtige Schritte zu einer Reform, etwa bei der Strafbarkeit von Ehebruch, Homosexualität und Vergewaltigung gibt.

Mirjam Künkler zeichnet schließlich die Stellung der iranischen Rechtsanwaltskammer und ihr Ringen um Erhalt ihrer Stellung als unabhängiges Organ der Rechtspflege von Beginn des 20. Jahrhunderts bis heute nach.

Abschließend sei allen gedankt, die an dem Zustandekommen dieses Bandes mitgewirkt haben, vorab den Autoren und Autorinnen, aber auch dem Verlag Peter Lang, in dem dieser Band wiederum in bewährter Weise betreut wurde.

Freiburg/Berlin im Oktober 2017 Die Herausgeber

Inhaltsverzeichnis

Vorwort der Herausgeber 5

Rudolph Peters
"Fossilized Sharia": Law, Violence and the Caliphate of Raqqa 11

Firouz Mahmoudi Janaki
The Aims of Punishment in Islamic Criminal Law and their Reflection in the Iranian Criminal Justice System 23

Seyed Emadeddin Tabatabaei
Schmähungen von *muqaddasāt* im iranischen Strafrecht 55

Benedikt Naarmann
Von *Macaulay* zu *Zia ul-Haq* - Das pakistanische (Religions-)Strafrecht zwischen kolonialem Erbe und Islamisierung 71

Afrooz Maghzi Najafabadi
Challenges to the Regulation of Sexuality under Iranian Criminal Law 99

Mirjam Künkler
Rule of Law or Rule by Law? Iran's Bar Association as a pawn in Islamic-republican contestations 133

Autor*innen des Bandes 155

“Fossilized Sharia”: Law, Violence and the Caliphate of Raqqa

Rudolph Peters, Amsterdam

1. Introduction

In some Muslim states the domain governed by Sharia law has recently been expanded: Countries like Pakistan and Iran have extended the application of Sharia law from family law to other fields, such as penal and fiscal law. This was done by codifying pre-modern Sharia doctrines. In drafting these new law codes the legislators had to choose from alternative doctrines and norms existing in the corpus of pre-modern Islamic jurisprudence. This selection was informed, not so much by technical legal factors, but rather by political and cultural ones. The re-introduction of Sharia penal law, for instance, had a clear symbolic ideological function of opposing Western thought.[1] Here I would like to introduce the term “fossilized Sharia” as a metaphor for a modern type of selective Sharia law defined by a state and consisting of big chunks of obsolete and anachronistic doctrines and norms excavated from the pre-modern Islamic religious and legal texts. I call such doctrines and norms “fossilized” because they were not “alive” anymore, since, for a long time, they had not been applied and, therefore, were stagnant and did not develop. Usually, the selection of the doctrines and norms are motivated not only by purely religious reasons, but also to justify state policies. Now, the Islamic State[2] is one of the polities that has used “fossilized Sharia” at an extensive scale. And its most conspicuous characteristic of its enforcement is its justification of cruel and violent practices in governance, warfare and, especially, the administration of justice. The atrocities that are carried out in public and are widely disseminated through the media are part of a deliberate policy. In the following I will try to analyze the way the Islamic State is using “fossilized Sharia”. After a brief exposé of the

---

1 See for a discussion my *Crime and punishment in Islamic law: Theory and practice from the sixteenth to the twenty-first century*, Cambridge: Cambridge University Press, 2005, chapter 5 (Islamic criminal law today).

2 The “Islamic State” refers here to the organization once known as the Islamic State of Iraq (ISI, October 2006-April 2013), the Islamic State of Iraq and Sham or the Islamic State in the Levant (ISIS, ISIL April 2013-June 2014), and the Islamic State (IS, June 2014-present). This usage conforms to its followers’ own shorthand for it.

origins and history of the Islamic State I will expound how Sharia law is enforced by the Islamic State. Finally I will analyze the instrumentality of this violent and ruthless practice justified by "fossilized Sharia".

2. The emergence of IS[3]

The Islamic State is only one of the warring rebellious parties in Iraq and Syria. However, it has distinguishing features that make it different from the other rebel organizations. The latter fight first and foremost for a regime change within the existing national borders, whereas the Islamic State's main objective is to establish an Islamic state with unspecified borders, exclusively enforcing Sharia law. It fights both the regimes in power and rebel militias in order to carve out territory for setting up the intended Islamic state.

The Islamic State was created in Iraq in 2006 when the local branch of Al-Qaeda and some jihadi groups merged into an organization that was first called the Islamic State in Iraq (ISI). It was headed by a certain Ḥāmid Dāwūd Khalīl al-Zāwī with the battle name Abū 'Umar al-Baghdādī, about whose personal background is not very much known. He succeeded in establishing the rudiments of the Islamic State that until 2015 controlled a considerably large territory in North West Iraq and North East Syria. One of the main features of this organization is its deep enmity towards the Shi`ites, which, originally, made it attractive to Iraqi Sunnites. This was a result of the change in the balance of power in Iraq after the American occupation. Under Saddam Hussein the political elite was Sunnite and Arab, although they represented only a minority in the country. After the occupation, political power shifted toward the largest community, the (Arab) Shiʿites. At the same time the Americans dissolved the two main props of the ancient regime, the army and the Baath Party. Many Iraqi Sunnites, therefore, resented the new, mainly Shiʿite government and the Shiʿites in general. This resentment was expressed in both political and theological terms: The Sunnites opposed the Shiʿites not only as "usurpers" of the political power in Iraq, but also as an expansionist power, striving, together with Iran and Hezbollah, at conquering a slice of the Middle East stretching from Iran to Lebanon. On the level of religion, many Sunnites, referring to Shiʿites with the pejorative term Rāfidites ("Rejectionists"), regarded them as

3 For the origins and development of IS, see Weiss, M., and Hassan, H. 2015, *ISIS: Inside the army of terror*. New York: Regan Arts; Stern, J., and Berger, J.M. 2015. *ISIS: The state of terror*. New York: Harper Collins Publishers; Atwan, Abdel Bari. 2015. *Islamic State: The digital caliphate*. London: Saqi Books.

non-Muslims. In Iraq, these sectarian feelings of resentment helped reinforce the military power of the Islamic State because of the support of former followers of Saddam Hussein, now converted to Islamism: the Baathists, the former military, and disaffected Sunnite tribes. When, since the beginning of 2013, the Islamic State started its operations in Syria, it could also recruit soldiers and civilians there because of religious opposition against the Alawites, to which the ruling elite of Assad belonged, and against the Shiʿites, since the Syrian regime was assisted by Iran and the Hezbollah.

Abū ʿUmar al-Baghdādī was killed in 2010 and succeeded by Ibrāhīm ʻAwwād Ibrāhīm ʻAlī al-Badrī with the sobriquet of Abū Bakr al-Baghdādī. The military strength of the Islamic State now greatly increased by the influx of foreign volunteers from the Arab world, Central Asia and Western Europe and its economy by the Islamic State's control of oil wells. In the first months of 2013, the Islamic State extended its operations to North Syria. Within one year the Islamic State controlled northern regions of Syria with the towns of Deir el-Zor as well as Raqqa, which became the capital of the Islamic State. In Iraq the city of Mosul was conquered by Islamic State in June 2014. By the summer of 2014 the Islamic State was ruling over a large area in Syria and Iraq, with some eight million inhabitants. The conquest of Mosul, the first large city under control of the Islamic State, was regarded as an opportunity to proclaim the Islamic State as a Caliphate. On 29 June 2014 the Shūrā (Consultation) Council of the Islamic State appointed Ibrāhīm Abū Bakr al-Baghdādī and swore allegiance (*bayʿa*)[4] to him as the caliph of all Muslims, having examined his qualifications for the office. In accordance they requested that all Muslims, wherever they live, pledge allegiance to him and emigrate (*hijra*) to the state to offer support.[5]

In the course of 2013 and the first half of 2014, the state structure became more articulated and the Islamic State carried out more and more state duties via 'ministries' (*dīwāns*). The number of ministries grew in the course of time. There were a total of fourteen in the summer of 2014.[6] The territory of the

4 For the term *bayʻa*, see Wagemakers, Joas. 2015. "The Concept of Bayʻa in the Islamic State's Ideology." *Perspectives on Terrorism* 9 (4):98-106.

5 The English translations of the proclamation is published in: http://triceratops.brynmawr.edu/dspace/bitstream/handle/10066/14242/ADN20140629.pdf (accessed 19 April 2017); Cook, David. 2015. *Understanding jihad*. 2nd ed. Berkeley etc.: University of California Press. pp. 224-237.

6 These were religious affairs: the Ministry of Spreading of Islam, Mosques and Religious Foundations (*Dīwān al-Daʻwa wa-l-Masājid wa-l-Awqāf*), the Ministry of Administration of Justice and Complaints (*Dīwān al-Qaḍāʼ wa-l-Maẓālim*), the Ministry of the Religious

Islamic State was divided into provinces (*wilāyat*), where local departments of the ministries function.[7]

3. Enforcement of Sharia

The organization of the Islamic State shows that the enforcement of Sharia law is regarded as the raison d'être of the state. There are five ministries that directly deal with Sharia. The Ministry of Fatwas and Research handles the theoretical side: It publishes treatises about topics related to Islam and Sharia and fatwas on practical matters, such as Islamic taxation, the treatment of prisoners of war, travelling, games, the behavior of women, smuggling, prescribed clothing, rituals and organ transplants.[8] On a doctrinal level, the Ministry of Education is also important. This ministry 'purges' the curricula of schools of non-Islamic matters and develops study programs consistent with version of Islam propagated by the Islamic State. The Ministry of Spreading of Islam, Mosques and the Religious Foundation controls the mosques and makes sure that no preacher propagates ideas contrary to religious doctrines of the Islamic State. There are two ministries charged with the direct application of Sharia: that of the religious police (*ḥisba*) and that of the administration of justice and complaints. The *ḥisba* falls under the Sharia courts and deals with public morality and religious behavior. For instance, religious police officers enforces that people

Police (*Dīwān al-Ḥisba*), the Ministry of Research and Fatwas (*Dīwān al-Buḥūth wa-l-Iftā'*) and the Ministry of Education (*Dīwān al-Ta'līm*); there are three that mainly deal with financial and economic affairs: the Ministry of Finance (*Dīwān Bayt al-Māl*), the Ministry of Mineral Resources (*Dīwān al-Rikāz*) and the Ministry of Agriculture (*al-Zirā'a*). There are two ministries for Warfare (*Dīwān al-Jund*) and one Ministry of Security (*Dīwān al-Amn al-'āmm*); and finally four for specific government duties: the Ministry of Information (*al-'Alāqāt al-'āmma*), the Ministry of Bedouin Tribes (*Dīwān al-'Ashā'ir*), the Ministry of Public Health (*Dīwān al-Ṣiḥḥa*) and the Ministry of Public Services (*Dīwān al-Khidamāt*). See the references mentioned in the previous note.

7 Tamimi, Aymenn Jawad al-. 2014. "The Dawn of the Islamic State of Iraq and ash-Sham." *Current Trends in Islamist Ideology* 16:5-16; Al-Tamimi, A.J. 2015, "The Evolution in Islamic State Administration: The Documentary Evidence", *Perspectives on Terrorism,* Vol. 9, No. 4, http://www.terrorismanalysts.com/pt/index.php/pot/article/view/447/html; Caris, Charles C., and Reynolds, Samuel. 2014. "Islamic State governance in Syria." In *Middle East Security Report, 22, July 2014*: Institute for the Study of War; Abu Haniyeh, Hassan. 2014. "Daesh's Organisational Structure." AlJazeera Center for Studies. http://studies.aljazeera.net/en/dossiers/decipheringdaeshoriginsimpactandfuture/2014/12/201412395930929444.htm (accessed 19 April 2017).

8 Bunzel, Cole. 2015. "32 Islamic State fatwas." *Jihadica: Documenting the Global Jihad*, 2 March 2015: http://www.jihadica.com/32-islamic-state-fatwas (accessed 19 April 2017).

wear Islamically prescribed clothing and that men and women do not mix in public. They also monitor shops and checks that they are closed during prayer.[9] There is also a special female police corps called the *Al-Khansā'* brigade. This brigade mainly oversees that women wear the prescribed clothing and that they behave decently in public. Women infringing upon the rules are arrested or flogged on the spot.[10]

Non-religious courts have been banned on the Islamic State territory and have been replaced with Sharia courts. These courts are authorized to settle civil and family disputes and to try criminal cases, which often end in harsh sentences of corporal punishment and mutilation such as lashing, amputation, stoning and crucifixion.[11] Protection of public order and security is the duty of the security services, which fall under the Ministry of Public Security (Dīwān al-Amn al-ʿāmm, often referred to as Amni or Emni). These services are responsible for the security of the person of the caliph and the implementation of his decisions and the execution of criminal sentences of the Sharia courts. They also carry out political murders, kidnappings and extortion.[12] More than other ministries, the Ministry of Public Security is dominated by officers from the former security services of Saddam Hussein. This explains that the police and the security services are used the same torture methods as were applied under Saddam Hussein.[13] In the following I shall sketch how Sharia is enforced in some of the domains of state activity.

---

9 Atwan, "*Islamic State.*" pp. 129, 139.

10 Winter, Charlie (transl. and analysis). 2015. *Women of the Islamic State: A manifesto on women by the Al-Khanssaa Brigade*. Quilliam Foundation: https://therinjfoundation.files.wordpress.com/2015/01/women-of-the-islamic-state3.pdf (accessed 19 April 2017).

11 Van Ostaeyen, Pieter (2013), *'Amnesty International, ISIS and Islamic penal law'* (28 December 2013): https://pietervanostaeyen.wordpress.com/2013/12/28/amnesty-internati onal-isis-and-islamic-penal-law/ (accessed 15 April 2017); Van Ostaeyen (2014), *'ISIS crucifies two prisoners in ar-Raqqa'* (30 April 2014): https://pietervanostaeyen.wordpress.com/2014/04/30/isis-crucifies-two-prisoners-in-ar-raqqa (accessed 15 April 2017); Van Ostaeyen (2014), *'An Official Islamic State statement on Shar'i punishments'* (16 December 2014): https://pietervanostaeyen.wordpress.com/2014/12/16/an-official-islamic-state-statement-on-shari-punishments/ (accessed 15 April 2017).

12 Abu Haniyeh, "Daesh's Organisational Structure".

13 Amnesty International, 2013, 'Syria: Harrowing torture, summary killings in secret ISIS detention centres' (19 December 2013): https://www.amnesty.org/en/latest/news/2013/12/syria-harrowing-torture-summary-killings-secret-isis-detention-centres/ (accessed 19 April 2017).

There is a document ascribed to Abū ʿUmar al-Baghdādī, called *ʿAqīdatunā* (Our Creed), which summarizes the principal points of faith of his movement and, at the same time, contains a declaration of war and a license to kill. The text is published on YouTube[14] in spoken form and also as a written text on the Internet.[15] In July 2014 a revision of this document appeared under the title "This is our credo and our method" (*Hādhihi ʿAqīdatunā Wa-Manhajunā*).[16] The contents in both documents seem to be purely theological; however, almost all issues addressed in these documents have political consequences since the theological definition of unbelief entails the permission or obligation to kill. That the foreign troops of the American-led coalition ("Crusaders") in Iraq are lawful targets goes without saying and is not even mentioned in the document. More important are the statements on the local Muslims. Here I follow the older document that is most detailed in this respect. Eight of its nineteen sections deal with the theological question of apostasy and, especially, what are the acts, beliefs, and utterances that excommunicate a Muslim (*takfīr*). The consequences are extremely serious since apostates, according to this Creed, must be killed. The criteria for being regarded as a Muslim by the Islamic State are very strict and leave out many of those who see themselves as believers. According to this document, beliefs that make a Muslim an apostate are being a Shi'ite (section 2), submitting legal disputes to courts adjudicating according to man-made law or tribal custom rather than Sharia (section 5), impairing the dignity of the Prophet, his relatives, and the first caliphs by building shrines on their graves and allowing believers to venerate them (section 6), following secular ideologies such as Baathism and communism (section 7), collaborating with the occupier (section 8), with the rulers and the military of all Muslim countries, since there the laws of idols (*ṭāghūt*) are enforced and not the Sharia (section 10,) and, finally, the soldiers of Iraqi army and police officers and members of related organizations (section 11). This Creed, therefore, justifies the killing of nearly

---

14 E. g. https://www.youtube.com/watch?v=kwYPdIaoGio (accessed 15 June, 2015)

15 Arabic text: https://goostmmb.wordpress.com/2014/01/23/%D8%B9%D9%82%D9%8A%D8%AF%D8%A9-%D8%A7%D9%84%D8%AF%D9%88%D9%84%D8%A9-%D8%A7%D9%84%D8%A5%D8%B3%D9%84%D8%A7%D9%85%D9%8A%D8%A9-%D9%84%D8%A3%D9%85%D9%8A%D8%B1%D9%87%D8%A7-%D8%A3%D8%A8%D9%88%D8%B9/ (accessed 19 April 2017). English translation in Peters, R. 2016. *Jihad: A history in documents*. Princeton: Markus Wiener Publishers, pp. 196-200.

16 Arabic text and English translation in Al-Tamimi, A.J. 2015, *'This is our Aqeeda and This is our Manhaj: Islam 101 according to the Islamic State'*: http://www.aymennjawad.org/2015/10/this-is-our-aqeeda-and-this-is-our-manhaj-islam (accessed 19 April 2017).

all Iraqi civilians and soldiers – the Shi'ites, the soldiers of the regular army, police officers, non-Muslims – and actually permits the killing of all citizens of Iraq since all of them would fall under the description of those who submit their disputes to state courts, espouse secular ideologies, or collaborate with the occupiers.

For the Islamic State there are many apostates who could lawfully be killed. However, massacres at that scale are not regarded viable. Therefore, the Islamic State has excavated a procedure from classical *fiqh*, which allows them to spare the lives of apostates after indoctrination and repentance. Under classical Sharia, apostates may not be executed until offering them the opportunity to repent and return to Islam. This offer is called *istitāba* (i.e. asking a person to repent). The Islamic State has introduced a bureaucratic form of *istitāba* for those who are regarded as apostates by the Islamic State, but are willing to embrace the Islamic State version of Islam. They have to follow an indoctrination course of usually two months and pass an examination, after which they are handed an official certificate stating that they are not anymore regarded as an unbeliever. This is in general voluntary but mandatory for defectors from the regular army or other oppositional militias, for all teachers and personnel of educational institutions in the Syrian parts of Islamic State territory, and for people who return to Islamic State territory for a journey abroad.[17]

According to most schools of law, the head of state of the Muslims may choose what to do with prisoners of war: they may be set free, be enslaved, be ransomed

---

[17] See for the order that persons who had been attached to regular armies or other rebellious groups have to follow the *istitāba* courses with regard to Deir al-Zor (Wilayat al-Khayr), the journal *Arabi21*: http://arabi21.com/story/824870/%D9%81%D9%8A-%D9%85%D8%B9%D9%87%D8%AF-%D8%A7%D8%B3%D8%AA%D8%AA%D8%A7%D8%A8%D8%A9-%D9%84%D8%AA%D9%86%D8%B8%D9%8A%D9%85-%D8%A7%D9%84%D8%AF%D9%88%D9%84%D8%A9-%D8%AA%D8%AA%D8%B3%D8%A7%D9%88%D9%89-%D8%A7%D9%84%D9%86%D8%B5%D8%B1%D8%A9-%D9%88%D8%A7%D9%84%D9%86%D8%B8%D8%A7%D9%85-%D9%81%D9%8A%D8%AF%D9%8A%D9%88 (accessed 19 April 2017). See also the order of 11 July 2014 from the Bureau of Security Deir el-Zor. (A photograph of this document is shown in this website after a great number of horrendous pictures of torture and atrocities): http://www.lebwindow.net/2014/07/%D8%A3%D8%B1%D8%B4%D9%8A%D9%81-%D8%A7%D9%84%D8%AE%D9%84%D8%A7%D9%81%D8%A9-%D8%A7%D9%84%D8%AC%D8%B2%D8%A1-%D8%A7%D9%84%D8%AB%D8%A7%D9%86%D9%8A-%D9%81%D8%B6%D8%A7%D8%A6%D8%AD-%D8%AF%D8%A7/ (accessed 19 April 2017); and also Website Rozana Radio, 14-6 2015: http://rozana.fm/ar/node/13048 (accessed 19 April 2017).

or be killed.[18] The Islamic State has massively executed their prisoners, often by slaughtering them with knives. And some of them were burned alive, such as the Jordanian pilot, whose punishment was justified in a fatwa as retaliation for his bombing attacks.[19] The execution was filmed and put on the internet.

In August 2014 the Islamic State conquered the region of Sinjar in Northern Iraq inhabited mainly by Yezidis. In the Ottoman Empire, these Yezidis were protected as *dhimmī*s just like Christians and Jews. The Islamic State, however, followed a contrary legal opinion[20] and refused to offer the Yezidis protection. Following this interpretation, the Islamic State justified taking the lives and properties of the Yezidi men, and enslaving women and children. The captured women (just like movable property) were part of the booty of war: they became the property of the military who had participated in the battle that resulted in their captivity.[21] These soldiers would acquire ownership after the distribution of the booty to the individual soldiers by the commander. Usually, however, these slaves and goods were not distributed in kind but sold in auctions (in which the soldiers could bid and buy booty for reduced prices) and the money was distributed among the soldiers. Enslaving the several thousands of captured women was, from the Islamic State perspective, a practical solution: the prisoners would be taken care of and guarded by their masters, and they could meet the sexual needs of the fighters. The Islamic State, thus, has revived slavery and the captured women, by virtue of the norms of Sharia, were forced to have sex with their owners. In order to inform the new slave owners of their rights and duties, the Ministry of Research and Issuing Fatwas (*Dīwān al-Buḥūth wa-l-Iftā'*) published a booklet in the fall of 2014, summarizing the relevant rules of Sharia.[22] This was a practical publication, since these rules are

---

18 Ibn Rushd, 1960. *Bidāyat al-mujtahid wa-nihāyat al-muqtaṣid.* Cairo: Maktabat Muṣṭafā al-Bābī al-Ḥalabī. Vol. 1, p. 382.

19 For a photograph of this fatwa and English translation, see https://pjmedia.com/blog/isis-issues-fatwa-to-justify-burning-of-jordanian-pilot (accessed 19 April 2017).

20 The jurists held that all non-Muslims could enter a treaty of protection, *dhimma*, except the Shafi'ite school of jurisprudence, which held that only the Jews, Christians, and Zoroastrians were entitled to do so. Ibn Rushd, *Bidāyat*, vol. 1, p. 389.

21 See Peters, R., "Booty," in Fleet, Kate, and Krämer, Gudrun, et al. (eds.), *Encyclopaedia of Islam Three*. Leiden: Brill, 2007.

22 *Su'āl wa-jawāb fī 'l-saby wa-l-riqāb* (Questions and Answers about Captives and Slaves). 2014. Published by Maktabat al-Himma, al-Dawla al-Islāmīyya, Muḥarram 1436 [October-November 2014]. 5 pp.: https://ia902701.us.archive.org/25/items/SabiReqab/Sabi_Reqab.rar. (accessed 19 April 2017). English translation in Peters, R., *Jihad: A history in documents*. 2016, pp. 211-216.

not arranged in one single chapter in the books on jurisprudence, but spread over several chapters, such as those on marriage, penal law, sale, emancipation, succession, and so on.

The Islamic State conquered regions and towns where non-Muslim subjects lived. Under Sharia law, Jews and Christians (The People of the Book) could enter a treaty of *dhimma*, by virtue of which they were entitled to the legal protection of their lives, their property, and freedom (i.e. they could not be enslaved). In exchange, they had to pay a special tax, *jizya,* and were obliged to abide by certain regulations demonstrating in public life that their status was inferior to the one of Muslims. One of the oldest and most important text of such treaties is the pledge of Caliph ʿUmar concluded with (or granted to) the inhabitants of Jerusalem in 638.[23] Its contents became exemplary for the doctrine of *fiqh.* In modern times, however, nation states in the Middle East have abolished the *dhimma*-system, and regard, ideally, all citizens as equal before the law, regardless of their beliefs. Now, section 12 of the Islamic State Credo *ʿAqīdatunā* by the Abū ʿUmar al-Baghdādī (see above) stipulates that the non-Muslim minorities have violated their original agreements of protection by not paying *jizya* tax and not abiding by the stipulations imposed upon them under Sharia law and are therefore lawful targets of violence, unless they conclude a new agreement with the Islamic State. The same is mentioned in the "Pledge to the Christians of Raqqa", proclaimed in February 2014.[24] Many Christians

[23] The text of ʿUmar's pledge has been transmitted in several versions with widely varying wordings. The Islamic State text is closest to the one included in *Tārīkh Dimashq* by Ibn ʿAsākir (d. 1175), except that the Islamic State text is a letter written by Caliph Abū Bakr al-Baghdādī to the Christians of al-Raqqa, whereas Ibn ʿAsākir's version is a letter written by the Christians of Jerusalem to ʿUmar. Ten out of the twelve stipulations are adopted from ʿUmar's pledge as presented by Ibn ʿAsākir. See for the different versions: https://ar.beta.islamway.net/article/38931/%D8%A7%D9%84%D8%B9%D9%87%D8%AF%D8%A9-%D8%A7%D9%84%D8%B9%D9%85%D8%B1%D9%8A%D8%A9-%D8%A7%D9%84%D9%86%D8%B5%D9%88%D8%B5-%D8%A7%D9%84%D9%88%D8%A7%D8%B1%D8%AF%D8%A9-%D9%88%D9%85%D9%86%D8%A7%D9%82%D8%B4%D8%AA%D9%87%D8%A7 (accessed 19 April 2019).

[24] See "The Pledge to the Christians of Raqqa", proclaimed in February 2014, which partly follows ʿUmar's pledge. Arabic text in: http://www.alarabiya.net/ar/arab-and-world/syria/2014/02/28/%D8%B5%D9%88%D8%B1%D8%A9-%D8%A3%D9%88%D9%84-%D8%B9%D9%87%D8%AF-%D8%B0%D9%85%D8%A9-%D8%A3%D8%A8%D8%B1%D9%85%D8%AA%D9%87-%D8%AF%D8%A7%D8%B9%D8%B4-%D9%85%D8%B9-%D9%85%D8%B3%D9%8A%D8%AD%D9%8A%D9%8A%D9%86-%D9%81%D9%8A-%D8%B3%D9%88%D8%B1%D9%8A%D8%A7-.html (accessed 19 April 2017). English Translation in Peters, R., *Jihad: A history in documents.* pp. 207-210.

fearing that their lifes and properties were in danger, left the Islamic State territory, often forced to leave their properties behind.

The administration of justice is the monopoly of Sharia courts. They settle civil disputes, but not very much is known how they function. This is different with regard to the administration of criminal justice.[25] Although we do not know very much of the trials, the punishments of the transgressors are well-known. It is the policy of the Islamic State to carry out penalties in public and disseminate photographs and videos. On the internet there are thousands of appalling videos and photographs of persons who are being crucified before being killed, whose hands or feet are being amputated, who are being beheaded with a sword or killed by throwing them off from the roof of a high building (for homosexuals) and the like. Crucified bodies are left hanged for some time, with notices of their crimes hanging from their necks. The heads of decapitated persons are sometimes put on the spikes of fences in public places. In view of the frequency of such penalties, it is implausible that the Sharia courts take into account the strict conditions for convicting persons for *ḥadd* offences or killing (*qiṣāṣ*). Many of the local observers doubted whether the Sharia courts in criminal trials did notactually pay attention to the requirements of evidence and procedure. Often persons are summarily sentenced and punished on the spot.[26] The religious police (*ḥisba*) and the women *al-Khansa' Brigade*, operate in the same way: if they see offences against morality or religious norms, they act immediately and flog or arrest the transgressors. Among the religious norms that are strictly enforced are the ban of smoking, of wearing T-shirts with certain pictures, of playing football and of raising pigeons on the roofs of houses. Women must wear a face veil in public and must be accompanied by a male relative (*maḥram*).

---

[25] For an Arabic and English translation of the Islamic State version of Sharia penal law, see Van Ostaeyen, Pieter, 2014, *'An Official Islamic State statement on Shar'i punishments'* (16 December 2014), https://pietervanostaeyen.wordpress.com/2014/12/16/an-official-islamic-state-statement-on-shari-punishments/ (accessed 15 April 2017). The statement includes as capital crimes casting insult on Allah/the Divine, casting insult on the Messenger, insulting the faith, adultery for the married, homosexuality, spying for the infidel, apostasy and banditry with killing. Flogging (with or without expulsion from the country) is the penalty for drinking alcohol, adultery for the unmarried and masturbation. Theft and banditry with theft is punished with amputation of the right hand or both the right hand and left foot. The statement is certainly not meant to be complete, since it does not list killing or wounding or slander (*qadhf*).

[26] Birke, Sarah, *How the Islamic State rules*. NY Review of Books, 5 Feb., 2015. http://www.nybooks.com/articles/archives/2015/feb/05/how-isis-rules/ (accessed 5 April 2017).

4. Conclusions

As we have seen, violence and brutal governance are essential characteristics of the Caliphate of Raqqa. This is not amazing, in view of the ambiance of relentless repression of the regimes of Saddam Hussein and Bashar al-Assad. There are differences, however, between these regimes and the Islamic State: the killing and torturing of the former regimes were carried out behind the prison walls, regarded as an unpleasant necessity in order to protect the regime. The Islamic State, to the contrary, executes its brutal repressive practices in public and justifies them as the enforcement of the Sharia. This legitimation by Sharia is a result of cherry picking: The religious leaders of Islamic State have selected the most ruthless Sharia doctrines and opinions in, for instance, the fields of *takfīr*, the treatment of prisoners of war and non-Muslims and for the criminal procedure of imposing *ḥadd* penalties. The ruthless acts and policies carried out by the Islamic State are framed as religiously desirable and as evidence that a really Islamic state is being established. Enforcement of this Sharia, coupled with violence and relentless governance, is the crucial base of the Caliphate of Raqqa. It is my contention that the way Sharia has been excavated by the Islamic State from the classical corpus of *fiqh,* and then shaped and applied, is first and foremost informed by its use for the legitimation of its infrastructure of brutal repression. However, in addition to this, the strict enforcement of Sharia is presented as the only correct version of Islam and, therefore, the justification of the existence of the Islamic State.

The Caliphate of Raqqa presents itself deliberately as a violent power, bloodily suppressing its subjects, and especially the non-Muslims. This constitutes also a message of shock and awe to the enemies, hoping that the enemy troops prefer desertion rather than being caught by the Islamic State and being bloodily slaughtered as a prisoner of war. Emphasizing its relentless power that crushes its enemy creates the image of invincibility. This triumphalism added to the attractiveness for foreign volunteers of joining the IS. However, the defeats that the Islamic State has suffered during the last year must have undermined this image of triumphalism. At the present (October 2017), the Islamic State has lost its cities and its territory has shrunk considerably.

The Islamic State claimed to be a genuine Islamic state, the only one now in existence and organized in order to enable Muslims to live the life of a good Muslim. This was one of the foremost propagandistic aspects addressed to its subjects and also, specifically, to the potential jihadist volunteers from abroad. In addition, the Islamic State positioned itself as a real anti-Western defending Islam against the attacks of the Western states, referred to as "Crusaders". Being anti-Western, then, implies contempt of universal human rights principles since these are seen as a totally Western invention. For the Islamic State – as well as for other Salafi groups – they are no part of the divine law, but rather made by man. And although Westerners assert that human rights are universal, this is hypocrisy according to the Islamic State scholars: human rights are not universally and justly applied: They are invoked only in order to weaken political enemies by charging them with human rights violations, which they condone if committed by Western states of their allies. Contempt of human rights standards is an intentional ideological tool to legitimize the Islamic State as a really anti-Western and Islamic state. The Islamic State deliberately violates human rights standards and the norms of international law of war, not only for practical reasons – observing these rules makes it more difficult to brutally repress its subjects –, but also for ideological motives. The Islamic State has instrumentalized brutal government and violation of human rights principles, not only for oppressing its subjects and scaring its enemies, but also as an ideological messaging stating that the Islamic State is defending Islam against Western military and ideological aggression. And in order to justify this policy of relentless cruelty, the leaders of the Islamic State have molded a very particular appalling version of the Sharia, consisting of "fossilized" opinions and doctrines, excavated from the rich and diverse corpus of Islamic jurisprudence.

The Aims of Punishment in Islamic Criminal Law and their Reflection in the Iranian Criminal Justice System

Firouz Mahmoudi Janaki, Teheran

Abstract

Punishment is one of the principles of criminal law that is related to criminalization and criminal responsibility. The three are considered as the basic elements in criminal law. A philosophy of punishment is necessary both to provide a theory of criminalization and also to give feature to penal responsibility. Punishment has unique features in Islamic criminal law, on the one hand because of the unchangeability of some crimes, and on the other hand because these crimes are regarded as specific to Muslims and Islamic society. It is common to consider four objectives of punishment, retribution, incapacitation, rehabilitation, and the protection of society. However, in the case of *ḥudūd (sg. ḥadd)* and *qiṣāṣ* crimes retribution is the main purpose, while in case of *ta'zīr* crimes deterrence is considered the main purpose. In the case of punishments under the Islamic criminal Code of Iran, reform or rehabilitation is considered the central objective in most cases. However, within the system of Islamic criminal law, punishment is not the unique means for reaching the utilitarian objectives, especially rehabilitation and deterrence; repentance, forgiveness, atonement and otherworldly punishment, concepts that are founded in belief and true faith in God and the Hereafter, are the other flanks of the reactive system which have pervasive operation, and do not apply differently or stand apart from other punishments. As Islamic jurists suppose that some Islamic punishments are fixed and can in principle not be dispensed with or changed to other sentences, philosophical perspectives and social changes cannot have a deep influence on criminal theory as a whole, unless a new approach can show that altering these punishments and their theoretical foundations is possible. By contrast, in case of *ta'zīr* punishments which comprise the main part of Islamic criminal law, the way is open to provide a criminal theory, especially a normative theory of punishment and bind the state to the consequences of such a theory. The current penal system has predominantly considered the formal aspects of Islamic religious law and therefore could not realize and recognize the social facts and needs in a changing human life. Such a penal system cannot not react properly to individual and social requirements for reaching its systematic goals.

1. Introduction

There are three important stages in the criminal law process whose theoretical justification and explanation is necessary in every legal system: criminalization, criminal responsibility and sentencing. Although these three are different issues and separable phases they touch upon and are related to each other, so they cannot be dealt with in a different way citing different foundations in their theoretical explanation and justification. Perhaps for the general public and also for most of the professionals in this field, the question why punishment is applied is one of the oldest and meanwhile the most basic questions in criminal law philosophy that has been answered in different and sometimes similar ways. This issue has a particular importance for Islamic criminal law in our era, first due to the lack of proper debate on the philosophy of punishment in this system and secondly due to its blend with customary criminal law in some Islamic countries and most importantly in Iran. Apparently, Islamic criminal law categorizes punishments based on the significance of the forbidden behavior and has determined fixed punishments for some actions. Furthermore it has given authority to the government to determine the types of forbidden behavior and the amounts of punishment in other cases, determining of general criteria for some of them. Do all these punishments follow one goal or do they have various goals? Are the goals in this legal system different from other penal systems? Is/are goal(s) of punishment in line with the goal of criminal law as a whole or not? Can Islamic jurists justify punishment in Islamic criminal law or should they restrict themselves to a proper explanation of punishment, especially for fixed punishments? Are prescribed goals in this legal system appropriate to the mechanisms that it provides for? Can it be expected that these goals (or these mechanisms?) are changed when the Islamic system of punishment enters a new political-social context?

The necessity of this type of questions is due to the fact that penal law is criticized and evaluated more than other branches of law because of its character as the most severe type of reaction against wrongful behavior and, for the offender, resulting in a high degree of limitation of individual freedoms and rights.

All these issues would call for a deep study about the mentioned triple levels, this article, however, limits itself to briefly evaluate and criticize the viewpoints proposed on the goals of punishment. A point which is necessary to explain is that this article due to criminalization of behavior in Islamic religious law and in the better world doesn't evaluate the criminalization theory in this legal system directly unless it is necessary to explain and criticize the punishment theory. Furthermore not every single punishment is discussed because it is generally assumed that these punishments have been accepted as a legal truth in this system and consequently in the criminal law of Iran. However, entering into this discussion needs further research independent of this article.

2. Theories of Punishment

Scholars and philosophers have not always agreed on the goal for punishments. They determined the goal of punishment depending on how and on what principle they have accepted a right of the government to punish and its moral foundations. Punishment may be inflicted on the offender because he deserves it; an offender receives punishment for a crime based on this idea. If the response and the reaction to the crime have to be appropriate and just, any concern about the effects of punishment in the future is irrelevant. Punishment is a reaction to a crime that happened in the past. So it is retrospective and the offender receives his punishment as a reward for what he has done to make amends to society and for unjustifiable advantage to be retrieved from him. This theory has been codified as a deontological approach to punishment not as a teleological or consequential one. By contrast, some theories justify punishment according to the consequences of punishment. "A consequentialist view holds that the rightness or wrongness of any action or practice depends solely on its overall consequences. It is right if its consequences are good (at least as good as those of any available alternative), and wrong if its consequences are bad (worse than those of some available alternative)".[1] The main utility of punishment is preventing the offender from repeating the crime or putting him as example for others to learn and not to commit a crime. Also reforming and rehabilitating the offender or making him incapable of committing a crime are other benefits which are considered in this type of theories

1 *Duff, R. A. and Garland, D.* (1994), Introduction: Thinking about Punishment. In Duff, R. A. & Garland, David, A Reader on Punishment, New York 1994, 1-44, 6.

so that maintaining public order and protecting society against crime, and, in the words of many Islamic jurists, against "corruption", can be considered the profit caused by punishment. All these explanations are looking forward while the first type is looking back.

The aim of introducing these two general categories of theories – that can be found in philosophical and legal texts – is to understand how Islamic thinkers and jurists have justified or explained punishment by referring to the principal Islamic texts and sources. Did they interpret punishment within the framework of retribution or utilitarianism? Is it possible to consider other interpretations apart from these for punishment? In this case, what are the features of this new classification?

2.1. Deontological approach and its background in the goals of punishment in the Islamic criminal system

The first goal of punishment is administration of justice. This theory – which in Western philosophy mostly stemmed from Kant's and Hegel's ideas and thoughts – has always had some advocates, but it has also encountered a wave of criticism; in this view the reason for punishment of crime is just because the offender has obtained an undeserved advantage by committing the crime. A thief who steals the property of another person has appropriated an illegal property that he could not achieve legally.

Some Islamic thinkers express that *ḥudūd* punishments and *qiṣāṣ* (retaliation) are applied to restore the balance which has been disturbed and also to realize justice.[2] In this justice-centered theory it is not important whether the offender commits a crime again or learns his lesson from suffering punishment, but what is important is the administration of justice to the degree the offender deserves it. The result of the punishment is not worthy of reflection, what is important is the duty of society to punish him, that is, he is punishable and blameworthy ethically. As Easton and Piper mentioned, "on the retributivist theory a wrong action should be met by a sanction appropriate to the action and deserved by the offender, so it is argued that: (i) punishment should be given in response to its being deserved; (ii) the penalty should be appropriate to the wrong action; and (iii) the consequences of punishment are irrelevant."[3]

---

2 *Al-'Arīs, H.*, Shakhsiyat 'uqūbāt al-ta'zīr fī 'l-Sharī'a al-Islamiya. Beirut 1417/1997, 129.

3 *Easton, S. and Piper, Ch.*, Sentencing and Punishment. Oxford 2005, 49.

Retributivists have a distinctive approach to humans; in Kant's viewpoint, a person is a rational agent for whom the law has an imperative function not a coercive one, because an individual himself recognizes and accepts law and thus some commitments and obligations are imposed on him. Intellect is a fundamental criterion and a basis for ethical regulation (by law). Kant considers autonomy or independency of the individual and intellectuality as the most fundamental features of human beings. Independency of intrinsic and inner action of a person requires to treat him as an independent creature with dignity and respect. Ethical law and regulation requires people to be treated equally.[4]

From the point of view of some Islamic jurists, however, the basis of the right to punish is God's decree that has been considered to emanate from divine mercy. It is mercy like the father's crackdown in the education of child.[5] From this point of view, although the administration of justice is sufficient to justify punishment, there is a higher justification than that as the basis of legitimation is the divine decree and people's acceptance can be based on the belief in that. Such obedience, however, is expected from believers, not unbelievers. Therefore, in the Islamic penal system, the goals of punishment should be based on the legislator's order and faithful acceptance. If punishment in the traditional approach seemed to be a mercy, it follows from the faith-centered nature of the religious law that its regulations are accepted due to faithful willingness and desire more than due to force and coercion. In this context, punishment, if imposed in an ideal Islamic society, can of course be mercy in the view of believers and for believers.

We cannot find a statement in Quran and *Hadith* that clearly indicates a specific goal of the legislator concerning punishments. What has been mentioned is an impression that scholars, commentators and Islamic jurists have concluded from verses of the Quran and *Sunna*. Some of these evidences are general in topic and some others are specific to *ḥudūd*. The following word of God is usually referred to in order to explain one of the aims of punishment: "penalty of evilness is likewise evilness" (Sura al-Shūrā: 40). This verse can guide us to two points: First, reaction to evilness is a behavior like that. Thus, punishment is an evil like an offence, which is also an evil. The second point is that evilness can be a behavior that has not only been branded as a sin but also considered as a crime in the religious law and there is punishment or retribution for that. In this explanation, the emphasis of

4 *Sullivan, R.*, Akhlāq dar falsafa-yi Kant. Tehran 1380/2001, 62-70.

5 *Abū Zahra, M.*, al-Jarīma wa-'l-'uqūba fi 'l-fiqh al-Islāmī. N.p., n.d., 7.

Islamic jurists is more on equality and proportionality that have high importance in the retribution theory.

This means that the offender is punished because he has committed an evil and a sin. He deserves a reaction that corresponds to his conduct (Sura Al-Nahl 126). Based on this famous impression, the Quran considers evilness – which we interpret as punishment – as a penalty, or quid pro quo, for evilness.

As to the *ḥudūd* crimes, the aim of retribution is more significant than other aims. Some reasons can be given for this assertion: first, based on the traditional theory in Islamic law, *ḥudūd* are considered as fixed in the religious law as regards two aspects: one, in terms of the values whose violation has been criminalized and the other, in terms of the punishments for them. Islamic branches of thought agree that the criminalization of such behavior has always existed and that it applies regardless of time and place. However, the unchangeability (*thābitangārī)* of these crimes by itself cannot indicate that the aim behind punishment is retribution because discussing what behavior should be a crime is an area within the theory of criminalization that is not the purpose of this article. However there is consensus among Islamic jurists and lawyers that *ḥudūd* crimes are in essence considered a right of Allah, except in the case of *qadhf* (falsely alleging illegal sexual intercourse) and *sirqat* (theft) (before bringing the case to the court or proving it) and that they are fixed due to that reason. Kasani in his famous book says, when defining *ḥudūd* crimes: "these crimes are legally forbidden actions for which God punishes their perpetrators with certain punishments that they deserve".[6] Mohammad Avva has interpreted God's right in *ḥudūd* crimes in this way, noting that the "benefit of executing *ḥudūd* is for all people and, in today's words, a public good".[7] Although this analysis is utilitarian, believing such crimes to be unchangeable and based on the right of Allah makes punishment the ethical retribution for the crime. The stability of *ḥudūd* crimes is considered to be based on the importance of the values that Islamic religious law wants to protect because they have been considered the base of the Islamic community: Religion, soul, property, honor and wisdom.

The second point is that the unchangeability of punishments can be considered a sign of accepting the retribution viewpoint in *ḥudūd*. The explanation about this issue lies in the assumption of the stability of punishment and in the refusal of diagnosis and discretion of the judge to increase or reduce the punishment, it being

---

6 *Al-Kāsānī al-Ḥanafī, A.*, Badā'i' al-sanā'i' fī tartīb al-sharā'i', vol.7. Beirut 1402/1982,56.

7 *Al-'Awā', M. S.*, Darāmadī bar uṣūl-i niẓām-i kaifarī-yi Islām. Qom 1385/2006, 94.

a feature of the retribution-based theories that the extent and type of punishment for each crime should be determined in the legal text in order to minimize the possibility of inequality, inconsistencies or discrimination in applying punishments. Here, the punishment is laid down by law by reference to the crime, not the offender. This means that the *ḥudūd* crimes would fall under a theory of penalization where the basic argument that guides the legislator in determining the type and amount of the punishment is the seriousness of the crime, thus observing the behavior, not the person's penal responsibility. Of course, these two elements have been combined with each other in new readings of the retribution theory.[8] However the fixed punishment shows the acceptance of the goal of retribution. As we noted above, the second principle gained from the analysis of this verse is that emphasis is not on equality or proportionality in terms of penalty, but on the level of badness of punishment, it being equal to the crime; because by reference to the Quran the response to evilness is to be evilness to a like degree. This can also lead us to another rule: punishment should be the last resort, because it is in itself an evil and we should avoid it when other alternatives are available. Further, God has mentioned "punishment" as the penalty for a criminal action or sin in the mentioned verse and in some other verses on the topic of punishment it can also be interpreted as the "penalty" for an action. For instance, the author of Al-Mizan has made such a comment in interpreting verse 38 of al-Mā'ida.[9] The following verses are examples that punishment has been interpreted as *jazā'*, that is a recompense or response to crime in view point of retributive approach (5: 33, 34; 5: 38). However, *jazā'* has another positive meaning as a recompense for good and good doers (5: 85; 39: 34).

Third, accepting the principle of toting up punishments for various crimes or in cases where punishments are not the same is another sign of *ḥudūd* punishments being based on a retributive aim.

Fourth, if *ḥadd* is to be proven by *bayyina* (witnesses with special conditions) according to Islamic jurists there is no way to change, convert, intercede with or forgive the punishment, or to avoid it through repentance. It is true that repentance makes it possible to forgive the perpetrator of a *ḥadd* crime in case of repentance before proceedings are initiated or the perpetrator is arrested, or in some cases when the *ḥadd* crime is proven by confession. However, after the trial there is no

---

8 *Von Hirsch, A.*, Censure and Sanctions. Oxford 1995.

9 *Ṭabāṭabā'ī, S. M.*, al-Mizān fi tafsīr al-Qur'ān, vol. 5. Qom 1363/1984, 532.

route open to ignore the punishment for *ḥadd*. This shows the predominance of retribution among the aims behind the *ḥudūd*.

Fifth, some Islamic jurists consider *ḥadd* an inherent purification and atonement for sin; most of the Islamic jurists, such as the Shafei and Hanbali jurists believe that *ḥadd* is a purification for the perpetrator and removes eternal punishment.[10] This statement can be given a further justification, namely that *ḥadd* is a right of Allah and that God would only punish the perpetrator of the violation of his right one time, and not two times both in the world and in the Hereafter. Accepting this position implies a sense that a *ḥadd* punishment is really a penalty for the action and a person who is punishable for the commission of a crime, and has been punished for that, should not be reprimanded anymore. However, it cannot be ignored that there is a second position that does not regard *ḥudūd* punishments as atonement (*kaffāra*) according to some Quranic verses and Hadiths; such as verse 34 of al-Mā'ida, where God after expressing punishment for warriors against God says: "for them is shame in this world and a great punishment in the everlasting life".

By contrast, what according to this verse leads to the purification of the perpetrator is not the *ḥadd* punishment, but repentance: "except those who repent before you have power over them. For you must know that Allah is forgiving, the most merciful". Jalāl al-Dīn al-Khwārizmī, one of the Hanafi scholars, argues for the character of *ḥudūd* being deterrence, not atonement by stating that they are imposed on the perpetrator not because of his will and for this reason do not work to his credit. If he repents, he will be cleansed.[11]

Although *ḥudūd* punishments have many features of retributive punishments and their rules, some Islamic jurists and scholars believe that punishments, especially in case of *ta'zīr* (undetermined punishments), aim at reaching specific purposes like the prevention of crime by different functions of deterrence and reform.

---

[10] *Abū Ya'lī, M.*, al-Aḥkām al-sulṭāniya. Beirut 1403/1983, 275-276; *Al-Nawawī, A.*, Ṣaḥīḥ Muslim bi-sharḥ al-Nawawī, v. 11. Beirut 1392/1972, 224; *Al-Ainī, B.*, 'Umdat al-qārī sharḥ Ṣaḥīḥ al-Bukhārī. V. 1. Beirut 1399/1979, 157.

[11] *Al-Khwārizmī, J.*, Al-Kifāya 'alā al-hidāya, v. 5. N.p. n.d. 3.

2.2. Consequentialist approach of punishment

As mentioned above, theories that pay attention to the results of behavior and justify the punishment due to its consequences form a further spectrum of theories. After a short introduction of the features of each one, the following question has to be asked: what is the main consequence of imposing punishment? Islamic jurists mostly asked this question by referring to the main functions of punishment and sometimes by expressing its different final aim, like prevention of crime or protection of society.

2.2.1. General and specific deterrence and the protection of the Muslim community

Maybe the most important category of consequential approaches in classical concepts of criminal laws sees the goal of punishment in preventing the commission of a crime in the future through deterrence of the offender from committing the crime again or through deterring potential offenders or people more generally. In the first variant – which is called specific deterrence – the punishment is supposed to give a "lesson" to the offender to not follow the way of crime again. In the second variant – which is called general deterrence – the aim is that the "consequences of committing a crime" are shown to the people in order to "intimidate them". The effect of specific deterrence is realized as soon as the punishment is imposed and the effect of general deterrence is realized when the punishment and its enforcement gets known to the public.

Many Islamic jurists and lawyers regard *ḥudūd* as penalties that are imposed to prevent prohibited matters and the omission of fulfilling commands. These punishments are applied against the perpetrator so as to stop him from committing a crime again. For people who have not committed a relevant crime, the *ḥudūd* punishments are a deterrent from committing a crime due to the awareness about them; for offenders they are considered deterrent due to suffering of them.[12] *Al-Māwardī*, a Shafei scholar, expresses the opinion that "punishments are deterrents that God imposed to prevent people from committing what is forbidden and omitting what should be conducted".[13]

The same expression can be clearly found in the sayings of other Islamic jurists so that some of them, such as Qarāfī, one of the Maliki scholars, and many of the

[12] *Ibn al Humām al-Hanafī, K.*, Sharḥ fatḥ al-Qadīr, vol. 5. Beirut n.d, 212.

[13] *Al-Māwardī al-Shafi'ī, A.*, al-Aḥkām al-sulṭāniya wa-'l-wilāya al-dīniya. Cairo 1973, 221.

Shiite jurists see the goal of executing punishment not only in the elimination of corruption caused by crimes but also in preventing offenders from the commission of further crimes and also preventing others from their commission.[14] Some others such as Kamal Ibn Ḥumām, one of the Hanafi jurists, see the target in the intimidation of people, pointing out that although it is true that the offender is deterred from committing a crime again by suffering the punishment, the emphasis on, and strict prescription in religions law that punishments be executed publicly are a sign and a basis for the opinion that public deterrence is a consideration.[15] Rejecting the testimonies of those against whom a *ḥadd* punishment has been applied is a further reason that can be mentioned as showing that there is an approach of public deterrence in Islamic law. However the reasoning behind rejecting the testimonies can be explained on the basis that these offenders have lost the quality of being just, which is one of the conditions for a witness to be admitted. Another reason for the view that deterrence is an aim is that in traditional criminal law there had been a belief that harsh and severe punishments are more fear-inspiring.

Some jurists in arguing for the deterrent aim of punishment said that one of the meanings of the term *ḥadd* is "prevention" or "forbiddance"[16] and punishments have been named *ḥadd* because they prevent people from committing a crime and a sin[17] and it is a right that belongs to God not to people to forgive the perpetrator.[18]

However, these references cannot disprove the viewpoint of Shah Vali Allah Diḥlawī who citing the verse 7 in the Surah al-Mā'ida, "so that he may taste the weight of the recompense of his action", said: *Ḥudūd* and atonement are all preventive of crimes.[19] Some Islamic jurists also argue in a similar way about *ta'zīr*. According to them, *ta'zīr* depends on the discretion and ijtihad of the Imam

---

14 *Al-Qarāfī, A.*, al-Furūq, v. 1. Beirut n.d., 213; *Abū Ya'lī, M.,* al-Aḥkām al-sulṭāniya. 275-276; *Al-Qastalānī, A.*, Irshād al-sārī li-sharḥ ṣaḥīḥ al-Bukhārī, v. 1. Beirut n.d, 101; *Ṭabāṭabā'ī, S. 'A.*, Riyāḍ al-masā'il, vol. 12. Qom 1422/2001, 415; *Al-Juba'ī al-Āmilī (al-Shāhid al-Thānī), Z.*, Masālik al-afhām fī sharḥ al-sharā'i al-Islām, vol. 14. Qom 1419/1998 325).

15 *Ibn al Humām al-Hanafī, K.*, Sharḥ vol. 14, 112.

16 *Al-Juba'ī al-Āmilī (al-Shāhid al-Thānī), Z.*, Masālik al-afhām v. 9, 11; *Al-Rāwandī, Q.*, Fiqh al-Qur'ān, v. 2,. Qom 1405/1985, 366.

17 *Al-Najafī, M.*, Jawāhir al-kalām fī sharḥ sharā'i' al-Islām, vol. 41. Beirut 1983, 254-258; *Al-Gulpayigānī, S. M.*, Dār al-manḍūd, vol. 1. Qom 1412/1992, 19.

18 *Al-Zuhailī, W.*, al-Fiqh al-mālikī al-mu'āṣir, vol. 2. Dimashq and Beirut 1420/2000, 390.

19 *Al-Dihlawī (Shah Walī Allāh), A.*, Ḥujjat Allah al-bāligha, vol. 1. Beirut 1418/1997, 16.

to determine what is appropriate based on the amount and seriousness of sin and aggression as well as the audacity of the perpetrator.[20]

The word "*ta'zīr*" has also been mentioned as meaning "prevention".[21] We understand from this meaning that *ta'zīrāt* (pl. of *ta'zīr*) prevent the offender from committing a crime again. Sarakhsī, when speaking about the salient features of *ta'zīr* has expressed that *ta'zīr* means discipline and that its purpose is to prevent a person from committing a crime again. The effect of the imposition of *ta'zīr* is different from person to person: some are prevented from further crimes by an exhortation by the judge, some by the obligation to restitute damages and some others by imprisonment.[22]

Some scholars argue that the basis of punishment in Islamic law is equality between a crime and its punishment, and that the legislator has had regard to abstract truth and human virtues in imposing punishment. Crime is opposition to ethical rules. For crimes that contain the oppression of life, property and dignity of people, the worldly punishments have been provided for and for other crimes only punishments in the life hereafter exist.[23] In the case of *ḥudūd* crimes, the strengthening of virtues and the provision of security has been considered as a right of God and anyone who violates those principles is considered violating God. However, *ḥudūd* crimes are differentiated based on the strength or weakness of the specific right that is violated; some rights belong absolutely to Allah, others have dual aspects and sometimes there is a dominance of the aspect of people's right such as in the case of *qadhf*. Other authors have considered the support of social interests as a goal of the commandments in Islamic religious law besides the target of deterrence from committing a crime. Hence they have summarized these purposes of religious law – influenced by Imam Al-Harmain Jovini and his student Imam Muḥammad Ghazālī – as religion, soul, property, wisdom and origin, sometimes reputation. Acts that violate these purposes are considered *mafsada*, corrupting, and acts that promote them are *maṣlaḥa,* good, because Ghazālī in defining *maṣlaḥa* has said: "it is the achievement of benefit and removing exorcising or setting back harms and disadvantage".[24] This group of scholars

---

[20] *Ibn Hajar al-Makkī al-Haithamī, S.,* Al-Fatāwā al-kubrā al-fiqhiya 'alā madhhab al-Imām al-Shāfi'ī, vol. 4. Beirut 1417/1997, 210.

[21] *Al-Najafī, M.*, Jawāhir al-kalām, v. 41, 254; *Al-Khwānsārī, S. A.*, Jāmi' al-madārik fī sharḥ mukhtaṣar al-nāfi', vol. 7. ed. by 'A. Ghaffārī. Tehran 1405/1985, 2.

[22] *Ibn al Humām*, Sharḥ, v. 5, 345.

[23] *Abū Zahra, M.,* al-Jarīma, 12-13.

[24] *Al-Ghazālī, M.*, al-Mustaṣfā fi 'ilm al-uṣūl, vol. 1. Beirut 1983, 286.

believes that commandments of religious law have been legislated to prevent people from committing this type of corruption.

This means that in line with punishing the offender in order to prevent him from corruption, there is a more basic target which is called protection of Islamic community. Although *prima facie* punishment is causing inconvenience and harm for him, it is in fact in his interest to not follow sin and corruption. Therefore punishments are inconvenient by their nature, but they are applied in order to remove corruption and promote social order. Al-Māwardī also considers *ta'zīr* punishments to have such a status when he says: "they are for disciplining, correcting and deterring" so that "they are differentiated as to their targets, taking in to account the difference of the sins".[25]

Likewise, some other Islamic jurists also state the target of these punishments to be the protection of the community against corruption and its cleansing from sin, and regard the severity of the *ḥudūd* punishments as a mercy, as they prevent people from committing crimes that are in fact oppressing them and making the community insecure. However, this implies making the proof of such crimes more difficult in order to not execute *ḥudūd* punishments so easily.[26] Some authors have considered preventing future crime and preventing damage to the community as the ultimate and final target of the *ḥudūd* crimes and they reiterated that the important factor in *ḥudūd* crimes is the protection of the Islamic community.[27]

In this case it cannot be said anymore that *ḥudūd* crimes are only retributive but they are also considered to follow, through retribution, a consequential approach, which consists of the protection of the Islamic community against corruption and harm. Some Islamic jurists also regard as acceptable and derivable from religious texts on punishment two obligations that have been considered in the new criminal law; first, the ethical obligation to educate and rehabilitate the offender to not commit a crime again, and second, the social obligation to support the community against the offender and his crime.[28]

To sum up the above explanations, it can be concluded that some jurists regard deterrence of committing crime as the target of punishments and they consider both the specific and general aspects of deterrence. Although this aim is common to

---

25 *Al-Māwardī al-Shafi'ī, A.* al-Aḥkām al-sulṭāniya, 236.

26 *Al-Zuhailī, W.*, al-Fiqh al-Islāmī wa-adillatuhu, Dimashq 1404/1984, 14.

27 *Al-Sha'rāwī, M.*, al-Fatāwā al-kubrā. Beirut 1422/2002, 614-615.

28 *Bahnasī, A. F.*, al-Siyāsa al-jazā'iya fī 'l-sharī'a al-Islāmiya. Beirut and Cairo 1409/1988, 270-271.

current criminal laws, Islamic jurists before that had tried long ago to theorize such purposes for punishment in an Islamic penal system. Besides this group of scholars, there were others who consider, based on their interpretation, that its aim is deterrence in line with a more general purpose, which consists of protecting the Islamic or Muslim community. However, they have considered the aim of punishment to be only correcting the offender or observed its final purpose to be correcting the offender and protecting the Islamic society.

2.2.2. Rehabilitation of the criminal

Some do not consider retribution and deterrence but rehabilitation of the criminal the aim of imposing punishment. Several reasons can be provided for this theory some of which can be found in sayings of Islamic jurists and lawyers.

a) Acceptance of repentance

Some Shiite commentators have defined the concept that is closest to "repentance" in Islamic law, *tawba*, as a dual concept that encompasses both *tawba* by God, i.e. forgiveness, which is a return to the human because of mercy, and *tawba* by the human, i.e. repentance, which is a return to God by retraction and abandoning sin.[29] Reversion from sin, return to obedience and contrition for sin[30] also have been mentioned in the definition of repentance. In most of the definitions that have been provided for repentance in religious law, we find reversion to God, obedience and refraining from sins. It is a systematic feature that crime or sin has divine aspects in a more general interpretation. As al-Qurtubī has told, repentance is not due to fear or in order to gain an advantage, but is purely for the sake of God, as the repentant feels ashamed before God[31] and does not only resolve to do righteous works but also carries them out as he understands the indecency of sin; as the Quran says: "and, o believers turn to Allah all together, in order that you prosper" (24: 31). Also, he mentions repentance and its signs and speaks about them as purification: "...except he who repents and believes and does good works, Allah will change their evil deeds into good deeds; Allah is ever forgiving and merciful" (25: 70); "...he who repents and does good works truly turns to Allah in repentance (25: 71)".

---

29 *Ṭabāṭabā'ī, S. M.*, al-Mizān v. 1, 133; idem, v. 4, 246.

30 *Ṣāliḥ, Ā.*, Al-Tawba fī daw' al-Qur'ān al-Karīm. Jidda 1419/1998, 18.

31 *Al-Qurtubī, A.*, Tafsīr al-Qurtubī: al-jāmi' li-aḥkām al-Qur'ān, v. 5. Cairo 1987, 91.

Imam Muḥammad Ghazālī believes that repentance is formed by three matters: recognition, status (*ḥāl*) and acting. Recognition is the identification of the sin and its danger; status is pain and suffering in the repentant's soul from such harm that is called regret, and acting is refraining from sin and doing what is possible to repair the damage in the future.[32] The Quran at (66:8) defines real repentance, *naṣūḥ*, which can, in brief, be interpreted as the repentant avoiding sin for the sake of God through identifying the indecency of sin and its harm on himself, being regretful about the past because of the sin that he has committed knowingly or unknowingly and deciding to not return to that sin and to do good works, exert obedience and ask God's servants to forgive him through paying their claims or satisfying them in another way.[33]

According to al-Ghazālī, the importance of repentance is so high that Islamic jurists and theologians are in consensus to regard it as obligatory for believers.[34] Repentance of sin is considered possible, from the context of the verses in the Quran and from the Hadiths, irrespective if the crime is major or minor, intentional or unintentional and committed knowingly or unknowingly: "when those who believe in our verses come to you, say: 'Peace be upon you. Your Lord has decreed mercy on himself, if any one of you commits evil through ignorance, and then repents and mends his ways, then he is forgiving, most merciful'". So it was not without reason that Quran promised believers that their sins will be changed to good deeds if they repent and correct themselves. An important condition of repentance is doing good deeds and continuing them (4:18; 3:135).

As to verses and Hadiths about repentance, they indicate the effect of repentance on these sins and show that this effect is purifying. In the verses about the punishment of *muḥāraba* or *hirāba*, the Quran mentions repentance as an excuse that exempts the perpetrator from the *ḥudūd* punishment (5: 34; 4:16).

This article does not intend to discuss legal and jurisprudential issues relating to repentance, e.g. for which crimes or sins it has been accepted and the reasons for that in the quotes of various sayings. What matters here is that, considering famous quotations of Islamic jurists that accept repentance in case of minor sins based on texts and reasons, and also considering above all its acceptance in case of major sins and given that it has been prescribed in Islamic criminal law for all *ḥudūd* crimes except, in certain circumstances, for the *ḥadd* of *muḥāraba*, we see that

32 *Al-Ghazālī, M.*, al-Wajīz fī 'l-fiqh al-Shāfi'ī, vol. 2. N.p. n.d. 3.
33 *Ṣāliḥ, Ā.*, Al-Tawba, 21.
34 *Al-Ghazālī, M.*, al-Wajīz, v. 4, 5.

repentance as one of the features of Islamic criminal law emphasizes the rehabilitation of the offender. It is also relevant that repentance is embedded into a legal system whose basic reference points are divine and transcendent. Basically, crime is considered in the first rank a sin and a violation of the commandments of God and in the second rank a violation of the rights of humans and Islamic society. Its penal system contains these commandments that have intertwined heavenly-earthly features. In this system, punishment is not the only way of deterring from sin or crime, because sin or crime are considered disassociation between human beings and God. God has made repentance a means for believers to return, and it appears that the Quran rarely mentions sin without also mentioning the possibility of repentance and retraction. When the offender is judged in this world there are efforts not to punish him with a *ḥadd* punishment so far as this is possible. This is apparent in the principle of *Dara ul-ḥadd*, which means the non-enforcement of *ḥadd* punishment in cases of doubt and difficulty of proving the crime. In a social context in which most people accept the commandments of religious law because of their belief in God and not due to the force or fear of punishment, rehabilitation and return to God is considered the basis of repentance and due to this the Quran has mentioned it as being close to rehabilitation by describing repentance as converting sins into good deeds.

Another important fact is that repentance must be accepted before the initiation of the prosecution or arrest, or, if after that, in any event before the testimony of witnesses, and that it has to follow a confession. The impossibility to accept repentance except in these cases shows that a true repentant is regretful about his action and is trying to compensate for his sin and his crime.[35] Accordingly, he must not be punished before a judgment or other conditions have been fulfilled. All acts of repentance have to take place before the initiating proceedings or the hearing of evidence. After that, repentance cannot be accepted and the perpetrator has to be punished. Perhaps it can be said that the legislator in the community of Muslims and believers seeks two types of aims in *ḥudūd* crimes: rehabilitation through encouraging repentance and return before initiating proceedings, and taking evidence and exacting retribution after having taken evidence. Some people say that an offender who has repented has in fact corrected himself because repentance is a sign of rehabilitation and of the purification of the offender. Therefore, punishing him is useless because the aim of punishment is also rehabilitation, an aim then already achieved through repentance. This statement can be criticized because it does not go far enough: as repentance has a purifying effect in Islamic

[35] *Shīrī, 'A.*, Suqūṭ-i mujāzāt dar ḥuqūq-i kaifarī-yi Islām va Īrān, Tehran 1372/1993, 55-94.

religious law, the repentant cannot be called offender anymore. What is more, repentance converts sins into good deeds according to the statement of Quran. In this case a punishment is not merely useless, but it is even unjust. If we only call it useless, this suggests that there remains a right to punish the offender, but that a choice is made not to exercise that right because the aim of punishment, namely rehabilitation, has been achieved beforehand. However, as the offender in such a case has been purified based on Quranic rules, and thus cannot be called an offender anymore, it is even contrary to the law and unjust to punish him. Of course, this statement does not conflict with the idea that the basis of punishment is the rehabilitation of the offender.

The opinion that rejects repentance after the arrest of the perpetrator (according to a quotation) or after the taking of evidence may be due to the fear that an offender who knows that there is evidence against him makes a declaration of his repentance in order to escape punishment because every perpetrator will after being arrested try to find a legal loophole to escape from punishment.

Considering the attention that God has paid to repentance, how have criminal laws dealt with it? Section 5 of the Islamic Penal Code deals with the repentance of the offender. Article 114 addresses repentance in case of *ḥudūd* punishments:

> In the case of offences punishable by *ḥadd*, with the exception of *qadhf* and *muḥāraba*, if the accused repents any time before the commission of the offense is proved, and his regret and correction is certain in the eyes of the judge, the *ḥadd* punishment shall not be given. In addition, if the abovementioned offenses, except for *qadhf*, are proved by confession, if the offender repents, even after the commission of the offense is proved, the court, through the Head of Judiciary, can apply for pardon of the offender by the Leader.

However, according to explanatory note 1 to this article, "If a *muḥārib* repents before he is arrested or held in custody, the *ḥadd* punishment shall not be given". This reflects an encouraging policy in the criminal laws of many countries in the field of crimes against public security, that encourages the disclosure of crimes and the effective cooperation in crime detection. In the cases of *zinā* (adultery) and *liwāṭ (sodomy)*, where the offense is committed by force or coercion or deception of the victim, if the offender repents and the *ḥadd* punishment is not given according to this article, he shall be sentenced to a *ta'zīr* imprisonment or to *ta'zīr* flogging, or both, of the sixth degree (Note 2 of article 114).

In *ta'zīr* punishments, which consist of almost all crimes except those categorized as *qiṣāṣ*, *diyāt* and *ḥudūd* (10 offences), repentance is accepted according to article 115 if the crime is of one of the lesser degrees: "In the case of *ta'zīr* offenses of the sixth, seventh, or eighth degree, if the offender repents and his regret and correction is certain in the eyes of the judge, the punishment shall not be given. In other *ta'zīr* offenses, [if the offender repents], the court can apply the provisions relating to mitigation of the punishment.

Note 1- The provisions relating to repentance shall not be applied on individuals to whom the provisions of re-offending of *ta'zīr* offenses are applicable.

Note 2- Provisions of this article, as well as paragraph (b) of article 7 and paragraphs (a) and (b) of article 8, and also articles 28, 39, 40, 45, 46, 92, 93, and 105 of this law shall not be applicable to *ta'zīr* offenses prescribed in Shari'a".

Sheikh Baha'i, like many Islamic jurists, regards repentance as abortive of *ta'zīr* punishment absolutely and without any obligation and condition.[36] A further interesting fact is that the Mu'tazilite reading of verse 31 in Sura an-Nisā' considers that avoiding major sins leads to the forgiveness of minor sins.[37] This point of view within Islamic criminal laws can serve as a source of change and in this view the above provision of the Islamic Penal Code of Iran is to be criticised, because it is limited to some of the *ta'zīr* crimes and does not provide a defense in relation to crimes that fall under the 1st to 5th degrees of punishment, which are more serious crimes than those where repentance is accepted. The legislature in Iran has usually tried to match the Islamic Penal Code with traditional Islamic criminal law in terms of the classification of crimes and punishments, but its steps in the adoption of institutions of mercy like repentance have been prudently and slowly. It seems that in this respect Iranian criminal law has operated in a discriminatory way and has taken on only part of Islamic religious law, not the whole of it.

If repentance is capable of cancelling *ḥudūd* punishments, why should it not have any effect on other punishments, especially serious *ta'zīr* punishments? As repentance must be accepted as an institution of Islamic law, why should we not clearly address the conditions of accepting repentance more in detail and discuss its acceptance by judges in cases where the defendant or offender refers to and cites repentance as a defense? According to recent judgments, the payment of damages to the injured person, the reaching of satisfaction for victims and the cooperation

36 *Al-'Āmilī (Sheikh Bahā'ī), B.*, Jāmi'-i 'Abbāsī. Tehran n.d., 429.

37 *Al-Qumī al-Nīshabūrī, H.*, Gharā'ib al-Qur'ān wa-raghā'ib al-furqān, v. 5. Beirut 1398/1978.

with judicial officials and officers are expressions of the regret of sins and proof of repentance.

As the last point, it is necessary to say that according to article 116 of the Islamic Penal Code, repentance is not considered a defense to *diya* and *qiṣāṣ* offences because *diya* (blood money) is an individual claim and, even though murder is a crime that violates both individual and public rights, *qiṣāṣ* as the main punishment for such an offence addresses mainly the right of victim or his family and has priority.

b) The possibility of forgiveness

Acceptance of forgiveness is the second element in some forms of punishment that can be regarded as related to the aim of correction. In several cases the Holy Quran has suggested to forgive the offender and the sinful. In this regard, the first and the most important verse of all is verse 40 of Sura al-Shūrā. Although the first sentence of this verse (as set out above), refers to retribution in punishments, it goes on to express that forgiveness has the aim to put matters in order and that, when it is applied, the aim of punishment is satisfied, too.

Some of verses and Hadiths about forgiveness are general and some are specific. In the case of *ḥudūd* crimes – which are to the most part absolute Rights of Allah – is considered permissible with the approval of the Imam in the case of repentance after confession. In *qiṣāṣ* and *diyāt* forgiveness is considered permissible if it is given by the next of kin or the victim because these crimes concern rights of people. In the case of *ta'zīrāt* it is considered a ground for exemption from punishment and in some cases a ground that leads to commutation of punishment (Articles 96, 97, 98, 219 of Islamic penal Code).

Forgiveness after repentance has the same effects as repentance, but forgiveness in relation to crimes that concern the rights of people, which is given by the victim, only leads to impunity or the commutation of punishment and does not have the purifying effect of repentance. Repentance is the inner transformation of a sinful person and a sign of his return to God while forgiveness is a sign of the valour of the complainant and rightful owner of the right to *qiṣāṣ* or *diya* and cannot have any other effect on the culprit than impunity or commutation of punishment. The importance of forgiveness in Islam shall be explained briefly with a principle in verse 40 of Sura al-Shūrā. As already mentioned, Islamic jurists have generally considered this verse to state that an evil must be compensated by its equal and not the same evil by a greater one; in other words, they deduce from this verse of the Quran the equality and proportionality of punishment with the crime. However, some Islamic commentators and mystics have interpreted the verse in another way. Islamic mystics do not deduce the principle of retaliation or equality in punishment from this Holy verse, but believe it to state that the reaction to sin and crime is likewise an evil. In other words, when speaking of evil against evil, it means that punishment is an evil pit against crime, which is an evil, too. In this line of thought, punishment should not exist unless in cases where God has stated it. It is for this reason that God after expressing this phrase says "if you forgive the offender, it will be a benefit. Benefit is in forgiveness and rehabilitation, not in punishment." Likewise, God said about the *qiṣāṣ* crimes: "He who is pardoned by his brother, let the ensuing be with kindness, and let the payment be with generosity. This is an alleviation from your Lord and mercy. He who transgresses thereafter shall have a painful punishment" (2: 178). Likewise, it is for the same reason that after stating the punishment of *qiṣāṣ* for murder, God says that it is better to forgive.

For this reason Ibn 'Arabī, one of the great theorists of theoretical mysticism, sees life in refraining from exercising a *qiṣāṣ* punishment, not in exercising it. This is because with the former another person – who is a creature of God – is not killed and survives through the forgiveness of the next of kin of the victim.[38] The late 'Allama Ṭabāṭabā'ī in interpreting verse 40 Sura al-Shūrā has regarded this quotation as the possible reason that the phrase of "Surely, He does not love the harm doers" might imply that the penalty for an evil is an evil, without considering similarity and equality.[39]

In a Hadith from the Holy Prophet of Islam it has been mentioned that it is upon a person to forgive. Forgiveness only increases the esteem of the person who forgives in the eyes of his fellow humans. It has been quoted from one of the Shiite Imams, that regret over forgiveness is better and easier than regret over punishment.[40] Accordingly, Islamic doctrine at the same time as suggesting forgiveness in relation to the rights of people, gives the Imam the authority to forgive an offender against the rights of Allah, after repentance and under the conditions that have been mentioned.

---

[38] *Faiż, 'A.*, Mafhūm-i kaifar dar 'irfān-i Ibn 'Arabī. In: Fażlnāma-yi Dānishgāh-i 'Ulūm-Islāmī-yi Razavī, No. 9 & 10. (2003), 39-57 (47-57).

[39] *Ṭabāṭabā'ī, S. M.*, al-Mizān fi tafsīr al-Qur'ān, vol. 18. Qom, 1363/1984, 94.

[40] *Kulainī, M.* Uṣūl al-kāfī, vol. 2. Tehran n.d., 8.

The difference is that forgiveness after repentance is actually founded on the rehabilitation of the offender, while forgiveness in relation to the rights of people is founded on the forgiving of the complainant and/or the person entitled to damages that can be a sign of the culprit's effort to change the situation and the conditions that have been caused by the crime. Obtaining satisfaction and forgiveness of the rightful owner can be a sign of that regret as it may be a ground for escaping from punishment. However, the justification for the fact that forgiveness can prevent executing punishment or lead to commutation in relation to crimes that concern the rights of people is that the offender could rehabilitate himself or rehabilitate the relation between himself and the victim. In both cases, there is no longer any need to apply punishment because of forgiveness. Of course, it is clear that in this case the justifying power of forgiveness for the rehabilitation aspect of punishment is limited only to those cases in which forgiveness is accepted, and not to other cases.

Acceptance of forgiveness is not only a basis for discerning an aim of reform or rehabilitation in Islamic law, but it has also been an important basis for developing the theory of restorative justice and mediation in the Islamic Penal Code of Iran (articles 82-84).

c) Exile and prison following acceptance of repentance in muḥāraba

Some supporters of rehabilitation as an aim of punishment influenced by quotations of many Islamic jurists such as Imam Muḥammad al-Ghazālī and Mardāwī [41] support continuing the exile punishment for the *Muḥārib* in Shafii and Shia jurisprudences, or the prison punishment in Hanafi jurisprudence until the "repentance of the offender or his rehabilitation" are proved.[42] The idea behind this statement is the same as that behind the theory of rehabilitation, and opinions from the field of criminology consider it a necessary condition of rehabilitation and treatment, namely to accept an uncertain condemnation so that the judge is able to continue rehabilitation measures until the rehabilitation of the offender is proved. This line of thought is completely contrary to the principle of legality of punishment that has been accepted in criminal laws.

Of course, criminal law has moderated itself influenced by this criminological point of view by accepting some institutions such as probation and suspension of

---

41 *Al-Ghazālī, M.*, al-Wajīz, v. 2, 179; *Mardāwī, A.*, al-Insāf fī ma'rifa al-rājiḥ min al-khilāf fī fiqh al-Imām al-Aḥmad, vol. 10. Cairo 1957, 298.

42 *Al-'Awā', M. S.*, Darāmadī bar uṣūl-i niẓām-i kaifarī-yi Islām, Qom 1385/2006, 39.

punishment and the like, but it did not desist from the principle of the legality of punishment. According to article 284 of the Islamic Penal Code, the duration of exile of a *muḥārib* is to be not less than one year but if he does not repent, the exile is to continue.

Looking at the legal argument more broadly, the availability of different punishments and the discretion of the judge in the selection of one of the punishments for the offence of *muḥāraba* have been regarded as signs that the target of rehabilitation is accepted in Islamic criminal law. Although this argument applies to specific cases and a general rule cannot be inferred from that, some Shafeis believe that the judge's discretion in the punishment of a *muḥārib* is not provided for to determine a proportionate punishment to the crime itself, but to choose the type of punishment that is most suitable to the offender with regard to the rehabilitation aspect.[43]

In fact, this theory as mentioned in some fatwas of Shiite jurisprudents such as Sheikh Tūsī, is able to tailor the punishment for the crime of *muḥāraba* to the offender and his conditions. However, it is Imam Al-Haramein Jovini who raises an interesting and delicate idea that has been very progressive for legal thought in the fifth century after the hijra, and that emphasizes that the individualization of penalties and the tailoring of punishment to the offender have a history of approximately 100 years in legal and criminological thought "… if it is assumed that a sanction that is in line with the crime does not prevent the culprit from committing the crime again, punishments such as execution should be not executed as the punishment of that crime and the sanction imposed on this offender are absolutely senseless".[44]

However, most people who consider rehabilitation a target for punishment are contemporary thinkers[45] and they mostly accept it for *ta'zīr* punishments. However, as it was mentioned above, even many Islamic jurists who had considered deterrence as target of religious law punishments regard the rehabilitation of the offender as the purpose.

At the end of this part, some points should be considered. In Islamic jurisprudence the aim of *iṣlāḥ* (rehabilitation) has not been clarified. If the purpose is to avoid committing crimes again or prevention of crime, how could we

---

[43] *Malik ibn Anas*, al-Mudawwana al-kubrā, vol. 16. Beirut n.d., 298-300; *Ibn Ḥazm al-Andalusī, 'A.*, Al-Muhallā bi-'l-āthār, vol. 11. Beirut n.d., 317.

[44] Quoted by *Al-'Awā', M. S.*, Darāmadī, 40.

[45] *Gurjī, 'A.*, Maqālāt-i ḥuqūqī, vol. 2. Tehran 1365/1986. V. 1: 65; *Al-'Arīs*, H., Shakhsiyat, 98.

distinguish between the consequences of deterrence and rehabilitation? It is possible that the offender does not commit a crime for fear of penalty and not due to regret and rehabilitation. It is possible that their purposes are discipline and re-compatibility with Islamic laws. In this case the framework is rehabilitation of a person's behavior. Again, in this assumption it is not clear how punishment which imposes only pain and affliction on the perpetrator (except in exceptional cases such as exile that provides an opportunity to think and change) can be a source of rehabilitation. A measure that has developed in modern times under the name of rehabilitation and treatment is imprisonment which has been introduced as the most important and effective method of rehabilitating the offender so that some facilities and opportunities are considered to rehabilitate the culprit. It seems unlikely that rehabilitation of an offender can be possible in case of the types of punishment that have been determined in *ḥudūd* and *ta'zīr* crimes, especially due to the character of the specific, fixed *ḥudūd* punishments the *ta'zīr* punishment of whipping in the traditional thought of Islamic jurisprudence. In this case, deterrence of the offender and others from the commitment of crime will be an acceptable and meaningful target.

Second, *qiṣāṣ* and execution in *ḥudūd* make the rehabilitation of an offender impossible, so such an aim is rendered impossible under these punishments. This claim is true in relation to *ta'zīrāt* based on the Islamic punishment law. However it can be accepted that in a new form of legislation concerning *ta'zīrāt*, the rehabilitation target may be included as one of the targets of punishments. The aim of rehabilitation has been supported in the new Islamic Penal Code of Iran by developing new correctional institutions like community-based punishments, parole, probation, suspension of punishment, the regime of "half release" (open prison) and the application of different security and correctional measures for adult and juvenile offenders.

3. Ultimate Review

3.1. Purpose or purposes

According to studies which have been done in the field of the philosophy of punishment, punishment can be considered to have one aim or multiple aims. Of course, this issue is not incalculable. It is different depending on the question which theory we adopt in other important philosophical issues. The aim of punishment cannot be different from and inconsistent with the theories and insights which we have in more fundamental issues. From the perspective of comparative study, there is not a single purpose of punishment, but different goals are considered, including retribution, deterrence, rehabilitation and defending and protecting society and public order. It was not traditional in the criminal system of many countries like Iran to mention the aim or aims of punishments, but this topic is discussed in scholarship and doctrine especially since this problem raises an aspect of penal philosophy in comparison with the aspect of legal technicality. However, in recent years we have seen a change whereby as far as possible some countries have tried to insert the purpose or basic purposes intended by the legislator into criminal legislation and to consider other, subsidiary aims. For example, in section 46 of the German Penal Code it has been provided that "the guilt of the offender is the basis for sentencing. The effects which the sentence can be expected to have on the offender's future life in society shall be taken into account". So, the primary aim in sentencing is guilt (retributive approach) and the rehabilitative aim stands in second place.[46] In some legal systems such as the Model Penal Code of America the aims are mentioned as a whole without considering superiority of one over another. Of course, each of these two approaches has its own implications and results that cannot be dealt with in this paper. Punishment can have more than one purpose, on the condition that it is justifiable in the context of a theory. For example, if we consider retribution as the main purpose of punishment, blaming the offender could be regarded as the formal expression of condemnation in criminal law; a blame that is embodied in punishment implies that certain types of behavior are false and the variety of punishments reflects the degree of blame. Humans as ethical agents are informed about the reasons for staying away from prohibited behavior. An offender is considered responsible for his behavior based on free will, in a way that he can

[46] According to the part 2 of section 46 "When sentencing the court shall weigh the circumstances in favour of and against the offender. Consideration shall in particular be given to:

- ✓ the motives and aims of the offender;
- ✓ the attitude shown by the offence and the degree of force of will involve in its commission;
- ✓ the degree of the violation of the offender's duties;
- ✓ the modus operandi and the consequences caused by the offence to the extent that the offender is to blame for them;
- ✓ the offender's prior history, his personal and financial circumstances;
- ✓ his conduct after the offence, particularly his efforts to make restitution for the harm caused as well as the offender's efforts at reconciliation with the victim."

understand the results of his actions, foresee them and understand the effects of punishment on him. Hence it is said that punishment can be considered a retribution to the offender and a deterrent factor at the same time. Therefore, the blame is based on the person's sense of ethical responsibility, but a human being is fallible and may be inclined to commit evil. Therefore, he needs more reasons to avoid the temptation to commit an evil or punishable behavior (crime). Punishment is known as a barrier against committing crime. A person who knows that he should not commit a crime, and also accepts this, may nevertheless be tempted to commit a crime. In such a case, punishment can be seen as an aid to behave properly. However, "the blaming function has primacy, the prudential disincentive function has only a secondary role, and the level of punishment should not be set too high or fear will displace the moral response".[47] In this justification, the retribution of the individual based on blameworthiness is the principal aim and deterrence is to be considered a subsidiary target. In this case, if we do not reach our deterrent aim, the theory could not be confronted with serious challenges, because deterrence, reform and rehabilitation, preservation of public order and community are result-oriented aims and impose punishment for palpable benefit. So, the evaluation of penal measures and the way in which criminal justice institutions operate should also be possible in this set of theories, and should be an integral part of the judgment. The logical result of the acceptance of such theories is the possibility and necessity of assessing and evaluating actions of the penal system. Criminological studies were undertaken and have evaluated the criminal law and its actions in this field. The result is also clear: adjustment, and probably a change in strategies, actions and adopted mechanisms against crime and delinquency, should be realized.

So, none of these goals may be accepted regardless of their logical implications. Acceptance of two or more targets for punishment, without giving priority to one of them, means to expect the consequences of punishments simultaneously and totally. But it seems that this will not be possible without establishing a logical and functional order and coherence among them. For example, retribution and reform cannot be both expected from punishment together. The first one is based on what the offender justly deserves and backward-looking, and the second one is to rehabilitate the offender and forward-looking. So, the rehabilitative aim, unlike the retributive one, would be assessable and its results can force us to changes that are not necessarily in line with the first aim, unless we justify the principle of

47 Easton and Piper, Sentencing, 62.

legitimacy of punishments with the first, and the degree of punishment with the second.

So, a simultaneous follow-up of targets is possible, if as much as possible one target is given priority and the other rests to be considered subsidiary. Of course, this does not prevent considering for specific crimes or offenders, such as children and adolescent, reform to be the main purpose and one of the other purposes to be subsidiary. The absence of a theoretical attitude to punishment as an institution and to the ways and methods they could be inflicted is one of the main problems in the theory of punishment in Islamic law.

3.2. The variety of aims of punishment

In the literature on the targets of punishments in Islamic criminal law which was mentioned above, less philosophical attempt can be seen to offer a coherent theory. Even Sunni jurists and lawyers of Islamic countries did not evaluate this sensitive issue but have tried, by referring to the original texts of Islamic law, to explain the likely purposes of punishment. Of course, this effort is valuable and useful. At least it suggests that the punishment of the offender, it being not only a matter of worship but also a formal governmental response to a social phenomenon, should be justified or explained. However, one cannot ignore that there exists an amount of general, deep philosophical discussion of the political and deep legal aspects and also the sociological subject matter that is considered vital and necessary to criminal law. To this extent, we have tried to answer the question of why we punish without asking ourselves a number of other questions: how much punishment is to be imposed? Which punishment would be effective? In which society and for which categories of offenders is it applicable? Can a theory be offered without considering the effect and importance of these basic components, and can it be expected to get the right answer and the expected results? It seems that an important part of the problems in the criminal justice system in Iran can be explained with the lack of such a theoretical coherence. We cannot regard criminal law, and especially its punishments, as incapable of being assessed under the pretext of legitimacy of the penal system while most of its aims that have been stated are assessable.

According to the first part of this paper, the idea was presented that *ḥudūd* punishments are at their core retributive and that they are implemented to achieve justice. This opinion is not popular among scholars and jurists who have written about it, because most of them primarily regard prevention of the offender and others from committing crime as the main purpose of punishments, including *ḥudūd*, *qiṣāṣ*, and *ta'zīr* punishments. Accordingly, some have considered the prevention of others from committing crime the primary and basic target of punishment. Some scholars have also considered other targets of religious punishments especially for *ta'zīr* punishments in addition to the target of deterrence. The most important of these is reform of the offender and the protection of the community of Muslims. Summing up all views it can perhaps be said that most of the jurists and scholars regard deterrence of crime to be the most important and most fundamental target of punishment, and other targets, such as the reform of the offender and the protection of the community, to be subsidiary targets. According to what was mentioned above, views that believe in deterrence in the case of *ḥudūd* cannot remain faithful to the results of this theory, because they believe that such punishments are fixed and unchangeable. Punishment cannot be fixed forever and be considered as a deterrent. This is because deterrence refers to the offender and the community in which he and others live as a general and special target, respectively. If then society or the offender regard a punishment for any reason, even contrary to that scholar's opinion, as unfair or inhumane, such a punishment cannot be assumed as a suitable means for reaching a utilitarian aim. The basis and the social role of punishments are different in every community, in every society. What is considered punishment in one society may be considered inhumane in another society. Thus, do we say this punishment is a deterrent in any social context, even for people who regard it as inhumane? Do we want to achieve a result by imposing a punishment that is not a repetition of crime? Not only pain and suffering may be effective.

If we expect punishment to reform and rehabilitate the offender, we cannot ignore the social opinion about the nature and functions of punishment and its place with regard to human dignity, the meaning and implication of which may change in the course of time. Maybe for this reason in article 225 of the new Penal Code the possibility of converting the punishment of stoning into a regular death sentence or into one hundred lashes has been prescribed. Hence it can be said that the *ḥudūd* crimes, are in essence based more on the retribution theory than on deterrence. In their case it can be said that other targets, such as deterrence and rehabilitation, are considered subsidiary targets.

Another point that should not be overlooked is the difference between the unchangeability of a value with the unchangeability of a reaction against the violation of that value. Religious law may prohibit or require, or regard as a red line, certain behavior for multiple reasons. If the reaction against it is considered to aim at preventing others from violating such a value, can we say that the reaction caused by this punishment is always uniform in all societies? If we pursue justice based on the acceptance of retribution, must we clearly explain what the meaning of justice is, what sources it inspire and whether, for example, collective wisdom can contribute to the understanding of justice and to determining what action is just or not? If the response to that last question is positive, we should accept the assessment of punishment and seek apply its consequences in practice. Punishment is one of the basic issues that all governments have to deal with as it plays an important role in social life. Therefore, as punishment is related to the political and social life of people and also to political theory governing policy, it is subject to targets and intentions. The views which have been taken by some Islamic jurists and scholars arguing that *ḥudūd* punishments are not applicable in an era where there is no infallible leadership (*aṣr-i ġaibat*),[48] do not seek to deny values that have been respected in Islamic criminal law or deny the necessity of criminalizing the violation of the values that are protected by *ḥudūd* punishments. But they believe that such punishments not only do not have any interest and utility, but are also in conflict with the final aims of inflicting punishment and the aims a harmonic system of criminal law tries to reach. Accordingly, for resolving this problem, we should make a distinction between the ideas behind the criminalization of breaching an unchangeable value on the one hand, and the unchangeability of punishments, or the reaction against such breaches, one the other hand.

In relation to *qiṣāṣ* punishments, the theory of specific deterrence or rehabilitation of the offender cannot be accepted unless pardon or forgiveness are made to be considered deterrent or corrective, either alone or with the help of the *ta'zīr* punishment. In this case, deterrence and rehabilitation are not the targets of *qiṣāṣ*, but also refer to forgiveness and *ta'zīr*. Accordingly, in the case of *qiṣāṣ* – like in the case of *ḥudūd*-retribution is considered the main aim of punishment and general deterrence can be considered the subsidiary target.

In the case of *ta'zīr* punishments – which are the punishments applying to most crimes and therefore require more and deeper attention in explaining the targets of punishment – because of the authority of the state to criminalize and punish

---

48 According to Twelver Shiite doctrine, Sufis, and some Sunni Muslims, the Twelfth Imam (Mahdi, al-Hujja) has been hidden and will return with Christ. He will reestablish the rightful governance of Islam and provide the earth with justice and peace. The term "aṣr-i ġaibat" describes that time of hiding, including the Present, during which no rightful governance by the Twelfth Imam exists.

wrongful behaviors, there is no major theoretic obstacle for providing a proper theory of punishment. *Ta'zīr* punishments are also based – as explained above – on the view that the main target is deterrence, although some voices have stated deterrence and rehabilitation as the targets of this set of punishments. It seems that so far the legislator has not followed a specific target in developing and deducting punishments by considering the development of the way of Islamic criminal law. Its amount, the kind of punishments enacted and the actions taken have not been systematic. Therefore it cannot really be said which theory has been followed. However, it can be said, that both the targets of deterrence and rehabilitation have been advanced in parallel, so that in some cases rehabilitation and in other cases deterrence has been superior to the other. For example in relation to prison sentences, taking into account the provisions of the Security and Corrective Measures Law and Regulations of the Prisons Organization approved on November 23, 2005 as well as the provisions relating to parole and suspension, the rehabilitation target is more prominent than deterrence, while in the case of flogging and fines it is the opposite.

3.3. Correlation of theories of punishment with other social and cultural factors

When we speak of punishment, our intention is not only a simple, formal reaction against the crime and the offender. Punishment needs a theory to justify it and that is in turn based on a theory that legitimates and justifies criminalization. Punishment and the form it takes is created, legitimated and implemented in an intertwined context of the criminal justice system that cannot be separated. It is not possible to accept some parts of it and to ignore others. The justification of punishment as a formal, coercive reaction against a wrongful conduct is more complex than explaining some possible aims by referring to semiotics in a religious context. This is because a proper, philosophical account of punishment requires acceptance of its logical or philosophical necessities. The Islamic criminal law system, as is clear, was legislated for a society that believes in Islam and accepts its rulings. It is expected that believers obey the religious laws and rules, ideally for the sake of the Lord, but at least for fear of eternal punishment more than for fear of the application of temporal punishment. Why should a sinner be presented to the Prophet or Imam Ali and despite their efforts to dissuade him from confession, confess to his sin repeatedly?[49] The answer can be found in a phrase that the offender has used regarding his faith and that is: "purify me by punishing". This is because he believed that punishment has a cleansing effect and saves him from divine retribution. Without the element of belief in God's

[49] *Nūrī Tabarsī, M.*, Mustadrak al-wasā'il, vol. 18. Qom 1407/1986, 377-381.

commandments punishment cannot not lead to its aim or aims. For this reason it is said that "According to the usual and acceptable definition of criminologists, sentencing can have a repairing and compensating effect for the community, but by this definition, punishment is never eligible for forgiveness and atonement in its Islamic meaning. Although the unbeliever may have suffered punishment, he will never feel the sense of forgiveness that a faithful person would do."[50] Punishment is essential to the protection of the rights of individuals and society. But when it is applied and implemented in the form of a legal right, the other organs and requirements of a criminal law system cannot be ignored. At first Islam tried to educate and teach its principal theoretical foundations, then to implement binding rules. "The Book," "justice" and "Coercion" have been laid down in the Quran, and have come together and not separately. They are worked out systematically and have effect on each other. The system of punishment in the law consists of atonement, repentance, forgiveness and finally imposes punishment subject to important conditions, such as the principle of rigor in proof. The criminal system cannot ignore some of these things or pay little attention to them and at the same time emphasize on the implementation of the punishment alone.

Islamic punishments were formed within a society which had a tribal structure and, by the formation of an Islamic state in Medina, it experienced the first steps of the birth of a city-state. Only the values, rules and regulations of Islamic law prevailed on this society in which the populace believed and which it regarded as necessary for a continuous unity of thought, conscience and ethic. For this reason many of those who spoke about the goals and philosophy of legal punishment have regarded the preservation of Islamic society and its values a final goal. For this reason, it can be said that its criminal system was more socially-oriented than individualistic.

Muslim persons had the obligation to protect this community and a violation of it was worthy of punishment and retribution. This manner and form of behavior in human societies, especially in the past and even in some of today's smaller communities, are not unprecedented but are also considered a major basis of communities. Rationality is not a phenomenon of today but is also specific for communities with high social cohesion and strong mechanical relationships. This is

---

50 *Faiż, 'A.* (2003), Kaifar, 45.

not only a means to scrutinize the criminal systems of those days, but it is also a sign of their vitality and intelligence that was used from all the social capabilities along with religious teachings to preserve its acceptable values. Our criticism, by contrast, is that the criminal system could not ignore the development that has occurred in Muslim communities that has been inevitable. Criminal law is obliged to adapt itself based on abilities in these communities as well as its traditional constraints to be able to achieve its goals. And this is not in conflict with the idea of assuming some fixed values that was mentioned above.

4. Final Remarks

Punishments in Islamic criminal law have followed almost the same goals that in other legal systems have been regarded as the purpose of the sentencing system. Both the deontological targets in the forms of retribution theory and consequentialist goals such as deterrence, rehabilitation and the preservation of social order can be taken for granted for punishments in Islamic law, with the difference that maybe one of the goals has priority and the others are secondary. The priority of theories in this paper has been based on the nature and features of each category of punishment. On this basis, it is likely that in the case of *ḥudūd* and *qiṣāṣ* punishments, retribution is the main purpose and deterrence is a subsidiary purpose, while in the case of *ta'zīr* punishments the set of these goals can be considered manifold. Where the punishment is imprisonment, the first goal may be rehabilitation, and deterrence and protection of the community may be subsidiary purposes, while in the case of corporal punishments and fines deterrence is the main goal. The system of punishments in the current criminal system does not have all features associated with the legal system, and is also not fully customary. Some of the angles and dimensions of a criminal act that are a sin in the Islamic legal system are not reflected in the criminal law today. The traditional criminal law, which was set for a small and monocultural society, is selectively transferred to a society that essentially does not have all of the features that the Islamic community had in the beginning of Islam. This selective transferring of criminal policy has closed the way to theoretical coherence in the current Iranian criminal justice system, especially with regards to punishment. Justifying punishment in current Islamic societies will not be possible without justifying their political systems. Not only do the efforts of Islamic jurists focus on the explanation of the aims of punishment rather than their justification, but they have also been completely silent about the state's legitimacy and the justification of its authority to punish. Therefore, focusing on the aims of punishment in Islamic countries like Iran should devote attention to political problematics, i.e. state authority and legitimacy.

Schmähungen von *muqaddasāt* im iranischen Strafrecht[1]

Seyed Emadeddin Tabatabaei, Freiburg i.Br.

Vorbemerkung

In rechtsvergleichenden Arbeiten ist die Wiedergabe von Fachbegriffen von zentraler Bedeutung. Darum gehört diese zu den ersten Punkten, die dabei zu beachten sind. Für den folgenden Beitrag bedeutet das, dass weder die Begriffe *sabb* und *tauhīn* im iranischen Strafrecht als genaues Gegenstück von Schmähung, Beschimpfung oder Beleidigung übersetzt werden können, noch dass sich das Wort *muqaddasāt* genau mit den Begriffen Heiligtümer, heilige Personen oder heilige Werte deckt. Aber dennoch kann der Begriff Schmähung eine Annäherung an die iranischen Begriffe bieten. Dagegen ist keiner der obengenannten deutschen Begriffe geeignet, für *muqaddasāt* benutzt zu werden; vielmehr muss hier wie auch bei anderen Begriffen aus dem islamischen Recht – wie z. B. *ḥadd* – der arabische Begriff unübersetzt bleiben.

Dieser Artikel wirft zunächst einen Blick auf die Stellung der Religion im iranischen Rechtssystem. Dann beschreibt er die Schmähung von *muqaddasāt* im iranischen Gesetz und berichtet schließlich einige Fälle der Schmähung von *muqaddasāt* in der iranischen Praxis.

1. Die Stellung der Religion im iranischen Rechtssystem

Wenn man über das islamische Rechtssystem spricht, behandelt man ein theoretisches System, das epistemologisch Gott zum zentralen Bezugspunkt hat. Das ist im Kern der Unterschied zu den Denksystemen, die auf den Menschen bezogen sind. Auf der moralphilosophischen Ebene wird dann statt vom Menschen und seinen Rechten von den durch die göttliche Offenbarung auferlegten Pflichten gesprochen. Das führt uns auf der rechtsphilosophischen Ebene zur entscheidenden Bedeutung des religiösen Rahmens. Es besagt, dass Rechte und Freiheiten ausschließlich im Rahmen der Religion anerkannt sind.

[1] Der vorliegende Beitrag ist die leicht überarbeitete und ergänzte Fassung des Vortrags, der auf der Jahrestagung der Gesellschaft für Arabisches und Islamisches Recht am 21.10.2016 in Freiburg i. Br. gehalten wurde.

Die iranische Verfassung wie das unter ihrer Geltung definierte Strafrechtssystem basieren auf diesen Grundlagen. Das Erkennen solcher Grundlagen ist die Voraussetzung, um die verfassungsrechtlichen und strafrechtlichen Vorschriften zu verstehen und zu interpretieren.

1.1. Die Religion in der iranischen Verfassung

Die Verfassung der Islamischen Republik Iran definiert ihre Identität durch die Religion des Islam. Die iranische Verfassung beginnt mit dem Vers 57/25 des Korans, um die Stellung der Religion und die Stellung der Menschen in dem neugegründeten politischen System zu betonen:

> Wir haben unsere Gesandten mit den deutlichen Zeichen gesandt und mit ihnen das Buch und die Waage herabkommen lassen, damit die Menschen für die Gerechtigkeit eintreten.[2]

Der erste Satz der Präambel danach lautet dann:

> Die Verfassung der Islamischen Republik Iran ist Ausdruck der kulturellen, gesellschaftlichen, politischen und wirtschaftlichen Institutionen der iranischen Gesellschaft auf der Grundlage islamischer Prinzipien und Grundsätze.[3]

Nach Art. 2 der iranischen Verfassung ist die Islamische Republik eine Ordnung auf der Grundlage des Glaubens unter anderem an:

1. den einen Gott („es gibt keinen Gott außer Gott"), dem Herrschaft und Gesetzgebung zukommen, und die Notwendigkeit, sich in sein Gebot zu fügen;
2. die göttliche Offenbarung und ihre grundlegende Rolle für die Erklärung der Gesetze.

Basierend darauf sieht Art. 4 der iranischen Verfassung vor, dass sich alle Gesetze und Vorschriften nach islamischen Maßstäben zu richten haben. In

---

2 Übersetzung von *Khoury, A.T.* http://tanzil.net/#trans/de.khoury/57:25 (aufgerufen am 29.8.2017).

3 Deutsche Übersetzungen von Verfassungsartikeln sind hier und im Folgenden entnommen aus *Tellenbach, Silvia*, Untersuchungen zur Verfassung der Islamischen Republik Iran vom 15. November 1979, Berlin 1985. Ein englischer Text der Verfassung findet sich unter http://www.iranonline.com/iran/iran-info/government/constitution.html (aufgerufen am 29.8.2017).

einer solchen religiösen Gedankenwelt ist der Mensch ein Wesen, das vor Gott Pflichten hat. Genau deswegen sind das Gebieten des Rechten und das Verbieten des Verwerflichen nach Art. 8 der iranischen Verfassung eine alle angehende und gegenseitige religiöse Pflicht. Es muss auch beachtet werden, dass bei der Garantie der Pressefreiheit in Art. 24 diese ausdrücklich dadurch begrenzt ist, dass die Grundlagen des Islam und der allgemeinen Rechte nicht verletzt werden dürfen.

Nach Art. 12 der iranischen Verfassung ist der Islam die offizielle Religion der Islamischen Republik Iran, und zwar die zwölferschiitische Konfession. Dieser Artikel erkennt aber auch andere islamische Bekenntnisse an. Er gewährleistet, dass andere islamische Bekenntnisse voll respektiert werden und die Anhänger dieser Bekenntnisse bei der Ausübung ihrer religiösen Zeremonien nach ihrem Recht frei sind. Ferner erklärt Art. 13 Zoroastrismus, Judentum und Christentum zu anerkannten Religionen.

Außerdem gewährleistet Art. 14 die Menschenrechte aller Bürger ungeachtet ihrer Religionszugehörigkeit oder ihres Glaubens. Es sollte aber berücksichtigt werden, dass die Bedeutung und Definition der Menschenrechte in diesem Artikel umstritten ist und nicht unbedingt dem westlichen Verständnis entspricht. Ein klarer Unterschied ist die Quelle der Menschenrechte. Während die Menschenrechte im westlichen Verständnis aus der Natur des Menschen selbst entstehen, sind die Menschenrechte nach islamischem Verständnis von Gott gegeben. Nun ist die Frage, ob diese von Gott gewährten Menschenrechte wieder durch göttliche Vorschriften zurückgenommen werden könnten. Die Antwort auf diese Frage trennt Asch'ariten und Mu'taziliten in der islamischen Geschichte; die ersteren vertreten die Meinung, dass alles, was Gott in seiner Allmacht tut, gerecht ist, die letzteren sind der Auffassung, dass Gott nur im Rahmen der Gerechtigkeit handelt. Dieser Rahmen der Gerechtigkeit wurde bei den Mu'taziliten als rational und religionsunabhängig angesehen. Diese Lehre hat die schiitische Rechtsschule nach dem historischen Untergang der Mu'taziliten in der islamischen Welt übernommen, die – neben dem Glauben an die Einheit Gottes, die Gesandten Gottes, den jüngsten Tag und die Auferstehung – eine der Grundlagen der schiitischen Konfession bildet. Dieses Gerechtigkeitsprinzip spiegelt sich auch in Art. 2 der iranischen Verfassung wider. Dort ist die Gerechtigkeit Gottes in Schöpfung und Gesetzgebung der vierte Punkt bei der Aufzählung der Grundlagen des Glaubens, auf welche die Islamische Republik gegründet ist. Als weiteres Resultat des mu'tazilitischen Erbes könnte der Versuch der iranischen Verfassung zu einer Versöhnung zwischen der göttlichen und der menschlichen Herrschaft erwähnt werden, der in Art. 56 folgendermaßen formuliert wird:

> Die absolute Herrschaft über die Welt und den Menschen ist Gottes. Er ist es auch, der den Menschen zum Herrscher über sein gesellschaftliches Schicksal gemacht hat. Niemand kann dem Menschen dieses göttliche Recht entziehen oder es in den Dienst des Vorteils eines einzelnen oder einer besonderen Gruppe stellen. Die Nation wird dieses gottgegebene Recht so ausüben, wie in den nachfolgenden Artikeln ausgeführt wird.

Deshalb muss sich die Verwaltung der Angelegenheiten des Landes in der Islamischen Republik Iran auf den Volkswillen stützen (Art. 6).

1.2. Die Religion in einem islamischen Strafrecht

Das iranische Strafrechtssystem umfasst heutzutage das islamische Strafgesetzbuch von 2013, das *ta'zīrāt*-Gesetzbuch von 1996 und viele besondere Gesetze. Im klassischen islamischen Strafrecht sind die Strafen in vier Kategorien klassifiziert: *ḥadd, qiṣāṣ, diya* und *ta'zīr*.

Das islamische Strafgesetzbuch von 2013 bestimmt neben den allgemeinen Vorschriften vier Kategorien von Strafen: *ḥudūd*[4] (Pl. von *ḥadd*), *qiṣāṣ*[5] und *diya*[6] (Sg. von *diyāt*) und *ta'zīr* (Sg. von *ta'zīrāt*). Ein statistischer Blick auf dieses Gesetz zeigt, dass nach 217 Paragraphen mit allgemeinen Vorschriften, die *ḥudūd*-Strafen mit 71 Paragraphen 10 Straftaten erfassen; dagegen regeln die Vorschriften zu *qiṣāṣ* mit 158 Paragraphen und zu *diyāt* mit 279 Paragraphen nur 2 Straftaten. Alle anderen strafrechtlichen Vorschriften, allen voran im *ta'zīrāt*-Gesetzbuch von 1996 mit 227 Paragraphen, aber auch in zahlreichen Nebengesetzen gehören systematisch zur Gruppe der *ta'zīrāt*. Ihre Zahl beträgt insgesamt ca. 1500 Straftaten. Die gesetzliche Definition von *ta'zīrāt* lautet in Art. 18 Islamisches Strafgesetz (IStG):

---

4 Art. 15 IStG: „*Ḥadd*-Strafe ist eine Strafe genannt, deren Art, Maß, sowie Art und Weise der Vollstreckung in der heiligen Scharia festgelegt sind."

5 Art. 16 IStG: „Vergeltung ist die Hauptstrafe für vorsätzliche Tötungs- und Körperverletzungesdelikte, die in der im Dritten Buch dieses Gesetzes beschriebenen Weise angewendet wird."
Bei Vergeltung (*Qiṣāṣ)* entspricht die Strafe der Tat des Täters nach dem Prinzip der Spiegelstrafe.

6 Art. 17 IStG: „Blutgeld (*Diya)* ist eine Vermögensstrafe in der heiligen Scharia, die für unvorsätzliche Tötungs- und Körperverletzungesdelikte oder für vorsätzliche Tötungs- und Körperverletzungesdelikte in den Fällen, in denen es aus irgendwelchen Gründen keine Vergeltung gibt, vom Gesetzgeber für eine Straftat festgelegt ist."
Diya ist vom Gesetzgeber für vorsätzliche Tötung oder Körperverletzung festgelegt und wird dem Opfer oder seiner Familie – und nicht dem Staat – gezahlt.

Die *taʿzīr*-Strafe ist eine Strafe, die keine *ḥadd*-, *qiṣāṣ*- und *diya*-Strafen umfasst und durch Gesetz für die Fälle des Verstoßes gegen Verbote der Scharia oder Vorschriften des Gesetzgebers festgelegt und angewendet wird. Ihre Art, Maß sowie Art und Weise ihrer Vollstreckung, Regelungen zu Milderung, Strafaussetzung, Erlöschen und weitere *taʿzīr*-Vorschriften werden durch Gesetz bestimmt.

2. Schmähungen von *muqaddasāt* im Gesetz

Auf die Schmähungen von *muqaddasāt* beziehen sich drei Straftatbestände, ein Tatbestand im Buch über *ḥudūd* und zwei im Buch über *taʿzīrāt*. Wir werden sie in ihrer zeitlichen Reihenfolge darstellen.

2.1. Art. 513 *taʿzīrāt*-Gesetz (1996)

Chronologisch betrachtet ist Art. 513 *taʿzīrāt*-Gesetzbuch von 1996 über die Beleidigung von Heiligtümern des Islam die am längsten geltende Vorschrift:

> Wer die *muqaddasāt* des Islam, einen der erhabenen Propheten, einen der sündenreinen Imame oder die Wahrhaftige Reine verunglimpft, wird mit dem Tode bestraft, wenn diese Verunglimpfung eine Schmähung des Propheten (*sabb an-nabī*) darstellt. Anderenfalls wird er mit Gefängnis von einem bis zu fünf Jahren bestraft.

Der Begriff *muqaddasāt* im islamischen Kontext umfasst ein breites Spektrum. Es gibt einen Kernbereich, der sowohl bei Schiiten wie bei Sunniten unumstritten ist. Dazu kommt ein Kernbereich, der für die Schiiten unumstritten ist. Um diesen Kernbereich herum lagern sich wie ein weiter werdender Kreis weitere Fälle, bei denen es sozusagen zunehmend von ihrer Entfernung vom Kern auch zunehmend umstritten ist, ob noch eine Schmähung von *muqaddasāt* und wenn ja, mit dem Gewicht einer Schmähung des Propheten vorliegt. Zum Kernbereich gehören:

- Personen, wie der Prophet Muhammed und die im Koran erwähnten Propheten bei allen Muslimen, dazu die sogenannten sündenreinen Imame bei den Schiiten,
- Orte, wie *Mekka* bei allen Muslimen, dazu für die Schiiten der heilige Schrein eines schiitischen Imams in *Nadschaf* oder *Karbalā,*
- Gegenstände, wie der Koran

- Umstritten dagegen ist die Eigenschaft als *muqaddasāt* bereits bei Werken wie *Nahǧ al-balāġa* und *ḥadīṯ*-Sammlungen, aber auch Gegenstände, die zu einem Heiligtum (*ḥaram)* gehören. Ja, nach Auffassung des Freitagspredigers in Mashhad sollte sogar ein Konzert in der heiligen Stadt als Schmähung von *muqaddasāt* gelten.[7]

Die Interpretation des Begriffes *muqaddasāt* sollte im Strafrecht aber beschränkt sein. Außer den Beispielen, wie dem Erhabenen Propheten und den sündenreinen Imamen, die die Vorschrift selbst erwähnt, zählt die Rechtsprechung den Koran dazu. Bei der Definition von „erhabenen Propheten" beschränkt sie sich aber auf Noah, Abraham, Moses, Jesus und Mohammed, ferner Maria, die im Koran als heilig angesehen wird. Im Gegensatz zur Mehrheit der Muslime stellen die Schiiten in diesem Sinn auch die Reihe der von ihnen als sündenrein angesehenen zwölf Imame dem Propheten Mohammed gleich. Dazu kommt auch Fatima, die Tochter von Mohammed und Mutter der Imame, die in der Vorschrift als die Wahrhaftige Reine bezeichnet wird.

In Art. 513 *ta'zīrāt*-Gesetzbuch von 1996 heißt es, wenn die Verunglimpfung eine Schmähung des Propheten (*sabb an-nabī)* darstellt, wird der Täter mit dem Tode bestraft, anderenfalls mit Gefängnis. Was *sabb an-nabī* bedeutet, sagt das Gesetz aber nicht. Bis zur Reform des Islamischen Strafgesetzbuchs im Jahr 2013 hatte auch kein anderer Gesetzestext den Straftatbestand Schmähung des Propheten – oder wie im *fiqh* genannt *sabb an-nabī* – definiert. Dann gab es über Jahre eine Diskussion zwischen den Juristen über die Grenze des Art. 167 der Verfassung.[8] Eine Gruppe meinte, dass der Richter gemäß diesem Artikel der Verfassung die Definition des Begriffs *sabb an-nabī* in den authentischen islamischen Quellen oder Rechtsgutachten finden müßte. Eine andere Gruppe war aber der Meinung, dass dieser Artikel der Verfassung nur außerhalb des Strafrechts zu interpretieren ist. Diese Unklarheit führte den Gesetzgeber dazu, den Begriff *sabb an-nabī* im Jahr 2013 als einen Straftatbestand in Art. 262 IStG zu definieren.

---

7 http://fa.euronews.com/2016/08/12/iran-mashhad-imam-alamolhoda-against-concert-and-tourism (aufgerufen am 28.8.2017).

8 Art. 167 Ver. IRI: „Der Richter ist verpflichtet, sich bei jeder Streitsache um eine Urteilsfindung anhand der geschriebenen Gesetze zu bemühen, und wenn er keines findet, ein Urteil in dem Prozess zu fällen, indem er sich auf authentische islamische Quellen oder Rechtsgutachten bezieht. Er kann nicht unter dem Vorwand des Schweigens, der Lückenhaftigkeit, zu summarischen Formulierung oder Widersprüchlichkeit der geschriebenen Gesetze die Prüfung der Klage und die Abgabe eines Urteils verweigern."

2.2. Art. 26 Pressegesetz (1986 i.d.F.v.2000)

In der Zeit der reformistischen Regierung im Iran zwischen 1997 und 2005 die immer noch Frühling der Presse genannt wird, gab es viele Fälle, für die die Rechtsprechung keine klare Antwort hatte. Einerseits genossen die Zeitungen und Zeitschriften politische Freiheit und dadurch wurden immer häufiger bisher nicht übliche religionskritische Artikel veröffentlicht und verbreitet. Andererseits übten die Konservativen immer mehr Druck auf die Judikative aus, damit die Richter strenger reagieren sollten. In den letzten Jahren der reformistischen Regierung und nachdem die Konservativen wieder die herrschende Mehrheit im Parlament gewonnen hatten, wurde im Jahr 2000 das Pressegesetz geändert. Art. 26 des neuen Pressegesetzes sagt nunmehr über die Beleidigung der heiligen Werte des Islam:

> Verunglimpft jemand im Wege der Presse die geoffenbarte Religion des Islam und ihre heiligen Werte, so wird, falls das einen Abfall vom Islam darstellt, gegen ihn ein Urteil wegen Abfalls vom Islam verhängt und vollstreckt. Stellt die Verunglimpfung keinen Abfall vom Islam dar, so wird der Täter nach dem Ermessen des Richters nach dem *ta'zīrāt*-Gesetz bestraft.

Abgesehen davon, dass der Begriff „die heiligen Werte des Islam" ein weiter und unklarer Begriff ist, ist interessanterweise auch der Abfall von Islam immer noch nicht gesetzlich definiert. So ähnlich wie die oben genannte Diskussion über den Begriff *sabb an-nabī* zwischen den Juristen gibt es immer noch die Frage, ob die Definition des Begriffs Abfall von Islam gemäß Art. 167 aus den authentischen islamischen Quellen oder Rechtsgutachten gefunden werden sollte und ob nur eine entsprechende Definition eine legitime Grundlage für eine Bestrafung sein kann.

2.3. Art. 262 Islamisches Strafgesetzbuch (2013)

Im Jahr 2013 und innerhalb der Neuordnung des iranischen Strafgesetzbuchs entschied der Gesetzgeber, die Schmähung des Propheten *(sabb an-nabī)* als einen eigenen Tatbestand und zwar als eine *ḥadd*-Straftat vorzusehen.

> Wer den erhabenen Propheten – Gott segne ihn und seine Familie und gebe ihm Heil – oder einen der erhabenen göttlichen Propheten beschimpft oder beleidigt[9] ist ein *sābb an-nabī*[10] und wird zum Tode verurteilt.

---

[9] In Farsi steht hier der Begriff *qaḏf* der eine Beleidigung/Verleumdung mit dem Inhalt eines illegalen Geschlechtsverkehrs beinhaltet.

> Gesetzliche Erläuterung: wer einen der sündenreinen Imame – der Friede sei mit ihnen – oder die hochverehrte Fatima Zahra – der Friede Gottes sei mit ihr – beleidigt, gilt als *sābb an-nabī.*

Im Art. 262 IStG werden beide, Beleidigung *(qaḏf)* und Beschimpfung, als mögliche Modalitäten der Straftat aufgeführt. Die mir zugängliche Rechtsprechung tendiert dazu, *sabb an-nabī* auf sexuelle Beschimpfungen zu beschränken, damit der Unterschied zwischen Art. 513 *ta'zīrāt*-Gesetzbuch und Art. 262 IStG deutlich wird. Durch diese Gesetzgebung werden also die als die schlimmsten geltenden Formen von Beschimpfung der Propheten als *ḥadd*-Straftat behandelt, die sonstigen strafbaren Formen der Beschimpfung der Propheten jedoch als *ta'zīr*-Straftat und gemäß Art. 513 *ta'zīrāt*-Gesetzbuch.

3. Schmähungen von *muqaddasāt* in der Praxis

Der Bericht über Schmähungen von *muqaddasāt* in der Praxis teilt diese in drei Kategorien ein:

a. Fälle, in denen der Staat durch die Justiz diesen Tatbestand als Instrument für die Unterdrückung Andersdenkender benutzt;
b. Fälle, in denen die Judikative passiv ist und gemäß der öffentlichen Meinung reagiert;
c. Sonstige Fälle.

Zu jeder Kategorie werden im Folgenden einige Beispiele aus der Rechtsprechung skizziert.[11]

3.1. Instrument der Unterdrückung

Die Kriminalisierung der Schmähungen von *muqaddasāt* kann vom Staat als Instrument zur Unterdrückung missbraucht werden. Die Geschichte der Islamischen Republik Iran zeigt, dass beispielsweise allein während der reformistischen Regierung des Präsidenten Chatami und als Reaktion der

[10] Der Tatbestand der Prophetenschmähung heißt *sabb an-nabī*, der Täter, der die Schmähung begeht, ist jedoch ein *sābb an-nabī* (mit langem a).

[11] Es ist anzumerken, dass die Urteile der Gerichte in Iran nicht regelmäßig veröffentlicht werden. Erst in den letzten Jahren begann die Judikative eine ausgewählte Reihe von Urteilen zu veröffentlichen. In diesem Artikel sind die beiden Fälle unter „sonstige Fälle" nirgendwo veröffentlicht, sondern durch Gespräche mit Richtern oder Lektüre von Akten gesammelt.

Judikative auf die reformistische Bewegung mehr als 20 Zeitungen sowie wöchentlich oder monatlich erscheinende Zeitschriften[12] durch richterliche Entscheidung und gemäß den obengenannten Paragraphen geschlossen worden sind. Als Beispiel von geschlossenen Zeitungen in diesem Zeitraum können die folgenden Fälle genannt werden:

a) Die Zeitung Ǧāmi'a[13]*:*

Der Staatsanwalt erhob gegen die Zeitung Ǧāmi'a unter anderem auch den Vorwurf der Veröffentlichung von Beiträgen gegen islamische Prinzipien.[14] Der Staatsanwalt nannte einen Artikel, veröffentlicht am 28.5.1998 auf Seite 7 dieser Zeitung, mit dem Titel „Wenn Sie an meinem Platz wären...".[15] Der Autor[16] kritisierte die Taliban in Afghanistan, aber argumentierte gleichzeitig auch, dass das Verhalten der Taliban auf einigen grundlegenden islamischen Lehren basiere. Er behauptete, dass, wenn die Schiiten auch heutzutage rein traditionell und gemäß den alten religiösen Auffassungen von den islamischen Vorschriften handeln würden, es nicht unwahrscheinlich wäre, dass die Ergebnisse dem Verhalten von Taliban in Afghanistan glichen. Dann erwähnte er in seinem Artikel einige Überlieferungen des Propheten Muhammad sowie der schiitischen Imame, die deutlich frauenfeindlich und diskriminierend sind.[17] Dementsprechend argumentierte er, dass alle Muslime außer den Taliban heutzutage diese Überlieferungen glücklicherweise nicht mehr berücksichtigten, dass aber solche Überlieferungen immer noch potenzielle Fundgruben für radikale Interpretationen seien. Der Staatsanwalt behauptete, der Autor hätte zeigen wollen, dass diejenigen, die den Prinzipien des *fiqh* folgten, „Fundamentalisten" seien. Deshalb sollten der Autor und die Zeitung gemäß Art. 26 des Pressegesetzes verurteilt werden.[18]

---

12 Als auf den Index gesetzten Zeitungen und Zeitschriften zwischen 1997 und 2005 können die Folgenden genannt werden: Zeitungen wie *Ǧāmi'a, Tūs, Našāṭ, 'Aṣr-i Āzādagān , Salām, Ḫurdād, Zan, Naurūz, Ǧumhūrīyat, Yās-i nau, Guzāriš-i Rūz, Bāmdād-i nau, Āftāb-i Imrūz, Payām-i Āzādī, Fatḥ, Āryā, Āzād, Ṣubḥ-i Imrūz, Mušārikat, Bayān, Aḫbār-i Iqtiṣād* sowie wöchentlich erscheinende Zeitschriften wie *Payām-i Hāǧar, Ābān, Arziš,* und monatlich erscheinende wie *Īrān-i Fardā*

13 *Ǧāmi'a* bedeutet „Gesellschaft".

14 *Pūrustād, Wahīd,* Muḥākama-yi *Ǧāmi'a* (The Trial of Jameah). Teheran 2001, S. 47.

15 *Ebd.*, S. 186.

16 Der Autor war *Muḥsin Sa'īdzāda*. Er ist selbst Kleriker und stellte sich im Artikel vor als Dozent der *Houze-ye Elmiye* (so viel wie geistliche Akademie) in Qom.

17 *Pūrustād, Ǧāmi'a* , S. 188.

18 *Ebd.*, S. 48.

Der Artikel war deutlich kritisch, aber auf keinen Fall eine Verunglimpfung der „geoffenbarten Religion des Islam und ihrer heiligen Werte“.[19] Trotzdem verurteilte die Geschworenenjury des Pressegerichts[20] am 8.6.1998 die Zeitung wegen dieses Beitrags, jedoch nur wegen Verunglimpfung und nicht wegen Abfalls vom Islam. Überdies erkannte sie noch eine Strafmilderung nach Art. 22 StGB als angemessen an[21] Das Urteil für diese Straftat war 3 Millionen Rial [zurzeit ca. € 850] anstatt 3 Monate Gefängnis samt 6 Millionen Rial [zurzeit ca. € 1200] als Geldstrafe.[22]

b) Die Zeitung Zan[23]*:*

In der Reihe der gerichtlichen Verfahren gegen die reformistischen Zeitungen und Zeitschriften konnte die Zeitung *Zan* am 14.12.1998 vor dem Pressegericht einen Freispruch erzielen.[24] Das war aber nicht das Ende der Verfolgung der Zeitung *Zan*. Am 7.4.1999 setzte das Revolutionsgericht die Zeitung *Zan* auf den Index. Eine der zwei Vorwürfe gegen die Zeitung war die Veröffentlichung einer Karikatur am 3.4.1999, in der das Blutgeld als islamische Strafe herabgewürdigt worden sein sollte. In der Karikatur trafen ein Mann und eine Frau einen Gangster mit der Pistole in der Hand, und der Mann sagte dem

---

19 Siehe ebd. S. 89 zur Verteidigung des Rechtsanwaltes gegen diesen Vorwurf.

20 Art. 168 Verf. IRI: „die Gerichtsverhandlung bei politischen und Pressestraftaten ist öffentlich und findet in Gegenwart einer Geschworenenjury vor den ordentlichen Gerichten statt. Wahlverfahren, Voraussetzungen und Kompetenzen der Geschworenenjury sowie Definition der politischen Straftat bestimmt das Gesetz aufgrund islamischer Kriterien.“
Das 1998 geltende Pressegesetz stammte von 1986. Aber das genannte Gesetz schwieg über den Mechanismus der Wahl der Mitglieder für die Geschworenenjury des Pressegerichts. Schließlich wurden die Mitglieder der Geschworenenjury gemäß Art. 31 des Pressegesetzes vom Jahr 1980 ausgewählt: „...Alle zwei Jahre im Monat Mehr (23 September bis 22. Oktober) versammelt sich auf Einladung des Ministers für die nationale Kultur ein Gremium aus den Gerichtspräsidenten der Städte und den Präsidenten der Stadträte (falls es keinen Stadtrat gibt, dem Bürgermeister) in Teheran, um die Geschworenenjury auszuwählen [...] Dieses Gremium wählt insgesamt 14 Personen aus, die das Vertrauen der Öffentlichkeit genießen und aus unterschiedlichen gesellschaftlichen Gruppierungen (Kleriker, Professoren der Universitäten, Ärzte, Autoren, Journalisten, Rechtsanwälte, Lehrer, [...]) kommen; 7 Personen als Mitglieder und 7 Personen als Ersatzmitglieder.“
Das Problem der Kombination der Geschworenenjury war damals, dass sie nicht als wahre Vertreter der öffentlichen Meinung anerkannt waren.

21 *Pūrustād, Ǧāmi'a*, S. 186, Fußnote.

22 *Ebd.*, S. 111.

23 *Zan* bedeutet Frau.

24 *Pūrustād, Wahīd*, Muḥākama-yi Zan (The Trial of Zan). Teheran 2001, S. 75.

Gangster „töte sie anstatt meiner, ihr Blutgeld ist günstiger."[25] Die Zeitung ist auch heute noch auf den Index, obwohl niemals Anklage gegen sie erhoben wurde[26] und vor allem das Revolutionsgericht für so einen Fall gar nicht zuständig ist.

Nach der reformistischen Regierung beschleunigte sich die Unterdrückung der Presse in der radikal populistischen Regierung von Ahmadinedschad. Mehr als 40 Zeitungen sowie wöchentlich oder monatlich erscheinende Zeitschriften wurden geschlossen.[27] Der Unterschied dieser zwei Regierungen für die Presse war, dass sie in der Zeit der Reformregierung durch die Judikative unterdrückt war und das Ministerium für Kultur und islamische Führung sie unterstützte, in der Zeit der radikal populistischen Regierung wurde die Presse jedoch durch die Pressestelle des Ministeriums unterdrückt. Solche administrativen Entscheidungen bleiben außerhalb dieses Artikels.

c) Hashem Aghadschari (Hāšim Āġāǧarī):

Außer in Bezug auf die Presse gab es im Jahr 2002 einen Fall, der deutlich von den damaligen politischen Spannungen verursacht und beeindruckt war. Der Reformpolitiker und Universitätsprofessor Hashem Aghadschari wurde vom Strafgericht der Provinz *Hamadān* aufgrund eines Vortrags, den er in dieser Stadt hielt, wegen Schmähung von *muqaddasāt,* wegen Schmähung des Propheten, aber auch wegen Abfalls vom Islam zum Tode verurteilt. Das Urteil war ein Schock für die Zivilgesellschaft. Aghadschari hatte in seinem Vortrag verschiedene Formen eines historisch bedingten religiösen Aberglauben kritisiert, die heutzutage von einfachen Menschen ernst genommen und als Teil der Religion angesehen werden und getadelt, dass trotzdem die Kleriker nicht darauf reagieren würden. Nach breitem Protest gegen das Urteil wurde es von dem Obersten Gerichtshof aufgehoben. Im Berufungsgericht wurden *sabb an-nabī* und Abfall vom Islam von der Anklage gestrichen. Schließlich wurde Aghadschari in der Berufung wegen Schmähung von *muqaddasāt* zu drei Jahren Gefängnis verurteilt.

---

[25] *Ebd.*, S. 92 und 107.

[26] *Ebd.*, S. 106.

[27] Als auf den Index gesetzte Zeitungen und Zeitschriften zwischen 2005 und 2013 können die Folgenden genannt werden: Zeitungen wie *Āyanda-yi Nau*, *Šarq*, *Hammīhan*, *Kārguzārān*, *I'timād-i Millī*, *Kalama-yi Sabz*, *Farhang-i Āštī*, *I'timād*, *Ārmān-i Ravābiṭ-i 'umūmī*, *Taḥlīl-i Rūz*, *Sarmāya*, *Ḥayāt-i Nau-i 'Iǧtimā'ī*, *Andīša-yi Nau*, *Bahār*, *Gul*, *Rūzagār*, *Haft*, sowie die Zeitschriften wie *Šahrvand-i Imrūz*, *Āftāb-i Luristān*, *Himmat*, *Mauǧ-i Andīša*, *Īrāndḫt*, *Sīnā*, *Sarw*, *Maġrib*, *Badr*, *Farhang-i Āmūziš*, *Madina-yi Guftugū*, *Bahār-i Zanǧān*, *Tališh*, *Čilčirāġ*, *Kayhān Kārīkātūr*, *Madrasa*, *Zanān*.

3.2. Druck der öffentlichen Meinung

Einige Fälle sind technisch betrachtet keine Schmähung von *muqaddasāt*, aber die Judikative reagiert auf den Druck der öffentlichen Meinung oder besser gesagt der Meinung des konservativen Teils der Gesellschaft, die solche Fälle als Schmähung ansieht und dagegen laut protestiert. Als Beispiele können die folgenden Fälle genannt werden:

a) Die Zeitung Bahār[28]*:*

Die reformistische Zeitung *Bahār* publizierte am 23. Oktober 2013 einen kritischen Artikel mit dem Titel „Der Imam: politischer Führer oder Vorbild im Glauben?“. Der Autor, *'Alī-Aṣġar Ġaravī*, Übersetzer, Forscher und Interpret des Koran, erklärte in seinem Artikel, dass der Imam Ali bei den Schiiten nicht unbedingt als ein politischer Führer, sondern als ein spiritueller Führer angesehen werden sollte. Der 23. Oktober war jedoch der Jahrestag des Ereignisses von *Ġadīr Ḫumm*. Bei diesem historischen Ereignis verkündigte der Prophet Muhammed unter anderem, dass „für diejenigen, für die ich der *maulā* bin, ist auch Ali der *maulā*“. Die Bedeutung des Begriffes „*maulā*“ ist zwischen den Muslimen umstritten, aber schiitische Muslime glauben, dass dies die Ernennung von Ali als Muhammads Nachfolger ist und feiern dieses Ereignis als ein großes Fest.

Die Veröffentlichung eines derartigen Artikels auf der ersten Seite der Zeitung an einem solchen Tag führte zu scharfen Reaktionen. Zwei *marǧa'-i taqlīd*[29] reagierten sofort darauf[30] und erklärten den Artikel als Schmähung von *muqaddasāt*. Ebenso verurteilten 30 Parlamentsabgeordnete, die Kleriker waren, den Artikel als Verzerrung der schiitischen Lehren. Um die Atmosphäre zu beruhigen, stoppten die Herausgeber die Veröffentlichung der Zeitung sofort von sich aus. Ebenfalls erklärten sie drei Tage später offiziell, dass die Veröffentlichung eines solchen Artikels ein unabsichtlicher Fehler gewesen sei. Trotz aller Abwiegelungsversuche wurde die Zeitung Bahār am 28. Oktober 2013 vom Aufsichtsrat der Presse auf den Index gesetzt. Der Autor wurde von dem Vorsitzenden Richter der 76. Strafkammer der Provinz Teheran, *Mudīr-Ḫurāsānī,* nach Art. 26 Pressegesetz zu sechs Monaten Gefängnis verurteilt. Die Zeitung wurde gemäß der gesetzlichen Erläuterung vom Art. 35 Pressegesetz[31]

---

[28] *Bahār* bedeutet Frühling.

[29] Die Bezeichnung für die höchsten schiitischen Religionsgelehrten.

[30] Großayatollahs *Nāṣir Makārim Šīrāzī* und *Ḥusain Nūrī Hamadānī.*

[31] Art. 35, Gesetzliche Erläuterung 5: Das Gericht kann bei Presse-Straftaten eine Gefängnis- und Auspeitschungsstrafe in eine der folgenden Strafen umwandeln: a) Geldstrafe von zwei Millionen Rial [zurzeit ca. € 50] bis fünfzig Millionen Rial [zurzeit ca. € 1.250]; b)

auch für sechs Monate auf den Index gesetzt. Das Urteil wurde vom 32. Senat des Obersten Gerichtshofs bestätigt.

b) Der Film Rūz-i Rastāḫīz[32]*:*

Dieser Film ist ein historisch-religiöser Film von *Aḥmad Riḍā Darwīš* über die Schlacht von *Karbalā* am Tag von *'Āšūrā'* und erzählt den Aufstand von *Ḥusain*, dem dritten Imam der Schiiten, im Jahre 680 nach Christus gegen den Khalifen *Yazīd*. Der Film gewann im Februar 2014 zehn von insgesamt 13 Preisen des 32. Fajr Internationalen Filmfestivals in Teheran. Der Film startete im Kino am 15. Juli 2015, aber noch am selben Tag wurde er wegen Protesten von höchsten Klerikern gestoppt. Drei *marǧa'-i taqlīd*[33] erklärten den Film als Schmähung von *muqaddasāt*. Der Grund einer solchen Reaktion war, dass der Film das Gesicht des Bruders von Imam Hussein, *'Abbās ibn 'Alī*, zeigte. Es gibt keinen Grund, der die Darstellung der Gesichter von heiligen Personen verbietet. Die einzige Ausnahme ist das Gesicht des Propheten Muhammad. Dieses Verbot beruht aber nicht auf einem religiösen Gebot, sondern hat einen kulturell-traditionellen Hintergrund. Diese Ausnahme verbreitet sich aber in der iranischen Kinoindustrie und umfasst ebenso die Imame der Schiiten. Andererseits gibt es seit Jahrhunderten die Tradition im iranischen „*ta'ziya*"-Theater, religiöse Geschichten zu inszenieren und es war bisher problemlos, die Gesichter der Schauspieler zu zeigen, die Imame darstellen. *'Abbās* ist aber weder Imam noch Prophet. Deswegen hat ein Protest gegen seine Darstellung mit Gesicht gemäß dem *fiqh* keine religiöse Begründung und viele Filme und Serien in Iran zeigten und zeigen das Gesicht verschiedener Propheten. Außerdem hatte einer der größten *marǧa'-i taqlīd*[34] schon vorher nach der Anfrage eines Gläubigen (*istiftā'*) dazu festgestellt, dass die Darstellung des Propheten Muhammed oder anderer Propheten oder Fatimas im Kino, Fernsehen und Theater unbedenklich seien, wenn der Grundsatz der Achtung und Ehrerbietung berücksichtigt und ihre geheiligte Person in der Vorstellung der Menschen nicht beschädigt wird."[35] Trotz allem ist der Film immer noch gesperrt.

Einstellung der Veröffentlichung bis zu maximal sechs Monate bei Zeitungen und bis zu einem Jahr bei anderen Publikationen; c) der Ausschluss vom Amt des verantwortlichen Redakteurs bis zu maximal fünf Jahren.

32 Der Begriff „*Rūz-i Rastāḫīz*" bedeutet wörtlich „Auferstehungstag". Der offizielle Titel des Films außerhalb von Iran ist aber „*Hussein, Who Said No*".

33 Großayatollahs *Ḥusain Waḥīd Ḫurāsānī*, *Nāṣir Makārim Šīrāzī* und *Saiyid Muḥammad 'Alī Ḥusainī 'Alawī Gurgānī*.

34 Großayatollah *Al-Saiyid 'Alī al-Ḥusainī as-Sīstānī*.

35 Frage 585 unter http://www.sistani.org/downloads/books_19_sistani.org.html (aufgerufen am 27.8.2017).

3.3. Sonstige Fälle

Es gibt sonstige Fälle, die weder mit dem politischen Kampf verbunden sind, noch in der öffentlichen Meinung eine große Debatte verursachen. Über diese Fälle gibt es kaum Statistiken, viel weniger als bei den beiden oben genannten Gruppen von Fällen. Aber trotzdem zeigt die Erfahrung, dass in solchen Fällen das Gericht versucht, die mildere Strafe zu geben, oder die Täter freispricht. In diesem Artikel seien die zwei folgenden Fälle genannt:

a) Der Fall Weblog:

Der Vorsitzende Richter der 41. Strafkammer des Berufungsgerichts Teheran im Jahr 2010, *Qanbarī*, erzählte mir von einem Fall von Schmähung des Propheten, als er Richter der 17. Strafkammer des Revolutionsgerichts war. Der Staatsanwalt hatte Anklage wegen Schmähung des zwölften Imams der Schiiten gegen einen Studenten erhoben. Da diese Tat eine Unterkategorie der Schmähung des Propheten ist, hatte der Staatsanwalt die Todesstrafe für den Angeklagten beantragt. Gemäß der Erzählung von Richter *Qanbarī* hatte es eine Diskussion über Weblog zwischen Studenten gegeben. Der Angeklagte war von seinen Freunden zu einer Zeremonie in einer Gemeinde eingeladen worden, in der der Geburtstag des zwölften Imams gefeiert werden sollte. In der Diskussion im Weblog hatte der Angeklagte geäußert, dass er nicht an die oberflächliche Interpretation von Imam Mahdi in dieser Gemeinde glaube, sondern dass Imam Mahdi für ihn ein Erlöser und ein befreiender Reformer sei. Gemäß dem Richter hatte der Staatsanwalt am Anfang versucht, zu beweisen, dass der Angeklagte die Existenz von Imam Mahdi geleugnet habe und deswegen vom Islam abgefallen sei. Dieser erste Versuch des Staatsanwaltes war aber erfolgslos gewesen, weil es eindeutig war, dass die Leugnung der Existenz des Zwölftens Imams, selbst wenn sie denn vorgelegen hätte, kein Beispiel des Abfalls vom Islam gewesen wäre. Dann hatte sich der Staatsanwalt umorientiert, um zu beweisen, dass der Angeklagte den Imam Mahdi verunglimpft und geschmäht hätte und deswegen die Todesstrafe verdiene. Dabei ist wichtig zu erwähnen, dass der Staatsanwalt in dem oben genannten Fall seinerzeit für die politisch motivierte Verfolgung von Reformaktivisten bekannt war. Schließlich lehnten alle drei Richter der Kammer die Anklage ab und sprachen den Angeklagten frei.

b) Familien-Video:

Der Vorsitzende Richter der 76. Strafkammer der Provinz Teheran, *Mudīr-Ḫurāsānī*, erlaubte mir, einen Fall aus dem Jahr 2009 zu lesen und Notizen zu machen. In diesem Fall waren vier Personen in Teheran wegen Schmähung des

Propheten Mohammed, Zerreißens des Korans und Trinkens berauschender Getränke angeklagt. Zu dem Verfahren war es gekommen, nachdem die Frau des Hauptverdächtigen und selbst eine der Angeklagten aus schlechtem Gewissen dem Staatsanwalt einen Film übergeben hatte. Gemäß diesem Film hatten die Angeklagten einige Jahren vorher auf einer Party während des Trinkens berauschender Getränke den Koran zerrissen, einer von ihnen hatte Seiten des Korans mit dem Penis berührt, sich dann auf ihnen selbstbefriedigt und das als Offenbarung bezeichnet. Der Staatsanwalt hatte daraufhin Anklage wegen Trinkens berauschender Getränke und Schmähung des Propheten erhoben.

Während die in diesem Fall beschriebenen Taten ohne weiteres als Schmähung des Propheten hätten angesehen und mit der Todesstrafe bestraft werden können, betonte der Vorsitzende Richter im Urteil, dass diese Taten kein Beispiel der Schmähung des Propheten wären und die Angeklagten daher nicht zum Tode verurteilt wurden. Die Angeklagten wurden aber wegen Schmähung von *muqaddasāt*, hier des Korans, gemäß Art. 513 des *ta'zīrāt*-Gesetzbuches zu Gefängnis, aber auch wegen des Trinkens berauschende Getränke zu 80 Peitschenhieben verurteilt. Der Richter äußerte in einem Gespräch mit dem Autor dieses Artikels, dass eine Vermeidung der Todesstrafe in diesem Fall nach dem, was in dem Film zu sehen war, nicht einfach war. Dennoch meinte er, die einzige Schuld der Täter wäre seiner Meinung nach ihre Dummheit, und die Strafe für Dummheit sei nicht die Todesstrafe.

Schlussbemerkung

Schmähung von *muqaddasāt* wird im heutigen iranischen Strafrecht unter zwei Kategorien, *ḥadd* und *ta'zīr,* klassifiziert. Unter *ḥadd* bedroht Art. 262 IStG *sabb an-nabī,* die Schmähung des Propheten, mit der Todesstrafe. Als *ta'zīr*-Straftat bestraft Art. 513 *ta'zīr*-Gesetz die Verunglimpfung von *muqaddasāt* mit bis zu fünf Jahren Gefängnis. Nur in schweren Fällen, in der Praxis solchen mit Sexualbezug, stellt sie die Schmähung von *muqaddasāt* der Prophetenschmähung gleich. Damit erfolgt implizit eine Verweisung auf Art. 262 IStGB. Schließlich spricht Art. 26 Pressegesetz von dem Fall, dass die Verunglimpfung einen Abfall vom Islam darstellt, ohne den Begriff Abfall vom Islam zu definieren und dessen Strafe zu beschreiben.

In einem Rechtssystem, das auf religiösen Werten basiert, ist die Strafbarkeit der Beleidigung und der Schmähung von Heiligen oder heiligen Werten vorstellbar. Dennoch, auch wenn man die Todesstrafe nicht für illegitim hält, ist sie doch für unsere Zeit nicht mehr zu empfehlen und bestimmt für eine solche Straftat auf keinen Fall angemessen. Das innere Potenzial für eine Reform in der diesbezüglichen Gesetzgebung ist nicht nur aus der praktischen Erfahrung der Islamischen Republik, sondern auch aus den theoretischen Quellen des *fiqh* zu erschließen.

Außerdem zeigen die geschichtlichen Erfahrungen, dass der strafrechtliche Schutz der heiligen Werte sehr einfach im politischen Machtkampf missbraucht werden und den Raum für die Kritik und die Meinungsäußerungsfreiheit immer mehr beschränken kann, sofern die Rechtsprechung keine klare Definition oder beschränkenden Rahmen für Begriffe wie Beleidigung und Schmähung sowie religiöse Werte formuliert.

Von *Macaulay* zu *Zia ul-Haq* Das pakistanische (Religions-)Strafrecht zwischen kolonialem Erbe und Islamisierung[1]

Benedikt Naarmann, Berlin

I. Das Rechtssystem Pakistans – rechtsvergleichende und verfassungsrechtliche Grundlegungen

Durchmisst man die rechtsvergleichende Literatur, wird Pakistan aufgrund des kolonialen Erbes üblicherweise dem Rechtskreis des common law zugeordnet, im selben Atemzug jedoch regelmäßig auf den Hybridstatus verwiesen, der sich aus der Einfügung islamischer Elemente in das Rechtssystem ergebe.[2] Der vergleichende Verfassungsrechtler *Ran Hirschl* zählt Pakistan zum Kreis der sog. „constitutional theocracies", die sich idealtypisch durch folgende kumulative Charakteristika auszeichneten: das Bekenntnis zu Elementen tradierter Verfassungsstaatlichkeit wie einer zumindest formalen Trennung zwischen politischer und religiöser Autorität oder dem Vorhandensein eines gerichtlichen Prüfungs- und Kontrollregimes (judicial review); die Anerkennung einer privilegierten bzw. „Staats"-Religion; die Maßgeblichkeit religiöser Rechtsquellen als *die* oder zumindest eine Quelle für Gesetzgebung und richterliche Gesetzesauslegung; und schließlich das Vorhandensein religiöser Spruchkörper und Tribunale neben der säkularen Gerichtsbarkeit.[3]

---

1 Der vorliegende Beitrag ist die leicht überarbeitete und ergänzte Fassung des Vortrags, den der Verf. am 21.10.2016 auf der Jahrestagung der Gesellschaft für Arabisches und Islamisches Recht e.V. (GAIR) in Freiburg i. Br. gehalten hat. Der Inhalt ist eine um aktuelle Entwicklungen (Stand: Januar 2017) ergänzte Verdichtung des Pakistan-Kapitels der Dissertationsschrift des Verf.: Der Schutz von Religionen und Religionsgemeinschaften in Deutschland, England, Indien und Pakistan – Ein interkultureller Rechtsvergleich, Tübingen 2015. Die Belege und Fußnoten beschränken sich daher auf das Nötigste, der Vortragsstil wurde bewusst beibehalten.

2 In diesem Sinne etwa Artikel Pakistan (*Chodosh, H.E. / Jilani, T.H.*). In: Legal Systems of the World – A Political, Social, and Cultural Encyclopedia (Vol. III), Santa Barbara 2002, S. 1247; *Ebert, K.H.*, Rechtsvergleichung – Einführung in die Grundlagen, Bern 1978, S. 123; ferner *Palmer, V.V.*, Mixed Legal Systems. In: Bussani, M./Mattei, U. (Hrsg.), The Cambridge Companion to Comparative Law, Cambridge 2012, S. 368, 381, der Pakistan dem Kreis der „mixed systems of common law and Muslim law" zuordnet.

3 *Hirschl, R.*, Constitutional Theocracy, Cambridge 2010, S. 38 f., zu den prägenden Merkmalen solcher sog. constitutional theocracies a.a.O., S. 2 f.

Gemessen an diesen Kriterien *Hirschls* erfüllt der status quo in Pakistan in der Tat alle Definitionsmerkmale einer „constitutional theocracy“: Ideologisch ist dessen Staatswerdung am 15. August 1947 unmittelbare Konsequenz der sog. „Zwei Nationen-Theorie“, welche sich die All-India Muslim League in einer im Februar 1940 in Lahore gefassten Resolution als offizielle Position zu eigen gemacht hatte. Demnach seien die Muslime Britisch-Indiens als eine eigene Nation anzusehen, die sich durch eine gemeinsame Religion, Kultur und Geschichte von ihrer hinduistisch geprägten Umgebung abhebe. Um der Gefahr einer Marginalisierung in einem zukünftig von Hindus dominierten Staat vorzubeugen, sollten sich diejenigen im Nordwesten und Osten gelegenen Provinzen Britisch-Indiens abspalten, in denen Muslime die Bevölkerungsmehrheit stellten und die gemeinsame Religion des Islam dabei das einigende Band innerhalb der Bevölkerung bilden.

Nach der Staatsgründung blieb allerdings deren exakte verfassungsrechtliche Position (bewusst) unklar: Während *Muhammad Ali Jinnah* (1876–1948), der „Gründungsvater“ und erste Generalgouverneur Pakistans, primär für einen von islamischen Werten inspirierten Staat plädierte, der gleichwohl die politischen Rechte aller seiner Bürger – auch der nichtmuslimischen – schützen sollte, fochten Zeitgenossen, insbesondere mehrere Organisationen islamischer Rechtsgelehrter, für einen wahrhaft islamischen Staat, der auf den Grundsätzen der Scharia basieren müsse.[4] Die im März 1949 verabschiedete sog. Objectives Resolution avisierte die Grundzüge des zu schaffenden Gemeinwesens als eines Amalgams von islamischen Staatsprinzipien und westlich-säkularem Verfassungsverständnis.[5]

---

4 Dazu im Detail *Lau, M.*, Islam and the Constitutional Foundations of Pakistan. In: Grote, R./Röder, T.J. (Hrsg.), Constitutionalism in Islamic Countries – Between Upheaval and Continuity, Oxford 2012, S. 171–186.

5 Vgl. dazu die Objectives Resolution (1949): „Whereas sovereignty over the entire universe belongs to Allah Almighty alone and the authority which He has delegated to the State of Pakistan, through its people for being exercised within the limits prescribed by Him is a sacred trust: This Constituent Assembly representing the people of Pakistan resolves to frame a Constitution for the sovereign independent State of Pakistan; wherein the State shall exercise its powers and authority through the chosen representatives of the people; wherein the principles of democracy, freedom, equality, tolerance and social justice as enunciated by Islam shall be fully observed; wherein the Muslims shall be enabled to order their lives in the individual and collective spheres in accordance with the teachings and requirements of Islam as set out in the Holy Quran and the Sunnah; [...] so that the people of Pakistan may prosper and attain their rightful and honored place amongst the nations of the World and make their full contribution towards international peace and progress and happiness of humanity.“ Nach einer unter *Zia ul-Haq* verfügten

Die derzeitige Verfassung aus dem Jahr 1973 enthält zwar typische Strukturelemente eines demokratisch-parlamentarisch-liberalen Verfassungsstaats (z.B. Gewaltenteilung, Grundrechtekatalog, judicial review), weist aber zugleich zahlreiche islamisch gefärbte Prägungen auf: Exemplarisch genannt seien die Bestimmung des Landesnamens als „Islamische Republik Pakistan" sowie des Islam als Staatsreligion (Art. 1 und 2), mehrere islamisch konturierte Staatszielbestimmungen, etwa zur Förderung des Islam in der Gesellschaft und der Einhaltung islamischer Moralstandards (Art. 31), zur Durchsetzung des Alkoholverbots für Muslime (Art. 37(h)) oder auch des schariatischen Wucherverbots (Art. 38(f)) sowie schließlich religiös gefärbte Grundrechtsvorbehalte, indem z.B. die in Art. 19 garantierte Redefreiheit ausdrücklich unter den Vorbehalt der „Ehre des Islam" gestellt wird.

Institutionell wachen mit dem Council of Islamic Ideology und dem Federal Shariat Court zwei Akteure über die Islamkonformität staatlichen Handelns. Während ersteres primär Regierung und Parlamente auf Bundes- und Provinzebene zur Vereinbarkeit von Gesetzen und geplanten Gesetzesvorhaben mit dem Islam berät (Art. 227–230), obliegen dem Federal Shariat Court und der beim Supreme Court angesiedelten Shariat Appellate Bench die Prüfung (und ggf. Niederschlagung) von Gesetzen als islam- bzw. nicht islamgemäß. Im Wege einer Popularklage, die den Nachweis einer qualifizierten Betroffenheit nicht verlangt, kann sich jedermann mit der Behauptung an das Gericht wenden, diese verstießen gegen islamische Prinzipien.[6] Zudem fungieren Federal Shariat Court und Shariat Appellate Bench als Rechtsmittelinstanzen in Verfahren unter den sog. Hudood Ordinances.

Dass darüber hinaus die Judikative gehalten ist, bei der Auslegung staatlicher Gesetze ebenfalls auf religiöse Quellen zu rekurrieren, ergibt sich einfachgesetzlich aus dem Enforcement of Shari'ah Act (1991)[7], daneben aber auch aus Urteilen des Supreme Court.[8]

Verfassungsänderung ist die Objectives Resolution nunmehr in Art. 2-A Teil des materiellen Verfassungsrechts.

6 Art. 203D.(1): „The Court may, either on its own motion or on the petition of a citizen of Pakistan or the Federal Government or a Provincial Government, examine and decide the question whether or not any law or provision of law is repugnant to the Injunctions of Islam, as laid down in the Holy Quran and the Sunnah of the Holy Prophet, hereinafter referred to as the Injunctions of Islam. [...]".

7 In diesem Sinne dessen section 4. Laws to be interpreted in the light of Shari'ah. For the purpose of this Act -
(a) while interpreting the statute-law, if more than one interpretation is possible, the one consistent with the Islamic principles and jurisprudence shall be adopted by the Court; and

Rechtssoziologisch lässt sich der Ist-Zustand damit als „state law pluralism" fassen, indem nämlich bereits in der Rechtsordnung selbst eine Parallelität verschiedener Rechtsquellen – säkular und religiös – angelegt ist.[9] Dass die für solche Gestaltungen typischen Phänomene der Instabilität und Konfliktimmanenz[10], die sich z.B. aus ungeklärten Hierarchieverhältnissen oder unpräzisen Bestimmungen der maßgeblichen religiösen Rechtsquellen ergeben können, in den letzten Jahrzehnten gerade auch die Verfassungswirklichkeit Pakistans geprägt haben, sei hier nur angedeutet.[11]

Vor dem Hintergrund dieses in aller Kürze skizzierten verfassungsrechtlichen Tableaus soll nun ein Blick auf das pakistanische Strafrecht – und dabei insbesondere das Religionsstrafrecht – geworfen werden. Letzteres zählt zu den rigidesten Regimes weltweit und sticht selbst unter den islamischen Ländern als außergewöhnlich hart hervor. So bestrafen neben Pakistan lediglich der Iran und Saudi-Arabien die Lästerung des Propheten Mohammed zwingend mit dem Tode.[12]

(b) where two or more interpretations are equally possible the interpretation which advances the Principles of Policy and Islamic provisions in the Constitution shall be adopted by the Court.

8 Supreme Court in Mst. Kaneez Fatima v Wali Muhammed, All Pakistan Legal Decisions 1993 (SC), S. 901, 912 f.

9 Zum Konzept eines solchen „weak pluralism" *Griffiths, J.*, What is Legal Pluralism? In: Journal of Legal Pluralism and Unofficial Law, London 24(1986), S. 1, 4–8. Dass daneben in Pakistan auch der sog. thick pluralism in Form von verhaltenssteuernden Systemen jenseits staatlich gesetzten Rechts weiterhin existiert, ist unbestritten – vgl. dazu exemplarisch *Chaudhary, M.A.*, Justice in Practice – Legal Ethnography of a Pakistani Punjabi Village, Oxford 1999.

10 *v. Benda-Beckmann, F.*, Pluralismus von Recht und Ordnung. In: Behemoth. A Journal on Civilisation, Freiburg 1(2008)1, S. 58, 64 f.

11 So etwa mit Blick auf die Kontroverse um die in Art. 2-A in den Stand materiellen Verfassungsrechts erhobene Objectives Resolution von 1949, der Gerichte teilweise den Status einer über sonstigem Verfassungsrecht stehenden Grundnorm beizumessen suchten, vgl. *Lau, M.*, The Role of Islam in the Legal System of Pakistan, The Hague 2005, S. 47–73; speziell zur Auslegung der „injunctions of Islam" durch den Federal Shariat Court und den dadurch auftretenden Konflikten mit der allgemeinen Gerichtsbarkeit *Cheema, S.A.*, The Federal Shariat Court's Role to Determine the Scope of 'Injunctions of Islam' and its Implications. In: Journal of Islamic State Practices in International Law, 9(2013)2, S. 92–111.

12 Dazu *Tellenbach, S.*, Blasphemie und verwandte Delikte in der Strafgesetzgebung muslimischer Länder – Ein Überblick, In: GAIR-Mitteilungen, Leipzig 5(2013), S. 195–205.

II. Das pakistanische (Religions-)Strafrecht

1. Historische Genese – von *Macaulay* über *Zia ul-Haq* zum status quo

Für die Anwendung des Strafrechts auf dem indischen Subkontinent markiert die Ankunft der East India Company Mitte des 18. Jahrhunderts eine wichtige Zäsur. Praktiziert wurde in deren Gefolge zunächst ein Dualismus verschiedener Rechtsordnungen: Kolonialbürger unterfielen englischem common law, die einheimische Bevölkerung je nach Region größtenteils islamischem, teils hinduistischem Strafrecht. Unzufrieden zeigte sich die Kolonialverwaltung jedoch vor allem mit der Anwendung des islamischen Strafrechts. Ihr Unbehagen speiste sich dabei insbesondere aus der geringen Anzahl an Kapitaldelikten, dem Begnadigungsrecht der Angehörigen bei Delikten gegen Leib und Leben und auch der starken Ermessensorientierung richterlicher Entscheidungsfindung.[13]

Geleitet von einem „väterlichen und aufgeklärten Despotismus"[14], der die Erarbeitung eines Strafgesetzbuchs durch eine Handvoll von Experten ohne die Notwendigkeit öffentlicher Beteiligung als klaren Vorzug des kolonialen Staates preist, wird 1833 unter Führung des schottischen Juristen *Thomas Babington Macaulay* (1800–1859) eine Indian Law Commission eingesetzt. Ziel und Mandat sind auf die Schaffung eines konsolidierten Indian Penal Code (IPC) im Geiste der Kodifikationsideen *Jeremy Benthams* gerichtet, Leitprämissen dabei Rechtsvereinheitlichung, Gleichheit und Vorhersehbarkeit – oder in den Worten *Macaulays*: „*Uniformity when you can have it; diversity when you must have it; but in all cases certainty.*"[15]

---

[13] *Peters, R.*, Crime and Punishment in Islamic Law – Theory and Practice from the Sixteenth to the Twenty-first Century, Cambridge 2005, S. 109–119.

[14] So explizit Macaulay im House of Commons, HC Deb 10 July 1833, c533: „As I believe that India stands more in need of a code than any other country in the world, I believe also that there is no country on which that great benefit can more easily be conferred. A code is almost the only blessing – perhaps it is thc only blessing which absolute governments are better fitted to confer on a nation than popular governments. […] A quiet knot of two or three veteran jurists is an infinitely better machinery for such a purpose than a large popular assembly divided, as such assemblies almost always are, into adverse factions. […] It is the work which especially belongs to a government like that of India – *to an enlightened and paternal despotism*" (Hervorhebung durch Verf.).

[15] *Macaulay, T.B.*, The Works of Lord Macaulay – Speeches, Poems & Miscellaneous Writings, Vol. I, London 1898, S. 582.

Macaulay formuliert jedoch eine klare Absage an präexistente Traditionen hinduistischen und islamischen Strafrechts. Aus dem Besten bestehender Gesetze und innovativen neuen Elementen sucht er eine Kodifikation zu schaffen, die zwar einerseits auf die Verhältnisse vor Ort abgestimmt sein, andererseits aber über Britisch-Indien hinaus allgemeine Geltung beanspruchen soll.[16] Im Gefolge des Sepoy-Aufstands tritt der Indian Penal Code schließlich im Jahr 1862 in Kraft und gilt auch nach Erlangung der Unabhängigkeit als Pakistan Penal Code (PPC) fort.[17]

Für die weitere Rechts- und Verfassungsentwicklung Pakistans markiert das Jahr 1977 eine prägende Zäsur: General *Zia ul-Haq* (1924–1988) putscht sich an die Macht. Im Schulterschluss mit islamistischen Parteien, insbesondere der Jamaat-e-Islami *Maulana Maududis*, beginnt er, einen Prozess der „Islamisierung von oben" ins Werk zu setzen. War *Zia* zwar auch persönlich von einer rigiden Frömmigkeit beseelt, suchte er den Islam aber vor allem als Instrument informeller Legitimierung für seine illegitim erlangte Herrschaft zu nutzen.[18]

Dies schlug sich in einer deutlichen Islamisierung der Rechtsordnung nieder, die insbesondere das Strafrecht betraf und nahezu ausschließlich die punitiven, drakonischen Aspekte der Scharia betonte. Pakistan setzte sich damit an die Spitze einer in den 1970er Jahren beginnenden Entwicklung, die zur Re-Islamisierung der Strafrechtsordnungen in zahlreichen weiteren muslimischen Ländern führen sollte.[19]

Ein zentrales Element der Reformen *Zias* war die Einführung der sog. Hudood Ordinances im Jahr 1979, mit der die koranischen Grenzstrafen für Eigentumsdelikte, Ehebruch, die unlautere Bezichtigung des Ehebruchs und Alkoholgenuss in die Rechtsordnung eingeschrieben wurden.[20] Auch der

---

16 *Macaulay, T.B.*, The Works of Lord Macaulay, a.a.O., S. 5–12.

17 Auf der Grundlage von section 18(3) des Indian Independence Act (1947) wurde die einstweilige Fortgeltung kolonialer Gesetze angeordnet.

18 *Manea, E.*, In the Name of Culture and Religion: The Political Function of Blasphemy in Islamic States. In: Islam and Christian-Muslim Relations, London 27(2016)1, S. 117, 123 f.; *Rahman, F.Z.*, State restrictions on the Ahmadiyya sect in Indonesia and Pakistan: Islam or political survival? In: Australian Journal of Political Science, London 49(2014)3, S. 408, 411–413, 416–418.

19 *Peters, R.*, Crime and Punishment in Islamic Law, a.a.O., S. 142 f., 155–160.

20 Dazu detailliert *Mehdi, R.*, The Islamization of the Law in Pakistan, Richmond 1994, S. 109–156; zu jüngeren Reformen, insbesondere im Bereich des Sexualstrafrechts, *Lau, M.*, Twenty-Five years of Hudood Ordinances – A Review, In: Washington and Lee Law Review, Lexington 64(2007)4, S. 1291, 1298–1314.

Bereich des Religionsstrafrechts – bis dahin ausschließlich kolonialer Provenienz – erfuhr erhebliche Umgestaltungen, die nachfolgend im Detail vorgestellt werden sollen:

2. Das pakistanische Religionsstrafrecht

Wie stellte sich dem Zeitgenossen *Macaulays* Mitte des 19. Jahrhunderts die Rechtslage im englischen Mutterland dar?

Im dortigen common law existierte ein Blasphemiedelikt, das ausschließlich die Dogmen der anglikanischen Staatskirche schützte. Durch die Verkoppelung von Staat und Religion wurde Blasphemie in die Nähe des Hochverrats gerückt, hatte mithin eine dezidiert politische Konnotation.[21] Zahlreiche Kritiker, unter ihnen auch *Lord Macaulay*, empfanden dies schon damals als anachronistisch. In Britisch-Indien bietet sich ihm nun jedoch die Gelegenheit, ein komplett neues – und nach seinem Empfinden „zeitgemäßes" und „modernes" – Religionsstrafrecht zu schaffen. Wegen der hier vorherrschenden religiösen Pluralität kann er aber, anders als in England, gerade keinen Wahrheitsanspruch einer bestimmten Religion voraussetzen. Anknüpfungspunkt ist für ihn daher das verletzte religiöse Gefühl der Betroffenen:

> „The question whether insults offered to a religion ought to be visited with punishment does not appear to us at all to depend on the question whether that religion be true or false. The religion may be false, but the pain which such insults give to the professors of that religion is real. It is often, as the most superficial observation may convince us, as real a pain and as acute a pain as is caused by almost any offence against the person, against property or against character. [...] All these considerations apply with peculiar force to India. There is perhaps no country in which the Government has so much to apprehend from religious excitement among the people. The Christians are numerically a very small minority of the population, and in possession of all the highest posts in the Government, in tribunals, and in the army. Under their rule are placed millions of Mahomedans, of differing sects, but all strongly attached to the fundamental articles of the Mahomedan creed, and tens of millions of Hindoos, strongly attached to doctrines and rites which Christians and Mahomedans join in reprobating. Such a state of things is pregnant with dangers which can only be averted by a firm adherence to the true principles of toleration."[22]

---

[21] Dazu House of Lords in Whitehouse v Lemon, [1979] A.C., S. 617, 633 f.

[22] *Macaulay, T.B.*, The Works of Lord Macaulay, a.a.O., S. 106–108.

Damit wird auch deutlich: *Macaulays* zentrale Prämisse für die Regelung der Religionsdelikte in Britisch-Indien ist das „emotive koloniale Subjekt", das religiösen Passionen unauflöslich verhaftet sei und auf jede Kränkung religiöser Ehre mit Aufruhr und Gewalt reagiere. Das übergreifende Ziel war damit „riot control", d.h. die Aufrechterhaltung des öffentlichen Friedens im kolonialen Herrschaftsraum.

In Kapitel XV des ursprünglichen Indian Penal Code („Of Offences Relating to Religion") wurden infolgedessen die Entweihung religiöser Plätze und Objekte (section 295 IPC), die Störung religiöser Versammlungen (section 296 IPC), die Entweihung von Grabstätten, Leichenschändung und die Störung von Begräbniszeremonien (section 297 IPC) und schließlich die Verletzung religiöser Gefühle durch Worte und Gesten (section 298 IPC) mit Strafe belegt. Später, in den Jahren 1898 und 1927, schuf der koloniale Strafgesetzgeber noch weitere Tatbestände gegen Volksverhetzung auch entlang religiöser Zugehörigkeiten (section 153-A IPC) sowie gegen die Kränkung kollektiver religiöser Gefühle (section 295-A IPC), nachdem sich die bis dahin geltende Rechtslage als defizitär erwiesen hatte.

Mit Erlangung der Unabhängigkeit 1947 wurde das Religionsstrafrecht zunächst in toto in den Pakistan Penal Code überführt, erfuhr dann aber unter der Ägide *Zia ul-Haqs* grundlegende Umgestaltungen:

Den Beginn im Jahr 1980 markierte die Schaffung eines Tatbestands zum Schutz der Ehre von Personen aus dem Umkreis des Propheten Mohammed und dem frühen Islam (section 298-A PPC), dem 1982 ein weiterer Tatbestand gegen die Schmähung des Koran (section 295-B PPC) folgte. Weitere zwei Jahre später wurde dann ein umfangreiches Sonderstrafrecht gegen die Ahmadiyya-Bewegung in Kraft gesetzt (sections 298-B und 298-C PPC) und im Jahr 1986 die Schmähung des Propheten Mohammed (section 295-C PPC) mit Strafe belegt.

Die unter *Zia* eingeführten Neuerungen zeichnen sich durch gemeinsame Charakteristika aus, die sie von der egalitären Tradition des Indian Penal Code *Macaulays* deutlich abgrenzen: Dies betrifft zunächst deren exklusive Fokussierung auf Personen, Dogmen und Objekte des Islam, sodann das hohe Maß an Unbestimmtheit bei der Formulierung der einschlägigen Tatbestände, zudem die rigiden Strafdrohungen und schließlich das Fehlen prozeduraler Sicherungen, die das koloniale Strafverfahrensrecht für ausgewählte Religionsdelikte noch vorgesehen hatte. Anhand von zwei Tatbeständen – der Schmähung des Propheten Mohammed (295-C PPC) und des Gerierens eines

Ahmadis als Moslem (298-C PPC) – soll dies im Folgenden näher verdeutlicht werden:

a) Section 295-C PPC: Use of derogatory remarks, etc. in respect of the Holy Prophet

> Whoever, by words, either spoken or written, or by visible representation, or by any imputation, innuendo, or insinuation, directly or indirectly, defiles the sacred name of the Holy Prophet Muhammad (peace be upon him) shall be punished with death, [or with imprisonment for life], and shall also be liable to a fine.

Schon bei kursorischer Durchsicht drängen sich hier unweigerlich zahlreiche Fragen auf: So ist mit Blick auf den objektiven Tatbestand erklärungsbedürftig, was als tatbestandliches „defilement" gelten kann. Es mag hier dem Wortsinn nach relativ eindeutige Beispiele für eine solche Beschmutzung bzw. Entweihung geben, etwa das Schlagen mit Schuhsolen auf Plakate, die Grußformeln an den Propheten Mohammed tragen.[23] Pakistanische Gerichte entschieden jedoch, ein „defilement" liege bereits dann vor, wenn ein Mangel an gebührendem Respekt nach außen hin manifestiert werde.[24] Das Folgeproblem liegt auf der Hand: Welcher Respekt dem Propheten Mohammed gebührt, ist höchst subjektiv gefärbt.

Auch das Erfordernis einer spezifischen beleidigenden Form ist im Tatbestand selbst nicht angelegt. Es kann also schon eine Respektlosigkeit genügen, die sich aus dem Inhalt der Äußerung ergibt, etwa eine bloße Abweichung von (vermeintlich) orthodoxen Lehrmeinungen. In *Malik Muhammad Mumtaz Qadri v The State* stellte der Supreme Court Ende 2015 allerdings klar, dass der Blasphemietatbestand selbst nicht sakrosankt sei, Kritik am status quo und der damit verbundene Ruf nach (prozeduralen) Reformen mithin keinen Fall einer strafbaren Lästerung darstellten:

> „In our country the offence of blasphemy has been defined in section 295-C, PPC and [...], thus, we have found it difficult to act in this case on the basis of a definition of blasphemy advanced by the learned counsel for the appellant which definition travels beyond the scope of the statutory definition of the same in the law of the land. Apart from that in a democratic

---

[23] Lahore High Court in Ranjha Masih v The State, 2007 Yearly Law Reports, S. 337, 338.

[24] Lahore High Court in Ayyub Masih v The State, Criminal Appeal No. 159/1998, Murder Reference No. 122/1998 (unveröffentlicht), S. 1, 25.

society citizens have a right to contend, debate or maintain that a law has not been correctly framed by the State in terms of the mischief sought to be suppressed or that the law promulgated by the State ought to contain adequate safeguards against its misapplication or misuse by motivated persons. *It goes without saying that seeking improvement of a manmade law in respect of a religious matter for better or proper enforcement of such law does not ipso facto amount to criticizing the religious aspect of such law.*“[25]

Ganz abgesehen von dem aus der Unbestimmtheit des objektiven Tatbestands resultierenden allgemeinen Missbrauchspotenzial sind damit unweigerlich Spannungen zwischen verschiedenen rivalisierenden Gruppen innerhalb des von hoher Binnenpluralität gekennzeichneten pakistanischen Islam vorprogrammiert: So sind für die puristisch gesonnenen Ahl-e-Hadith zahlreiche exaltierte Praktiken der Barelvis – etwa die Feier des Geburtstags des Propheten, die direkte Fürbitte bei ihm oder die Verehrung sufistischer Heiliger – Lästerung und werden als solche zur Anzeige gebracht.[26]

Unklar ist darüber hinaus, ob section 295-C PPC eine öffentliche Begehung erfordert. Obwohl der objektive Tatbestand selbst dazu schweigt, haben pakistanische Gerichte entschieden, dass bereits Äußerungen gegenüber einer einzigen Person tatbestandsmäßig sein könnten. Begründet wurde dies mit einer bei *Abū Dāwūd* überlieferten Prophetentradition:

„Der Prophet entdeckte vor seiner Moschee eine getötete Frau. Er fragte die Betenden, wer sie umgebracht habe. Ein Blinder erhob sich und sagte: ‚Ich. Sie ist meine Sklavin, und ich habe von ihr zwei Kinder, Perlen gleich. Doch gestern Nacht hat sie dich, Prophet Gottes, beleidigt. Ich forderte sie auf, dich nicht mehr zu beschimpfen, aber sie wiederholte das Gesagte. Ich konnte das nicht aushalten und habe sie umgebracht.’ Mohammed entgegnete: ‚Das Blut dieser Frau ist zu Recht geflossen!’“[27]

---

[25] Supreme Court in *Malik Muhammad Mumtaz Qadri v The State*, Criminal Appeals No. 210 and 211 of 2015, S. 23 (Hervorhebung durch Verf.), erhältlich unter *http://online.wsj.com/public/resources/documents/BlasphemyPak.pdf* (zuletzt besucht am 23.01.2017).

[26] Für eine exemplarische Fallschilderung siehe *Ahmed, A.A.*, Specters of Macaulay – Blasphemy, the Indian Penal Code, and Pakistan's Postcolonial Predicament. In: Kaur, R./Mazzarella, W. (Hrsg.), Censorship in South Asia – Cultural Regulation from Sedition to Seduction, Bloomington 2009, S. 172, 185–195.

[27] Lahore High Court in Bashir Ahmad v The State, 2005 Yearly Law Reports, S. 985, 991 f. (Übersetzung durch Verf.).

In dieser Entscheidung tritt exemplarisch die Ambivalenz der Praxis zutage, staatliches Recht unter Rekurs auf religiöse Rechtsquellen auszulegen, da dies – wie hier – zu einer deutlichen Verschärfung führen kann.

Die Unbestimmtheit von section 295-C PPC setzt sich bei der subjektiven Tatseite fort, die nicht näher konkretisiert ist. Wenngleich pakistanische Gerichte wiederholt klargestellt haben, dass ein implizites Vorsatzerfordernis in den Tatbestand hineinzulesen sei[28], wird in der Praxis regelmäßig keine bewusste bzw. wissentliche Schmähung verlangt. Dies manifestiert sich insbesondere in den (durchaus nicht seltenen) Fällen, in denen eine schwere geistige Störung des Täters naheliegt.[29]

Augenfällig ist schließlich auch das Strafmaß, nämlich die Todesstrafe für Lästerer des Propheten Mohammed. War in der ursprünglichen Fassung von section 295-C PPC noch die Alternativsanktion der lebenslangen Freiheitsstrafe vorgesehen, muss mittlerweile zwingend die Todesstrafe verhängt werden, nachdem der Federal Shariat Court 1991 entschieden hatte, dass islamischem Recht zufolge die Tötung des Lästerers geboten sei.[30] Trotz Fehlens eines entsprechenden parlamentarischen Aufhebungsaktes hat dieser Beschluss Gesetzeskraft, die Todesstrafe ist mithin einzig zulässige Sanktion.[31]

b) Sonderstrafrecht gegen die Ahmadis

Gegen die Ahmadis gerichtete Tatbestände sind ein weiteres Beispiel religiös geprägter Strafgesetzgebung und insofern verstörend, als hier eine gesamte Religionsgruppe unter Sonderstrafrecht gestellt wird. Die einschlägigen Gesetze

---

[28] Exemplarisch Lahore High Court in Muhammad Sharif v The State, 2008 Yearly Law Reports, S. 387, 389.

[29] *Husain, M.*, Blasphemy laws and mental illness in Pakistan. In: The British Journal of Psychiatry – Psychiatric Bulletin, London 38(2014)1, S. 40, 41–43. An sich gilt nach section 84 PPC (Act of a person of unsound mind): „Nothing is an offence which is done by a person who, at the time of doing it, by reason of unsoundness of mind, is incapable of knowing the nature of the act, or that he is doing what is either wrong or contrary to law."

[30] Federal Shariat Court in Muhammad Ismail Qureshi v Pakistan, All Pakistan Legal Decisions 1991 (FSC), S. 1, 26; zur Kritik an dieser Fehlinterpretation *Mazhar, A.*, Blasphemy and the death penalty: Misconceptions explained, The Dawn vom 02.11.2015, erhältlich unter *http://www.dawn.com/news/1215304/blasphemy-and-the-death-penalty-misconceptions-explained* (zuletzt besucht am 04.01.2017).

[31] So zuletzt Lahore High Court in Mst. Asia Bibi v The State & another, Murder Reference No. 614 of 2010/Criminal Appeal No. 2509 of 2010, Rn 18, erhältlich unter *https://assets.documentcloud.org/documents/2104047/lhc-verdict.pdf* (zuletzt besucht am 23.01.2017).

sind Kulminationspunkt fortwährender historisch und religiös begründeter Ressentiments, die nachfolgend kurz skizziert werden sollen:

Hauptstreitpunkt zwischen der Ahmadiyya und dem orthodoxen Islam ist das Verständnis der Finalität der Prophetenschaft Mohammeds. Die im Koran erwähnte zweite Ankunft des Messias wird von Ahmadis auf ihren Religionsstifter *Mirza Ghulam Ahmad* (1835–1908) bezogen. Anders als Mohammed habe er aber kein neues Gesetz stiften, sondern lediglich die Botschaft des Islam erneuern wollen. Nach dem orthodoxen Islam ist Mohammed jedoch das endgültige „Siegel der Propheten“[32], d.h. der letzte in einer langen Überlieferungskette.[33]

Von Beginn an sind die Ahmadis auf dem indischen Subkontinent auf eine breite Welle der Ablehnung gestoßen, die sich insbesondere aus ihrer Loyalität zum kolonialen Staat speiste. *Maulana Maududi*, der bereits erwähnte Gründer der islamistischen Jamaat-e-Islami, bezeichnete sie als „Krebsgeschwür“, das ausgemerzt werden müsse.[34] Premierminister *Zulfikar Bhutto* ließ die Ahmadis 1974 durch Einfügung eines Verfassungszusatzes ausdrücklich zu Nicht-Muslimen erklären.[35]

Bis in die Gegenwart sind sie – neben der institutionalisierten Diskriminierung – Opfer gezielter Tötungen und Attentate durch sunnitische Extremisten. So stürmten im Mai 2010 pakistanische Taliban eine Moschee der

---

[32] Vers 33:40: „Muhammad ist nicht der Vertreter eines eurer Männer, sondern Allahs Gesandter und *das Siegel der Propheten*; und Allah weiß alle Dinge“ (Hervorhebung durch Verf.). Alle Koranzitate nach der Übersetzung von *Henning, M.*, Der Koran, Stuttgart 2008.

[33] Zu den religiösen Lehren der Ahmadis und den Unterschieden zur Orthodoxie *Ahmed, M.D.*, Ausschluss der Ahmadiyya aus dem Islam – Eine umstrittene Entscheidung des pakistanischen Parlaments. In: Orient – Deutsche Zeitschrift für Politik, Wirtschaft und Kultur des Orients, Berlin 16(1976)1, S. 112–116.

[34] *Maududi, S.A.A.*, The Qadiani Problem, Lahore 2006, S. 40.

[35] Art. 260(3): In the Constitution and all enactments and other legal instruments, unless there is anything repugnant in the subject or context:

(a) 'Muslim' means a person who believes in the unity and oneness of Almighty Allah, in the absolute and unqualified finality of the prophethood of Muhammad (Peace be upon Him), the last of the Prophets, and does not believe in, or recognize as a Prophet or religious reformer, any person who claimed or claims to be a Prophet, in any sense of the word or of any description whatsoever, after Muhammad (Peace be upon Him); and

(b) 'non-Muslim' means a person who is not a Muslim and includes a person belonging to the Christian, Hindu, Sikh, Buddhist or Parsi community, a person of the Qadiani group or the Lahori group (who call themselves 'Ahmadis' or by any other name), or a Bahai, and a person belonging to any of the Scheduled Castes.

Ahmadis in Lahore und richteten ein Blutbad mit nahezu 100 Toten und Dutzenden Verletzten an.[36]

Die strafrechtliche Stigmatisierung dieser Religionsgruppe soll im Folgenden anhand von section 298-C PPC exemplarisch dargestellt werden:

Section 298-C PPC: Person of Qadiani group, etc., calling himself a Muslim or preaching or propagating his faith

> Any person of the Qadiani group or the Lahori group (who call themselves ‚Ahmadis' or by any other name), who, directly or indirectly, poses himself as a Muslim, or calls, or refers to, his faith as Islam, or preaches, propagates his faith, or invites others to accept his faith, by words, either spoken or written, or by visible representations or in any manner whatsoever outrages the religious feelings of Muslims, shall be punished with imprisonment of either description for a term which may extend to three years and shall also be liable to fine.

Hier ist einmal mehr eine beispiellose Weite des Tatbestands erkennbar, wenngleich der pakistanische Supreme Court Probleme fehlender Bestimmtheit ausdrücklich negiert hat. „Poses as Muslim" sei immer dann erfüllt, wenn Ahmadis auf traditionell muslimische Symbole zurückgriffen.[37] Fälle aus der Judikatur betrafen unter anderem das Aufnähen des islamischen Glaubensbekenntnisses auf die Kleidung[38], die Bezeichnung ahmadischer Gebetsstätten als „Moscheen", da dies allein orthodoxen islamischen Gotteshäusern vorbehalten sei oder die Errichtung solcher Gebetsstätten nach den für Moscheen geltenden architektonischen Bauprinzipien[39].

Zahlreiche religiös motivierte Handlungen, die klassischerweise dem forum externum der Religionsfreiheit unterfallen, etwa das öffentliche Bekenntnis zum eigenen Glauben oder auch die Werbung und Missionierung für diesen, sind auf der Grundlage von section 298-C PPC mit Strafe belegt.

---

36 *CNN*, Death toll rises to 98 after Lahore attacks, Meldung vom 29.05.2010, erhältlich unter *http://edition.cnn.com/2010/WORLD/asiapcf/05/28/pakistan.violence/* (zuletzt besucht am 05.01.2017).

37 Supreme Court in Zaheeruddin v State, Pakistan Law Journal 1994 (SC), S. 1, 43.

38 Supreme Court in Zaheeruddin v State, a.a.O., S. 1, 49.

39 Lahore High Court in Ata Ullah v The State, All Pakistan Legal Decisions 2000 (Lahore), S. 364, 378.

c) Vereinbarkeit des Religionsstrafrechts mit religiösen Rechtsquellen

Zia ul-Haq, der mit dem Versprechen angetreten war, das „System des Propheten“ in Pakistan zu etablieren, sollte an seinen eigenen Worten gemessen werden.[40] Ist er diesem Anspruch gerecht geworden und lässt sich der status quo tatsächlich auf islamische Rechtsgrundsätze zurückführen?

Mit Blick auf die Bestrafung der Lästerung des Propheten Mohammed, die hier pars pro toto herausgegriffen werden soll, stellt sich die Position im klassischen islamischen Recht nach mehrheitlicher Meinung wohl wie folgt dar:

Im Koran selbst gibt es keine textliche Fundierung für die Tötung des Lästerers im Diesseits. Die Prophetentraditionen sind ambivalent: So existieren einerseits Hadithe, in denen Mohammed eine Tötung seiner Lästerer billigte, andererseits aber auch solche, in denen er eine nachträgliche Begnadigung aussprach. Die dennoch rigide Position zur Schmähung Mohammeds scheint vor allem der islamischen Rechtsgelehrsamkeit zu entspringen, wobei hier das „Buch der Heilung durch Kundgabe der Rechte des Erwählten“ des *Qāḍī Iyāḍ* sowie *Ibn Taimīyas* „Scharfschneidendes, gezückt wider den, der den Gesandten Allahs schilt“ exemplarisch zu nennen sind.

Unter anderem auf diese beiden Werke stützte sich der Federal Shariat Court 1991 in seiner Entscheidung zur Gebotenheit der Todesstrafe für die Lästerung des Propheten, die er als zwingend bejahte.[41] Das Gericht schränkte jedoch ein, der Tatbestandsvorsatz müsse klar dargetan sein und erfordere ein Element böswilliger Verächtlichmachung, das sich z.B. aus dem Kontext der Äußerung ergeben könne. Entgegen der (in Pakistan herrschenden) hanafitischen Rechtsschule machten die Richter allerdings keinen Unterschied zwischen Muslimen und Nicht-Muslimen.[42]

Dass der status quo keinesfalls klaglos akzeptiert wird, sondern sich auch deutlicher innerislamischer Kritik ausgesetzt sieht, sei anhand einer Stellungnahme des auf dem indischen Subkontinent bekannten islamischen Rechtsgelehrten *Maulana Wahiduddin Khan* (geb. 1925) verdeutlicht. In seinem Traktat „Shatme Rasool ka Masla“ (Das Problem der Lästerung des Propheten),

---

40 In seiner ersten Fernsehansprache erklärte *Zia*: „Pakistan, which was created in the name of Islam, will continue to survive only if it sticks to Islam. That is why I consider the introduction of an Islamic system as an essential prerequisite for the country.“ (Zitat aus *Talbot, I.*, Pakistan – A Modern History, London 2005, S. 251).

41 Federal Shariat Court in Muhammad Ismail Qureshi v Pakistan, a.a.O., S. 10, 26.

42 Zu dieser notwendigen Unterscheidung *Mazhar, A.*, Blasphemy and the death penalty: Misconceptions explained, a.a.O.

das unmittelbar nach seinem Erscheinen in Pakistan verboten wurde, kommt der Maulana zu dem Schluss, die Todesstrafe für die Lästerung des Propheten Mohammed sei eine reine Innovation islamischer Rechtsgelehrter:

So gebe es dafür kein klares Mandat aus Koran und Sunna. Viele der zur Verteidigung angeführten Prophetentraditionen seien von zweifelhafter Authentizität und könnten nicht verallgemeinert werden, da sie sich häufig nicht auf bloße Schmähungen, sondern eher Fälle einer aggressiven Kriegsführung gegen den Islam insgesamt bezögen. Selbst wenn man sich aber auf diese zweifelhaften Traditionen stützen wolle, müsse die Vollziehung der Todesstrafe dennoch ausgesetzt werden. *Ibn Taimīya* selbst habe nämlich anerkannt, dass alle Handlungen zu unterlassen seien, die der Reputation des Islam schadeten – angesichts weltweiter Proteste gegen die Rechtslage in Pakistan schwerlich zu leugnen.[43]

Auch liege kein Fall des „Verderbenstiftens auf der Erde“[44] vor, denn dieses erfasse ausschließlich Akte des gewaltsamen Terrorismus. Schmähungen gegen den Propheten wirkten jedoch auf geistiger Ebene und würden allein durch Wort und Schrift begangen. Hier gebe es nur zwei islamkonforme Reaktionsmöglichkeiten: das Ignorieren der Schmähungen oder einen ausschließlich publizistischen „Gegenschlag“.[45]

d) Die Rationes des zeitgenössischen pakistanischen Religionsstrafrechts

Welcher Schluss ist aus diesen theologischen Disputen für das pakistanische Strafrecht zu ziehen? Basiert es möglicherweise allein auf einem religiösen Fundament, das gänzlich frei von zweckrationalen Erwägungen ist? Oder geht es auch um den Schutz innerweltlicher Rechtsgüter?

---

43 Siehe exemplarisch *Mara, D.*, Pope offers rare criticism of Pakistan blasphemy law, Deutsche Welle vom 10.01.2011, erhältlich unter *http://www.dw.com/en/pope-offers-rare-criticism-of-pakistan-blasphemy-law/a-14760222* (zuletzt besucht am 04.01.2017); *European Parliament*, Resolution of 27 November 2014 on Pakistan: blasphemy laws (2014/2969(RSP), erhältlich unter *http://www.europarl.europa.eu/sides/getDoc.do?type=TA&language=EN&reference=P8-TA-2014-0064* (zuletzt besucht am 04.01.2017).

44 Vers 5:33: „Siehe, der Lohn derer, welche Allah und seinen Gesandten befehden und Verderben auf der Erde betreiben, ist nur der, daß sie getötet oder gekreuzigt oder an Händen und Füßen wechselseitig verstümmelt oder aus dem Lande vertrieben werden. Das ist ihr Lohn hienieden, und im Jenseits wird ihnen schmerzliche Strafe.“

45 Die Wiedergabe dieser Argumentation basiert auf einer Korrespondenz, die der Verf. im Jahr 2010 mit *Maulana Wahiduddin Khan* geführt hat.

Wie bereits dargelegt, ist der öffentliche Friede seit der Kolonialzeit prägendes Schutzgut der Religionsdelikte. Auch in der zeitgenössischen Judikatur klingt dies an, indem pakistanische Gerichte insbesondere argumentieren, einer Aufhetzung zu Straftaten vorbeugen zu müssen:

> „It is the cardinal faith of every Muslim to believe in every Prophet and praise him. Therefore, if anything is said against the Prophet, it will injure the feelings of a Muslim *and may even incite him to a breach of peace*, depending on the intensity of the attack.“[46]

Darüber hinaus wird nachdrücklich auch die Notwendigkeit beschworen, Selbstjustiz zu verhindern:

> „The provisions of section 295-C of the P.P.C. have made it possible to bring the culprits to book through the judicial process and has [sic] set a trend in society to resort to the law. The registration of a criminal case under the above-referred section of the Pakistani Penal Code provides a lease of life to an accused with full opportunity to defend himself in a Court of law through a counsel of his choice and in case of conviction, to avail of the remedies of appeal, revision etc. in the higher Courts. No person, much less a Muslim, can possibly oppose this law as it curtails arbitrariness and promotes the rule of law. *If the provisions of section 295-C of the P.P.C. are repealed or declared to be ultra vires to Constitution, the time old method of doing away with the culprits at the spot would stand revived.*“[47]

Dieser Hinweis auf Vigilantismus und Lynchjustiz speist sich aus einschlägigen historischen Erfahrungen. In Britisch-Indien, das zu Beginn des 20. Jahrhunderts von schweren Auseinandersetzungen zwischen Hindus und Muslimen heimgesucht wurde, gab es mehrere Fälle, in denen Muslime die Verletzung der Ehre Mohammeds zu rächen suchten und seine Lästerer eigenhändig töteten.[48] Für diese Taten bezahlten sie mit dem Leben, erlangten aber im kollektiven Bewusstsein Märtyrerstatus als Vorbilder einer authentischen und grenzenlosen Liebe zum Propheten, die selbst das Opfer des eigenen Lebens einschließt. In

---

46 Supreme Court in Zaheeruddin v State, a.a.O., S. 1, 49 (Hervorhebung durch Verf.).

47 Sondervotum des Richters *M.N. Akhtar* in Lahore High Court in Riaz Ahmad and 3 others v The State, All Pakistan Legal Decisions 1994 (Lahore), S. 485, 502 (Hervorhebung durch Verf.).

48 Der bekannteste von ihnen war der 18-jährige *Ilam Din* aus Lahore, der 1929 den (vermeintlichen) Autor des gegen den Propheten Mohammed gerichteten Spottgedichts „Rangila Rasul“ erdolchte und dafür hingerichtet wurde.

dieser Traditionslinie, die bis heute wirkmächtig beschworen wird[49], steht auch der am 29. Februar 2016 hingerichtete Attentäter *Mumtaz Qadri*, der Anfang Januar 2011 den Gouverneur der Provinz Punjab erschoss, nachdem dieser Kritik an den pakistanischen Blasphemiegesetzen geäußert und sich für Reformen eingesetzt hatte.

Ein weiterer Rechtfertigungsstrang – vor allem im öffentlichen Diskurs – ist die Verknüpfung des Religionsstrafrechts mit der herrschenden Sozialmoral. Im Lichte deutscher Strafrechtsdogmatik und des strafrechtskritischen Rechtsgutsbegriffs sind Zweifel angebracht, ob dies überhaupt legitime Aufgabe des Strafrechts sein kann. Auch in der anglo-amerikanischen Rechtsphilosophie gab es dazu in den 1960er Jahren eine berühmte Debatte, die nach den beteiligten Protagonisten als *Hart*/*Devlin*-Kontroverse bekannt geworden ist: Der englische Lordrichter *Devlin* postulierte, das Überleben jedweder Gesellschaft hänge ab von einer gemeinsam geteilten Moral. Daher sei der Staat berechtigt, denjenigen zu bestrafen, der gegen allgemein geteilte moralische Überzeugungen verstoße. Der Rechtsphilosoph *Hart* hielt dagegen, das Strafrecht sei allein auf den Schutz personaler Kerninteressen beschränkt.[50]

In Pakistan ist *Devlinsches* Denken allerdings nach wie vor verbreitet und vollzieht sich entlang folgender Argumentationslinien:

1. Die gemeinsame Sozialmoral wird vom Islam gespeist.
2. Die Lästerung religiöser Objekte untergräbt diese gemeinsame Moral, indem so deren religiöses Fundament geleugnet wird. Dies gilt in besonderer Weise für den Propheten Mohammed, der zentraler Gewährsmann für die Wahrheit der göttlichen Überlieferung ist.
3. Aus diesem Grund darf der Staat Blasphemie bestrafen, um die Quellen der Sozialmoral rein zu halten und sich und die Gesellschaft vor Unmoral und letztlich Chaos zu schützen.[51]

Das *Pew Center* hat dazu Ende 2011 eine Meinungsumfrage durchgeführt: Demnach urteilten 75 % der Befragten in Pakistan, die dortigen Blasphemiegesetze seien notwendig, um den Islam zu schützen.[52]

---

49 Dazu *Rumi, R.*, Blasphemy it was not, The Friday Times vom 30.10.2015, erhältlich unter *http://www.thefridaytimes.com/tft/blasphemy-it-was-not/* (zuletzt besucht am 05.01.2017).

50 Zusammenfassung bei *Häyry, H.*, Liberalism and Legal Moralism: The Hart-Devlin Debate and Beyond. In: Ratio Juris 4(1991)2, S. 202–218.

51 Exemplarisch *Ghazi, M.A.*, The Law of Tawhīn-i-Risālat, In: Jan, T. et al. (Hrsg.), Pakistan: Between Secularism and Islam, Islamabad 2003, S. 219, 220–223.

e) Vom „law in the books“ zum „law in action“ – das Religionsstrafrecht in der Praxis

Richtet man den Blick vom „law in the books“, seiner Genese und Geschichte zum „law in action“, sind gravierende Defizite augenfällig. Zwei Problemkomplexe sollen hier exemplarisch herausgegriffen werden: das Viktimisierungs- und Eskalationspotenzial bestehender Blasphemiegesetze sowie die inhärenten Mängel bei der Durchführung von Blasphemieverfahren.

aa) Viktimisierungs- und Eskalationspotenzial der Blasphemiegesetze

Ein zentrales Argument der Apologeten ist gerade vorgestellt worden, nämlich die Behauptung, dass ohne ein strafrechtliches Verbot der Lästerung des Propheten Mohammed die Bevölkerung das Recht unweigerlich in die eigenen Hände nehme. Die Existenz einschlägiger Tatbestände diene mithin dem Schutz des Täters.

Das damit behauptete Befriedungspotenzial der Religionsdelikte lässt sich – vor dem Hintergrund einer zunehmenden Radikalisierung und religiösen Intoleranz in Pakistan – empirisch jedoch nicht belegen, vielmehr ist das genaue Gegenteil der Fall: Es stimmt zwar, dass auf Geheiß des Staates bisher keine Hinrichtungen stattgefunden haben. Verbürgt sind aber zahlreiche Fälle nichtstaatlicher Lynchjustiz. Findet sich für die Phase ab 1947 noch kein einziger solcher Fall, wurden im Zeitraum 1990 bis Mitte Juli 2012 nach Zählungen einer pakistanischen NGO 59 Personen, die im Verdacht der Blasphemie standen, ermordet.[53] Dies ist auch an vermeintlich sicheren Orten geschehen, etwa in Gerichten, durch Gefängnispersonal oder auch Mithäftlinge.

Darüber hinaus sind zahlreiche Fälle von Mob-Gewalt dokumentiert: So kamen in Gojra im Punjab Ende Juli 2009 nach einer christlichen Hochzeitsfeier Gerüchte auf, dort seien Papiere mit Koranversen verbrannt worden. Vor den Dorfrat zitiert stritt der Beschuldigte die Anschuldigungen jedoch ab. Kurz danach wurde von den Lautsprechern aller umliegenden Moscheen dazu

---

52 *Pew Research Center*, The World's Muslims: Religion, Politics and Society, 2013, S. 199, erhältlich unter *http://www.pewforum.org/files/2013/04/worlds-muslims-religion-politics-society-full-report.pdf* (zuletzt besucht am 22.01.2017).

53 *Center for Research and Security Studies*, Blasphemy Laws in Pakistan – A Historical Overview, Islamabad 2013, S. 44, erhältlich unter *http://crss.pk/wp-content/uploads/2010/07/Report-on-Blasphemy-Laws-.pdf* (zuletzt besucht am 04.01.2017); *Julius, Q.*, The Experience of Minorities Under Pakistan's Blasphemy Laws. In: Islam and Christian-Muslim Relations, London 27(2016)1, S. 95, 103. Die Zahl von 59 Toten gibt jedoch nicht mehr den aktuellen Stand wieder, es haben sich seitdem zahlreiche weitere Fälle von Lynchjustiz ereignet.

aufgerufen, den Christen eine Lektion zu erteilen und die Ehre des Koran wiederherzustellen. Nach mehreren Tagen der Verwüstung – unter den Augen einer passiven und überforderten Polizei – waren acht Christen aus Gojra tot, mehrere verletzt und etwa 120 Häuser und zwei Kirchen gebrandschatzt.[54]

Die Statistiken mehrerer NGOs belegen, dass es im Gefolge der Verschärfung der Religionstatbestände unter *Zia* zu einem massiven Anstieg der Verfahrenszahlen gekommen ist: Waren für den Zeitraum 1947 bis 1980 lediglich acht Verfahren unter den pakistanischen Blasphemiegesetzen verbürgt, belief sich diese Zahl im Zeitraum 1980 bis 2012 auf 1.246 Fälle. Das Befriedungsargument der Apologeten ist damit schlechterdings nicht haltbar.[55]

Nicht verschweigen sollte man auch die überproportionale Betroffenheit religiöser Minderheiten. Zwar sind nach absoluten Zahlen die meisten Opfer Muslime (v.a. Schiiten); angesichts eines Bevölkerungsanteils von zusammen lediglich ca. 3–4 % muss es aber verstören, dass ca. 40 % aller Verfahren Ahmadis und etwa 12 % Christen betreffen.[56]

bb) Schwere prozedurale Mängel bei der Durchführung von Blasphemieverfahren

Bezichtigungen eines Verstoßes gegen die Blasphemiegesetze – häufig von religiösen Eiferern oder Klerikern vorgebracht[57] – entwickeln regelmäßig eine Eigendynamik, die kaum zu kontrollieren ist.[58] Üblicherweise erfolgt auf der

---

[54] *Tavernise, S.*, Hate Engulfs Christians in Pakistan, New York Times vom 02.08.2009, erhältlich unter *http://www.nytimes.com/2009/08/03/world/asia/03pstan.html* (zuletzt besucht am 05.01.2017).

[55] Dazu ausführlich *Julius, Q.*, The Experience of Minorities Under Pakistan's Blasphemy Laws, a.a.O., S. 95, 100–104; ferner *Center for Research and Security Studies*, Blasphemy Laws in Pakistan, a.a.O., S. 43–52.

[56] *Julius, Q.*, The Experience of Minorities Under Pakistan's Blasphemy Laws, a.a.O., S. 95, 96–100.

[57] *Amnesty International*, „As Good as Dead" – The Impact of the Blasphemy Laws in Pakistan, London 2016, S. 11, 29, erhältlich unter *https://www.amnesty.org/en/documents/asa33/5136/2016/en/* (zuletzt besucht am 23.01.2017); speziell zur Vereinigung zur Finalität der Prophetenschaft Mohammeds, die für zahlreiche Anzeigen verantwortlich ist, siehe *Reuters*, Pakistani lawyers' group behind spike in blasphemy cases, Meldung vom 06.03.2016, erhältlich unter *http://www.reuters.com/article/pakistan-blasphemy-lawyers-idUSKCN0W905G* (zuletzt besucht am 23.01.2017).

[58] Zum Verfahrensmissbrauch detailliert *Amnesty International*, „As Good as Dead", a.a.O., S. 21–42; ferner *International Commission of Jurists*, On Trial: The Implementation of Pakistan's Blasphemy Laws, Geneva 2015, S. 25–27, erhältlich unter: *http://www.refworld.org/pdfid/565da4824.pdf* (zuletzt besucht am 23.01.2017).

Ebene der Instanzgerichte zunächst eine Verurteilung, die von den Rechtsmittelgerichten später wieder aufgehoben wird.

In zahlreichen Verfahren gibt es Indizien für eine persönliche Feindschaft zwischen Beschuldigtem und Anzeigendem, etwa vorausgegangene Streitereien, religiöse Dispute oder Auseinandersetzungen um Land. Dies führt dazu, dass der Beweiswert belastender Aussagen, die teilweise auch frei erfunden werden, deutlich entkräftet ist. Laut einer jüngst veröffentlichten Studie der International Commission of Jurists finden sich solche Verfahrenskompromate in 60 % der 25 einschlägigen Urteile pakistanischer Obergerichte aus den letzten Jahren.[59]

Die Neigung der Instanzgerichte, trotz unsicherer Beweislage dennoch zu Verurteilungen zu gelangen, lässt sich zunächst mit einer verbreiteten Einschüchterung der Beteiligten und einem daraus resultierenden Klima der Angst erklären. Häufig sind religiöse Eiferer anwesend, die vor oder im Gerichtssaal Slogans skandieren oder Drohungen aussprechen. 1997 wurde ein Richter des Lahore High Court ermordet, nachdem er christliche Angeklagte freigesprochen hatte, die der Schmähung des Propheten nach section 295-C PPC angeklagt waren.[60] Dasselbe Schicksal ereilte 2014 einen prominenten Rechtsanwalt, der vor allem Mandate in Blasphemieverfahren übernommen hatte.[61]

Eine effektive Verteidigung ist zudem regelmäßig erschwert durch die Furcht, die Wiederholung der inkriminierten Aussagen könne erneut als Blasphemie gewertet werden. Zudem vermag die Unbestimmtheit der Strafgesetze allzu leicht als Einfallstor für stark religiös gefärbte Überzeugungen bei Polizei, Staatsanwaltschaft und Gerichten zu fungieren. In diesem Kontext ist auch erwähnenswert, dass Verfahren unter section 295-C PPC von Gesetzes wegen vor muslimischen Richtern geführt werden müssen.

Es liegt auf der Hand, dass dies mit großem Leid für die Betroffenen verbunden ist.[62] Da in solchen Fällen eine gesetzliche Vermutung gegen die

---

59 *International Commission of Jurists*, On Trial, a.a.O., S. 25.

60 *Walsh, D.*, Pakistan's blasphemy laws have left even judges in fear of their lives, The Guardian vom 03.10.2011, erhältlich unter *https://www.theguardian.com/commentisfree/belief/2011/oct/03/pakistan-blasphemy-laws* (zuletzt besucht am 05.01.2017).

61 *BBC*, Pakistan 'blasphemy lawyer' shot dead in Multan office, Meldung vom 07.05.2014, erhältlich unter *http://www.bbc.com/news/world-asia-27319433* (zuletzt besucht am 05.01.2017).

62 Dies klar konzedierend Supreme Court in *Malik Muhammad Mumtaz Qadri v The State*, a.a.O., S. 25 f.: „It is an unfortunate fact which cannot be disputed that in many cases registered in respect of the offence of blasphemy false allegations are leveled for extraneous purposes and in the absence of adequate safeguards against misapplication or

Gewährung von Kaution besteht, bleiben sie üblicherweise während des gesamten Verfahrens in Haft. Das bedeutet regelmäßig zunächst zwei bis drei Jahre von der Verhaftung bis zum erstinstanzlichen Urteil und weitere vier bis fünf Jahre bis zum Urteil des Berufungsgerichts, bei Letztbefassung des Supreme Court auch noch einige Jahre mehr. In diesem Zeitraum werden die Betroffenen häufig in Einzelhaft gehalten und sind den Bedrohungen von Mitinsassen oder auch des Gefängnispersonals ausgesetzt.

f) Pakistanisches Religionsstrafrecht und völkerrechtliche Gewährleistungen

Seit 2010 ist Pakistan Ratifikationsstaat des Internationalen Pakts über bürgerliche und politische Rechte (IPbpR), dessen Garantien einen globalen menschenrechtlichen Grundkonsens reflektieren.[63] Stoßen menschenrechtlich fundierte Argumentationen in Pakistan selbst zwar regelmäßig auf Skepsis, weil sie allzu leicht als trojanisches Pferd des „Westens“ zur Unterminierung einer islamkonformen Lebensweise diskreditiert werden können, bilden sie gleichwohl einen verbindlichen völkerrechtlichen Maßstab, an dem sich der innerstaatliche Rechtszustand messen lassen muss. Im Lichte der Paktgewährleistungen sind jedoch zahlreiche Verstöße zu konstatieren[64], die neben dem materiellen Religionsstrafrecht insbesondere dessen Anwendung in der Praxis betreffen:

Als paktwidrig kann zunächst die strafrechtliche Privilegierung des Islam gelten, der durch zahlreiche Sondertatbestände – etwa die Entweihung des Koran oder die Schmähung des Propheten Mohammed – eigens geschützt ist. In Art. 26 IPbpR[65] wird ein umfassendes und autonomes Recht auf Gleichbehandlung verbrieft, das auf den unterschiedslosen Schutz aller im Staat lebenden Personen durch nationale Gesetze zielt und Ausnahmen vom Vorliegen objektiver und vertretbarer Gründe abhängig macht.[66] Der

---

misuse of such law by motivated persons the persons falsely accused of commission of that offence suffer beyond proportion or repair.“

[63] In diesem Sinne *Nowak, M.*, CCPR Commentary, Kehl 2005, Introduction, Rn 2: „most authoritative universal minimum standard of present international human rights law“.

[64] Dazu jüngst ausführlich *Amnesty International*, „As Good as Dead“, a.a.O., S. 53–59; ferner *International Commission of Jurists*, On Trial, a.a.O., S. 16–56.

[65] Art. 26 ICCPR: „All persons are equal before the law and are entitled without any discrimination to the equal protection of the law. In this respect, the law shall prohibit any discrimination and guarantee to all persons equal and effective protection against discrimination on any grounds such as [...] religion [...].“

[66] *Human Rights Committee*, General Comment No. 18, UN Doc. HRI/GEN/1/Rev.9, §§ 12 f.; *Schilling, T.*, Internationaler Menschenrechtsschutz, Tübingen 2010, S. 272 f.

Menschenrechtsausschuss hat diesbezüglich jedoch klargestellt, dass weder der Status als Staats- oder Mehrheitsreligion noch Tradition, Herkommen oder soziale Verwurzelung eine Differenzierung zu rechtfertigen vermöchten.[67] Daher kann – entgegen dem pakistanischen Supreme Court[68] – auch das gleichheitswidrige Sonderstrafrecht gegen die Ahmadis nicht mit historisch gewachsenen Ressentiments oder einem Schutz der Mehrheitsreligion gerechtfertigt werden.

Zudem verstößt die Todesstrafe als ausschließliche Sanktion für die Lästerung des Propheten Mohammed gegen Art. 6(2) IPbpR[69], dem zufolge deren Verhängung allein in Bezug auf eine (paktimmanent zu bestimmende) Kategorie der „most serious crimes" zulässig ist. Die seinerzeitige VN-Sonderberichterstatterin für die Problematik außergerichtlicher, summarischer und willkürlicher Tötungen, *Asma Jahangir*, stellte 2002 ausdrücklich fest, dass Verstöße gegen herrschende Moralvorstellungen oder religiöse Aktivitäten keinesfalls in diese Gruppe fielen.[70] Mittlerweile beschränkt der Menschenrechtsausschuss solche „most serious crimes" allein auf Fälle einer vorsätzlichen Tötung und betont zudem, die Todesstrafe dürfe – anders als bei der Schmähung des Propheten Mohammed in section 295-C PPC – niemals ausschließliche Strafandrohung (mandatory death penalty) sein.[71]

Das Problem fehlender Bestimmtheit – von pakistanischen Gerichten mit Blick auf das nationale Verfassungsrecht zurückgewiesen[72] – stellt sich aus

---

67 *Human Rights Committee*, General Comment No. 22, UN Doc. CCPR/C/21/Rev.1/Add.4, § 9.

68 Supreme Court in Zaheeruddin v State, a.a.O., S. 1, 38: Demnach seien sich die Muslime einig „that the birth of the Ahmadia community [...] was a serious and organized attack on its ideological frontiers. They consider it a permanent threat to their integrity and solidarity, because the socio-political organization of the Muslim society is based on its religion. In that situation their using the above given epithets etc., in a manner which to the Muslim mind looks like a deliberate and calculated act of defiling and desecration of their holy personages, is a threat to the integrity of 'Ummah' and tranquility of the nation, and it is bound to give rise to a serious law and order situation, like it happened many a time in the past."

69 Art. 6(2) ICCPR: „In countries which have not abolished the death penalty, sentence of death may be imposed only for the most serious crimes in accordance with the law in force at the time of the commission of the crime and not contrary to the provisions of the present Covenant [...]".

70 *Jahangir, A.*, Special Rapporteur on Extrajudicial, Summary or Arbitrary Executions, Report 2002, UN Doc. E/CN.4/2002/74, 9 January 2002, § 114.

71 *Joseph, S./Castan, M.*, The International Covenant on Civil and Political Rights – Cases, Materials, and Commentary, Oxford 2013, Rn 8.50 und 8.57 m.w.N.

72 Supreme Court in Zaheeruddin v State, a.a.O. (Fn. 37), S. 1, 42–45.

völkerrechtlicher Perspektive sehr wohl: Hier ist die Einschränkung von Kommunikationsgrundrechten nur bei einer hinreichend präzisen Formulierung des einschränkenden Tatbestands zulässig (Erfordernis des „prescribed by law“[73]). Dem Menschenrechtsausschuss zufolge bedeutet dies, dass sich die Kriterien der Strafbarkeit bereits direkt aus der zugrunde liegenden Bestimmung selbst ergeben müssten, staatlichen Stellen mithin keine unbeschränkte Ermächtigung zur Einschränkung des Grundrechts gegeben werden dürfe. Kritik an religiösen Führern oder auch die Kommentierung religiöser Glaubenssätze seien in jedem Fall straflos.[74]

Weitere Verstöße gegen Garantien des Zivilpakts liegen in prozeduraler und verfahrensrechtlicher Hinsicht vor: Art. 14 IPbpR garantiert verschiedene Facetten des Rechts auf ein faires Verfahren, u.a. die Unabhängigkeit und Unparteilichkeit der Gerichte[75], das Recht auf ein zügiges Verfahren sowie das Recht auf eine effektive Verteidigung.[76] Gehört zur Unabhängigkeit der Gerichte, wie der Menschenrechtsausschuss klargestellt hat, auch die Möglichkeit einer von Bedrohung durch private Akteure freien Entscheidung des Spruchkörpers[77], scheint dies in Pakistan angesichts der zuvor geschilderten, durchaus gängigen Einschüchterungspraktiken nicht gewährleistet. Mit Blick auf die regelmäßig überlange Haft- und Verfahrensdauer, die sowohl durch systemimmanente Faktoren, etwa die paktwidrige Verweigerung einer

---

73 Vgl. exemplarisch Art. 18(3) und 19(3) ICCPR.

74 *Human Rights Committee*, General Comment No. 34, UN Doc. CCPR/C/GC/34, §§ 25, 34, 48.

75 Art. 14(1) ICCPR: „All persons shall be equal before the courts and tribunals. In the determination of any criminal charge against him, or of his rights and obligations in a suit at law, everyone shall be entitled to a fair and public hearing by a competent, independent and impartial tribunal established by law. [...]“

76 Art. 14(3) ICCPR: „In the determination of any criminal charge against him, everyone shall be entitled to the following minimum guarantees, in full equality: [...] (c) to be tried without undue delay; (d) to be tried in his presence, and to defend himself in person or through legal assistance of his own choosing; [...].“

77 *Human Rights Committee*, General Comment No. 32, UN Doc. CCPR/C/GC/32, § 25: „The notion of fair trial includes the guarantee of a fair and public hearing. Fairness of proceedings entails the absence of any direct or indirect influence, pressure or intimidation or intrusion from whatever side and for whatever motive. A hearing is not fair if, for instance, the defendant in criminal proceedings is faced with the expression of a hostile attitude from the public or support for one party in the courtroom that is tolerated by the court, thereby impinging on the right to defence, or is exposed to other manifestations of hostility with similar effects“; ähnlich *Nowak, M.*, CCPR Commentary, a.a.O., Art. 14 CCPR, Rn 26.

Freilassung gegen Kautionsleistung[78], aber auch durch die Unwilligkeit der Verfahrensbeteiligten bedingt ist, sind zudem Garantien auf einen zügigen Verfahrensabschluss verletzt. Kompromittiert ist auch das Recht auf eine effektive Verteidigung in Anbetracht der Schwierigkeiten, Anwälte für solche Personen zu finden, die schwerer Blasphemieverbrechen angeklagt sind und diese auch vor Einschüchterungsversuchen von dritter Seite zu schützen.[79]

Auf der Grundlage von Art. 10(1) IPbpR[80] ist schließlich eine humane Behandlung von Gefangenen während der Haft sicherzustellen, deren stringente Gewährleistung angesichts aus pakistanischen Gefängnissen häufig berichteter Übergriffe auf die Betroffenen bis hin zu deren Tötung klar in Frage steht.

Folgerichtig wird daher eine fehlende Völkerrechtskonformität des Religionsstrafrechts Pakistans konstatiert und auch aus diesem Grund die Abschaffung der einschlägigen Tatbestände gefordert:

> „Blasphemy laws, Hudood Ordinances, and anti-Ahmadi laws, as well as any other discriminatory legal provisions, should be repealed and replaced with provisions in conformity with Pakistan's Constitution and the international human rights law instruments to which Pakistan is a party."[81]

---

78 Art. 9(3) ICCPR: „[...] It shall not be the general rule that persons awaiting trial shall be detained in custody, but release may be subject to guarantees to appear for trial, at any other stage of the judicial proceedings, and, should occasion arise, for execution of the judgement."

79 Siehe Fn. 77.

80 Art. 10(1) ICCPR: „All persons deprived of their liberty shall be treated with humanity and with respect for the inherent dignity of the human person. [...]". Siehe dazu *Human Rights Committee*, General Comment No. 21, UN Doc. HRI/GEN/1/Rev.1, § 3: „Article 10, paragraph 1, imposes on States parties a positive obligation towards persons who are particularly vulnerable because of their status as persons deprived of liberty, and complements for them the ban on torture or other cruel, inhuman or degrading treatment or punishment contained in article 7 of the Covenant. Thus, not only may persons deprived of their liberty not be subjected to treatment that is contrary to article 7, including medical or scientific experimentation, but neither may they be subjected to any hardship or constraint other than that resulting from the deprivation of liberty; respect for the dignity of such persons must be guaranteed under the same conditions as for that of free persons." Zudem liegt ein Verstoß gegen Art. 9(1) ICCPR vor, dem zufolge auch das „right to security of person" als Schutz von „individuals against intentional infliction of bodily or mental injury, regardless of whether the victim is detained or non-detained" garantiert ist, vgl. Human Rights Committee, General Comment No. 35, UN Doc. CCPR/C/GC/35, § 9.

81 *Knaul, G.*, Report of the Special Rapporteur on the independence of judges and lawyers, UN Doc. A/HRC/23/43/Add.2 (2013), 4 April 2013, § 117.

3. Ausblick – Zur Reformfähigkeit des religionsstrafrechtlichen status quo in Pakistan

Existiert angesichts der zahlreichen Missstände jedoch tatsächlich eine realistische Reformperspektive?

Mit welch hohen Risiken eine Kritik am status quo verbunden ist, verdeutlichen zwei Attentate aus jüngerer Zeit:

Im Januar 2011 wurde der Gouverneur der Provinz Punjab, *Salman Taseer*, von seinem eigenen Leibwächter erschossen, nachdem er, *Taseer*, section 295-C PPC als „black law“ bezeichnet hatte. Auch hatte er angekündigt, eine Christin zu begnadigen, die gerade wegen Lästerung des Propheten Mohammed verurteilt worden war. Dasselbe Schicksal ereilte wenige Monate später den christlichen Minister für religiöse Minderheiten, *Shahbaz Bhatti*, der sich ebenfalls für eine Reform der Blasphemiegesetze ausgesprochen hatte. Während die für *Bhattis* Tod verantwortlichen, unter den pakistanischen Taliban vermuteten Hintermänner weiter flüchtig sind, wurde der Attentäter *Salman Taseers* Ende Februar 2016 wegen Mordes und Terrorismus hingerichtet. Etwa 100.000 Personen begleiteten sein Begräbnis in Rawalpindi, die Grablege hat sich zu einem vielbesuchten Wallfahrtsort für seine Anhänger entwickelt.[82]

Der das Todesurteil bestätigende Supreme Court bekräftigte noch einmal das ausschließliche Gewaltmonopol des Staates, das es allen Bürgern verbiete, Lynchjustiz zu üben.[83] Außerdem stellten die Richter klar, dass Kritik an den Blasphemiegesetzen und der Ruf nach Reformen nicht bereits ihrerseits tatbestandsmäßige Blasphemie seien.

Nimmt man mögliche Reformperspektiven in den Blick, sind abstrakt zwei grundsätzliche Optionen denkbar: zunächst die „große Lösung“ im Sinne einer

---

[82] *Boone, J.*, Thousands at funeral of Pakistani executed for murdering governor, The Guardian vom 01.03.2016, erhältlich unter *https://www.theguardian.com/world/2016/mar/01/funeral-pakistani-mumtaz-qadri-executed-salmaan-taseer; Pasha, A.*, Mumtaz Qadri's shrine: In memory of Salmaan Taseer's assassin, The Dawn vom 27.12.2016, erhältlich unter *http://www.dawn.com/news/1302289* (beide zuletzt besucht am 05.01.2017).

[83] Supreme Court in *Malik Muhammad Mumtaz Qadri v The State*, a.a.O., S. 37, 38: „The law of the land does not permit an individual to arrogate unto himself the roles of a complainant, prosecutor, judge and executioner. [...] If the asserted religious motivation of the appellant for the murder committed by him by taking the law in his own hands is to be accepted as a valid mitigating circumstance in this case then a door shall become open for religious vigilantism which may deal a mortal blow to the rule of law in this country where divergent religious interpretations abound and tolerance stands depleted to an alarming level.“

Änderung des materiellen Strafrechts, z.B. durch Egalisierung oder Abschaffung der islamschützenden Tatbestände; alternativ eine zumindest verfahrensrechtliche Einhegung, die auf Eindämmung der eklatanten Missbrauchsproblematik zielt.

Ersteres wird auf lange Sicht nicht möglich sein, da hier zäher Widerstand von Seiten konservativ-islamistischer „pressure groups" zu erwarten ist[84] und ein solcher Schritt zudem die Verwurzelung der Tatbestände im kollektiven Rechtsbewusstsein ignorierte. Auch der Supreme Court hält dies für unrealistisch.[85]

Eine wahrscheinlichere, wenngleich keinesfalls zwangsläufige Reformperspektive liegt in einer Veränderung des flankierenden prozeduralen Rahmens. Schon das koloniale Prozessrecht kannte Bestimmungen, nach denen die Exekutive bei der Strafverfolgung von Religionsdelikten ihre ausdrückliche, an Opportunitätsgesichtspunkten orientierte Zustimmung zum Verfahrensfortgang geben musste.[86] Diese Einschränkungen gelten aber nicht für die später unter *Zia ul-Haq* geschaffenen Tatbestände. Auf der Grundlage der Anfang 2005 in den pakistanischen Code of Criminal Procedure (CrPC) aufgenommenen section 156-A CrPC[87] sind Ermittlungen in Verfahren unter

---

84 *Hussain, Z.*, Islamists Rally for Pakistan's Blasphemy Laws, Wall Street Journal vom 10.01.2011, erhältlich unter *http://www.wsj.com/articles/SB10001424052748704482704576071701535155530* (zuletzt besucht am 22.01.2017); ferner *Reuters*, Pakistan arrests 150 Islamists trying to rally in support of blasphemy law, Meldung vom 05.01.2017, erhältlich unter *http://www.reuters.com/article/us-pakistan-protests-idUSKBN14P1ZE* (zuletzt besucht am 22.01.2017).

85 Supreme Court in *Malik Muhammad Mumtaz Qadri v The State*, a.a.O., S. 24: „Keeping in view the strong religious sentiments in our society it ought to be understood quite clearly that any call coming from serious quarters for reform in the laws regarding religion related offences can only be a call for introducing safeguards against misapplication or misuse of such laws by motivated persons and such call is ordinarily not to be construed as a call against the religious aspects of the offences covered by such laws."

86 Section 196 Code of Criminal Procedure (Prosecution for offences against the State): „No Court shall take cognizance of any offence punishable under Chapter VI or IXA of the Pakistan Penal Code (except section 127), or punishable under section 108-A, or section 153-A or section 294-A, or *section 295-A* or section 505 of the same Code, unless upon complaint made by order of, or under authority from the Federal Government, or the Provincial Governments concerned, or some officer empowered in this behalf by either of the two Governments" (Hervorhebung durch Verf.).

87 Section 156-A Code of Criminal Procedure (Investigation of offence under section 295C, Pakistan Penal Code): „Notwithstanding anything contained in this Code, no police officer below the rank of a Superintendent of Police shall investigate the offence against any

section 295-C PPC, der Lästerung des Propheten Mohammed, ausschließlich hochrangigen Polizeioffizieren zugewiesen, denen der Gesetzgeber höhere Professionalität und geringere Beeinflussbarkeit unterstellt; allenthalben wird jedoch beklagt, die Bestimmung bleibe in der Praxis weitestgehend außer Anwendung.[88]

In der Provinz Sindh ist im April 2015 eine Änderung des Sindh Mental Health Act (2013) beschlossen worden, der zufolge Personen, die der Begehung von „Blasphemie" beschuldigt werden, zwingend von einem Psychiater zu untersuchen sind, der seine Einschätzung dem Gericht mitteilt.[89] Fehlt es hier zwar bislang noch am Erlass notwendiger Durchführungsbestimmungen, könnte dies perspektivisch aber doch zu einer Sensibilisierung dahingehend führen, wegen Geisteskrankheit nicht verantwortlich handelnde Täter von Strafe zu verschonen, wie es geltendem Recht eigentlich ohnehin schon entspräche.[90]

Prominent im Kreis der Reformvorschläge ist darüber hinaus die Forderung nach harten Strafen für wissentlich falsche Anschuldigungen. Grundsätzlich hält das pakistanische Strafrecht dazu entsprechende Tatbestände bereit[91], die in solchen Fällen aber bis dato nicht zur Anwendung gelangt sind.[92]

Weitere Überlegungen gehen dahin, nicht länger Polizei und Staatsanwaltschaft, sondern einen Richter die Plausibilität der Anschuldigungen

---

person alleged to have been committed by him under section 295C of the Pakistan Penal Code, 1860 (Act XLV of 1860)."

88 *International Commission of Jurists*, On Trial, a.a.O., S. 14, 59.

89 Section 49 Sindh Mental Health Act (Cases of attempted suicide): „A person who attempts suicide including an accused of Blasphemy shall be assessed by an approved physiatrist [sic] and if found to be suffering from a mental disorder shall be treated appropriately under the provisions of this Act." Dazu *Ghori, H.K.*, Sindh makes mental assessment of blasphemy suspect mandatory, The Dawn vom 11.04.2015, erhältlich unter *http://www.dawn.com/news/1175196* (zuletzt besucht am 05.01.2017). Es fehlt eine Legaldefinition dessen, was „blasphemy" im Sinne des Sindh Mental Health Act konstituieren soll. Wahrscheinlich sind alle im einschlägigen Kap. XV Pakistan Penal Code genannten Religionsvergehen gemeint.

90 Siehe dazu die in Fn. 29 zitierte section 84 Pakistan Penal Code.

91 Vgl. sections 191–211 im Kap. XI Pakistan Penal Code (Of False Evidence and Offences against Public Justice).

92 *Abbasi, O.*, Rimsha Masih Case: Cleric set free for want of evidence, The Express Tribune vom 18.08.2013, erhältlich unter *http://tribune.com.pk/story/591745/rimsha-masih-case-cleric-set-free-for-want-of-evidence/* (zuletzt besucht am 05.01.2017).

prüfen zu lassen, bevor in einem zweiten Schritt dann förmlich Anklage erhoben werden kann.[93]

Inwieweit diese Bemühungen fruchten, müssen die kommenden Jahre zeigen, Erfolg ist ihnen aufgrund des immensen Leids für die Betroffenen in jedem Fall zu wünschen.

[93] In diesem Sinne die Review of the Blasphemy Laws Bill (2010) der Parlamentsabgeordneten *Sherry Rehman*, die jedoch angesichts massiver Proteste im Sande verlief.

Challenges to the Regulation of Sexuality under Iranian Criminal Law

Afrooz Maghzi Najafabadi, Freiburg

Abstract

Shortly after the Islamic Revolution of 1979, the new Iranian government began to Islamize the Iranian legal system, most significantly through the adoption of the Islamic criminal laws on *ḥudūd, qiṣāṣ* and *diyāt* punishments of 1982, which had a significant impact on sexual crimes. From its introduction, the Islamic law on sexuality was challenged by legal scholars and human rights activists both in and outside of Iran, for the criminalization of consensual hetero-sexual acts outside marriage, the criminalization of adultery and homosexuality, for the discriminatory nature of its sexual crimes, as well as for the harshness of punishments including lashes and death by stoning. In the 2013 reform of the Penal Code, the Islamic Republic, for the first time, tried to respond to some of the criticism. While the reformed Penal Code largely continues to adhere to the rules and principles of the old law on sexuality, it nevertheless brought about some changes, in particular related to the punishment of adultery, homosexuality and rape. Overall, the outcome of the reform presents a mixed picture. However, it might provide important groundwork for more ambitious challenges to Islamic criminal law in the future.

I. Introduction

The Iranian revolution of 1979 not only profoundly changed the political system of Iran, but also proved to be a turning point in many respects regarding the religious, cultural, sexual and gender policy of the country. Islamic clerics, by coming into positions of power, considered the „Islamization" of law and society as the crucial first step to realizing their vision of a moral and just society, and as a remedy against all social ills that were perceived as being the result of Western-style and imperialist policies of the previous regime.[1]

---

[1] *Mir-Hosseini, Z.*, Criminalizing sexuality: Zina Laws as violence against women in Muslim contexts. In: Mir-Hosseini, Z. and Hamzić, V. (eds.), Control and Sexuality: The

Therefore, by introducing what was called the „authentic Islamic way of life", the new powers called for a return of Islamic normative ideas to all aspects of society by introducing laws and social policies which were compliant with Islam.[2] Until 1979, especially following the Constitutional Revolution of 1906-1907 and the general policy to modernize society under the Pahlavi dynasty (1925-1979), Iran had adopted a legal system that was heavily influenced by European codifications based on secular laws. [3]

The first step was taken by declaring Islam (Twelver Ja'fari school of Shia Islam)[4] as the central paradigm and ultimate source of law in the Iranian Constitution of 1979. It emphasized that all legislation must be in conformity with Islamic norms.[5] Accordingly, in order to ensure this conformity, the Constitution envisioned the establishment of the Guardian Council of the constitution; a body consisting of *fuqahā / mujtahids* (high ranking Islamic scholars) and *ḥuqūqdānān* (lawyers), who would be responsible for supervising the conformity of parliamentary enactments with Islam and the Constitution.[6] As a part of this process, Islamic special courts were set up. As early as 1981, the courts began to apply Islamic criminal law and the first sentences of amputation and stoning were carried out.[7]

The integration of Islamic criminal law (the laws on *ḥudūd, qiṣāṣ* and *diyāt* punishments) into the criminal law of Iran in 1982 constitutes the most significant step in this process. Between the years 1982-1983, four laws of *ḥudūd* and *qiṣāṣ* (25-8-1982); *diyāt* (15-12- 1982); Islamic Punishments and general provisions (13-10-1982); and Provisions on *ta'zīrāt* (9-8-1983) were enacted to codify Islamic criminal law.[8] These laws with the exception of the

---

Revival of Zina Laws in Muslim Contexts, London 2010, pp. 19-48 (25, 26).

2 Ibid, p. 36.

3 *Entessar, N.*, Criminal Law and the Legal System in Revolutionary Iran. In: BC Third World LJ, Boston vol. 8(1988), pp. 91-101 (93).

4 Shia Islam is a branch of Islam the followers of which believe that Muhammad 's religious leadership, spiritual authority, and divine guidance passed to his descendants (imams), beginning with his son-in-law and cousin, Ali ibn Abi Talib. The Twelver Ja'fari school is one of the schools of Shia Islam.

5 The Constitution of the Islamic Republic of Iran (1979). Art 4.

6 Ibid, Articles 96 and 72.

7 *Alsoufi, R.H.A.,* Strategies for the Justifications of Ḥudūd Allah and Their Punishments in the Islamic Tradition, pp. 1-285,(220), http://hdl.handle.net/1842/7989, (accessed 12.06.2016).

8 *Tavana, M.*, Three Decades of Islamic Criminal Law Legislation in Iran. In: Electronic Journal of Islamic and Middle Eastern Legal Studies (EJIMEL), Zurich 2 (2014), pp. 24-38(27).

law of *ta'zīrāt* were incorporated into one Islamic Penal Code (IPC) in 1991. The law of *ta'zīrāt* later in 1996 was inserted as chapter five into the IPC.[9]

Influenced by sharia law, the IPC of 1991 reshaped also the way in which sexual crimes were understood as well as the punishments prescribed for sexual crimes. Most notably, any heterosexual relationship outside marriage and homosexuality in general are considered a crime. Depending on the nature of the offences, the marital status of the offender, and the nature of the evidence, various forms of punishments apply, reaching from lashes to death by stoning.

However, when rules on sexuality are designed and enforced based on Islamic law, they are regularly criticized on human rights grounds. Over the years, demands to reform the criminal law of the Islamic Republic not only came from the international human rights community and legal scholars, human rights and political activists inside the country, but also from some Islamic jurists and even political authorities themselves who tried to harmonize national and international legal standards. While many of these attempts were fended off by hardliners in the political and judicial establishment, the IPC of 2013 brought about some changes to sexual crimes.

This contribution will aim to review the structure of sexual crimes in Iran with regard to the reform of the law in 2013 and to explore to which extent the efforts in challenging the criminalizing of sexuality by different groups from civil society and international community were effective in the reforms of 2013.

The first section will examine the regulation of sexuality in the IPC of 1991 (general part, *ḥudūd, qiṣāṣ, diyāt*) and 1996 (*ta'zīrāt*). It aims to provide an understanding of how sexual acts are criminalized under the law of the Islamic Republic. The second section will illustrate the reformist discourse that preceded the 2013 reform and sketch its main arguments. The third section will evaluate the impact of reformist arguments on the 2013 reform, and in the light of this, assess the potential for further reform of Iranian law.

II. Criminalization of sexuality in Iran under the Islamic Penal Code 1991/1996

This section will briefly introduce the Iranian legal perspective on sexual crime throughout history with an emphasis on the two main legal landmarks of the penal codes of 1926 and 1982. It will then provide an overview of the different

---

9 Ibid.

categories of sexual crime under Islamic penal code and relevant specific evidentiary rules and procedural regulations of each category especially with regard to sexual crimes. The third section will detail the different acts which can be prosecuted under sexual offences.

1. Iranian legal perspective to sexual crime over the history

The regulation of sexual crimes similar to other areas of Iranian criminal law underwent significant changes over the last century, initially taking a step away from the traditional values, moving towards modern ideas of sexual autonomy under the penal code of 1926, and then again reversed to a more religious and traditional understanding of sexuality under the IPC of 1982.

Following the Constitutional Revolution of 1906-1907, Iran adopted a legal system that was heavily influenced by European codifications, in particular by French law, thereby effectively bringing to an end the existing bipartite system of adjudication. [10] Until then, in criminal matters, two systems of adjudication operated in parallel.[11] On one side, Sharia (Islamic law) courts run by clerics dealt with civil, family and criminal cases in applying Islamic law. While courts that operated under the control of the provincial or central governments dealt with particular public or political relevance, such as crimes against the state, against public order, and tax law.[12]

Following its general policy to modernize society, the Pahlavi dynasty (1925-1979) undertook the first comprehensive attempt to introduce secular laws. [13] As a result, the influence of Islamic law on the country's legal system was gradually mitigated.[14] Amongst other things, the definition of sexual and gender norms in line with modern ideas, were a priority of the Pahlavi regime. The Pahlavi period thus led to legal and cultural policy reforms, such as prohibiting the veil (1936-1941), promoting monogamous relationships, giving women autonomy over marriage choices, and raising the legal minimum age of marriage.[15]

With the 1926 penal code, and similar to other areas of the criminal law, the criminalization of sexuality experienced significant change. Inspired by European penal codes, crimes and the respective punishments became somewhat

---

10 *Entessar, N.*, Criminal Law and the Legal System, p. 93.
11 *Tavana, M.*, Three Decades of Islamic Criminal Law, p. 25.
12 Ibid, p. 26.
13 *Entessar, N.*, Criminal Law and the Legal System, p. 91.
14 Ibid.
15 *Afary, J.*, Sexual Politics in Modern Iran. Cambridge 2009, p. 217.

systematic.[16] Consensual sexual relationships outside marriage were decriminalized in 1926.[17] Further reforms of the penal code (1931, 1933, 1935 and 1975) led to changes of the punishment for adultery, incest and rape, abolishing execution (as provided for under Islamic jurisprudence) and introducing the secular punishment of imprisonment.[18] Moreover new crimes of sexual intercourse with a person under the age of 15 and also sexual intercourse with a person between 15 and 18 years age irrespective of the consent of the child were introduced into the penal code. During this period sexual crimes increasingly were not conceptualized as a crime of honour or morality, but as crimes against individuals. However, sexual crimes were still manifestly influenced by patriarchal traditions; in particular with regard to the exception of punishment provided for a husband who witnessed his wife having sexual intercourse with another man and therefore killed or injured his wife or both of them.[19] A mitigation of punishments was also provided for the brother or father, who killed a woman in the aforementioned circumstances.[20] Sexual crimes during this period included, rape, sexual intercourse with a person under the age of 15, sexual intercourse with a person between 15 and 18 years age irrespective of the consent of the child, incest, indecent assault, procuring the defilement of a person, abduction, aiding prostitution, living on the earnings of prostitution, running of brothels and sexual relationship of married individuals outside marriage.[21]

Iran's post-revolution government sought to islamicize the country through laws and policies that centred around gender and sexuality with the aim of reinstating authentic Islamic ways of life. Therefore, the criminal law constitutes one of the tools to regulate sexuality as part of the general policy of the Islamic republic regarding sexual and moral politics, in addition to other measures in the family laws, by strengthening patriarchal structures, imposing compulsory hijab on women, removing women from senior positions (such as large parts of the judiciary) and enforcing a broadly-defined policy of gender segregation.[22] Against this background, the rationale of sexual offences had again changed towards being crimes against honour or morality. The IPC of 1991 not only

---

16 *Tavana, M.*, Three Decades of Islamic Criminal Law, p. 94.

17 *Ḥaidarī, F.*, Barrasī-yi mabānī-yi ḥuqūqī-yi taḥawwul-i jarāyim-i- jinsī dar qānūn-i mujāzāt-i islāmī (A review of the development of sexual offences in the Islamic penal code) 2014 , pp. 1-84(24), available at: http://ganj.irandoc.ac.ir/articles/803100 p. 24 (accessed 12.06.2016).

18 Ibid.

19 The Iranian Penal Code (1926), Art 179.

20 Ibid.

21 Ibid, Arts. 207-213.

22 *Afary, J,* Sexual Politics, p. 265.

created entirely new sexual offenses that had not been treated as crimes under the provisions of the 1926 Penal Code, but also new punishments, notably whipping and stoning to death. Under the IPC any heterosexual relationship outside marriage and homosexuality in general are considered a crime. Furthermore, even non-physical contact such as flirting and verbal communication, or staying in a private place without legal cause can now be considered as a criminal sexual act.

2. General principles of sexual crime under the Islamic penal Code

The IPC of Iran consists of five books including the part of generalities, *ḥudūd, qiṣāṣ* and *diyāt* which were introduced in 1991 and the book of *ta'zīrāt* enacted in 1996. In 2013, the law of the general part and books on *ḥudūd, qiṣāṣ* and *diyāt* were reformed while the law of *ta'zīrāt* is still under revision. This part will illustrate the rules on sexual offences under the pre- 2013 law.

2.1. Categorization of sexual crime

In general, the IPC divides crimes into the four categories of *ḥudūd, qiṣāṣ, ta'zīr* and *diyāt* based on the type of punishment for each category of offense.

Ḥudūd, under Sharia, are rules stated in the Qur'an and the Sunnah, whose violation is deemed in Islam as a crime against God and therefore does not require an individual complaint for a prosecution to commence.[23] *Ḥudūd* crimes have specific evidentiary requirements and fixed punishments.[24] Besides various crimes such as the consumption of intoxicants and robbery, several types of illicit sexual acts are covered under the *ḥudūd* part of the IPC. These include crimes of *zinā (*any illicit heterosexual relationship outside marriage), *liwāṭ* (homosexuality), *qawwādī* (procuring a relationship between two or more persons for the purpose of *zinā* or *liwāṭ*, *ifsād fil-'arḍ* (sowing corruption on earth) and *qadhf* (libel by falsely accusing another of *zinā* or *liwāṭ*). The punishments of *ḥudūd* crimes including corporal punishment or death penalty are definitely fixed, leaving, in principle, no room for the judge to take mitigating or extenuating circumstances into account: Punishment can, under specific conditions, be averted, reduced, or replaced only through repentance and pardon. Furthermore, anyone found committing the same offence

23 *Ghassemi, G.,* Criminal Punishment in Islamic Societies: Empirical Study of Attitudes to Criminal Sentencing in Iran. In: European Journal on Criminal Policy and Research, University of Trento, Vol. 15 (2009), pp. 159-180(162).

24 Ibid.

punishable by *ḥudūd* will be subject to the death penalty, upon the fourth offence.[25]

Qiṣāṣ (equal retaliation) and *diyāt*, (blood money), are the second and third categories of crime, specified by Sharia *(Islamic law)*. *Qiṣāṣ* concerned with the punishment for crimes against the body (bodily injury) and crime against the person (homicide), which entitles the victim or the heirs of the victim – with the exception of the spouse – to seek retaliation.[26] The crimes that are punishable by *diyāt* are concerned with accidents or semi-intentional act that caused bodily harm or death. [27] *Diyāt* is also applicable to cases where such acts were caused intentionally but a sentence of retaliation could exceptionally not be pronounced. [28] Under *diyāt* a particular amount of money as defined by law is paid to the victim. In the present context, it has to be noted that under *qiṣāṣ* law, a husband is exempted from retaliation in case he kills his wife and her lover in flagrante.[29] Furthermore, in the part of *diyāt*, the legislator has provided compensation for a woman who is the victim of rape.[30]

The last category, *ta'zīrāt*, is comprised of all other sinful acts or forbidden conducts which are not explicitly mentioned in the original Islamic sources but can be criminalized by the state in the name of public order.[31] To a large extent, today's *ta'zīrāt* law still contains the crimes that were already contained in the 1926 Penal code.[32] Furthermore, a number of new offences were added to the old code's content, notably offences related to women's dress and to Islamic moral behavior.[33] Sexual crimes are mostly contained in chapter eighteen of the *ta'zīrāt* section of the IPC (Article 637-641), which outlines the crimes against public morality and chastity.[34]

In practice, due to the practical difficulty for courts to meet the stringent evidential requirements of *ḥudūd* crimes, only a relatively small number of offences in Iran's criminal justice system are sanctioned by *ḥudūd* punishments,

---

25 *Ghassemi, G.*, Criminal Punishment in Islamic Societies, p. 164.
26 Ibid, p. 163.
27 Ibid.
28 Ibid.
29 IPC (1996), Art 630.
30 IPC (2013), Art 231.
31 *Ghassemi, G.*, 'Criminal Punishment in Islamic Societies, p. 164.
32 *Mir-Hosseini, Z.*, Sharia and National Law in Iran. In: Otto, J.M. (ed.), Sharia and National Law: Comparing the Legal Systems of Twelve Islamic Countries, Cairo 2010, pp. 319-371(358).
33 Ibid.
34 Ibid.

and the great majority of cases are dealt with as *ta'zīrāt* crimes, which is true even for sexuality-related crimes.[35]

2.2. Procedural Rules on Sexual Crime

In accordance with Islamic law on *ḥudūd*, the IPC also contains some procedural rules, some of them being especially applicable to sexual crimes. The doctrine of *shubha* (doubt, ambiguity) states that, in the case of the slightest doubt, the investigation of a complaint is unwarranted.[36] For instance pregnancy of an unmarried woman is not considered a sign for the committing of an illicit sexual relationship in the IPC.[37] Furthermore, an uncorroborated accusation (*qadhf*) does itself constitute a *ḥudūd* crime, and is punishable by eighty lashes, which also can apply to witnesses if their testimony is not based on eyewitness accounts, and even in case that the number of witnesses does not meet the number required by law.[38] Most importantly according to Islamic jurisprudence which is also reflected in the IPC investigation for uncovering the crimes of adultery and sodomy and other crimes against chastity is prohibited.[39] In order to be prosecuted, the offence must have happened in public or somebody must have been harmed or the perpetrator itself confesses to committing the sexual crime.[40]

2.3. Evidentiary rules

Special evidentiary requirements apply to sexual crimes under the *ḥudūd* section, i.e. those crimes considered to be offences against God. These offences can be proven only by means of confession, testimony or the „knowledge of the judge"; each of these means of evidence must further meet particular requirements. In case of testimony by witnesses, the latter must fulfil certain special personal criteria, e.g. the must qualify as being „pious" (*'ādil*).[41] More importantly, the witness must have personally observed the act of penetration in the cases of *zinā* (sexual relationship outside marriage) and *liwāṭ*

35 *Tavana, M.*, Three Decades of Islamic Criminal Law, p. 31.

36 *Naubahār, R.*, Ahdāf-i mujāzāthā dar jarāyim-i mustaujib-i ḥadd dar ḥuqūq-i kaifarī-yi Islām (Aims of Punishment for Sexual Crimes in Islamic Penal Law). In: Nama-yi mufīd, Qum, vol. 23 (2000), pp. 133-162(139).

37 Ibid.

38 IPC (1991), Art 73 and 76. IPC (2013), Art 200.

39 The Criminal Code of Procedure(1999), Art 43.

40 IPC (2013), Art 241.

41 Ibid, Art 199.

(homosexuality).[42] Furthermore, for proving sexual crimes under *ḥudūd* it is an additional requirement that four male witnesses have to testify in exactly the same way; testimony of women is accepted only in respect of a few crimes, and only when testifying in conjunction with male witnesses. In case of *zinā* (adultery), which is punishable by flogging, the testimony of two just men and four just women is deemed sufficient.[43] A valid confession requires that it is repeated four times in front of the judge the cases of *zinā, liwāṭ, tafkhīẕ,* and *musāḥaqa.*[44] However, the most important type of evidence in Iranian law is called the „knowledge of the judge". According to this rule, the knowledge of the judge suffices to prove a crime when such knowledge is resulting from manifest evidence brought before him, even if the required conditions of confession and testimony would not be met in the case. As meeting the requirements of confession and testimony for proving sexual crimes under the *ḥudūd* regulations is almost impossible, the knowledge of the judge appears to be the only way that such crimes could be established.[45] It is also noticeable that the lack of evidence for *ḥudūd* does not necessarily exonerate the accused of his criminal liability, as he/she could still be liable for *ta'zīrāt* crimes, which however have a lesser punishment.[46]

Ta'zīrāt crimes, however, follow general rules of evidence, contained in the Iranian Code of criminal procedure. Here, different standards apply, following a more modern understanding of criminal law, e.g. allowing for the use of expert and in particular forensic evidence.

3. Various criminalized sexual acts under the Islamic Penal Code

Given the mostly general and vague definition of sexual offences in the IPC, the application of the law in the courts has to be considered in order to understand what sexual conducts can fall under the heading of sexual offences. However, there is little information regarding the procedural practice of the courts in the cases of sexual offences as the judiciary system of Iran has not disclosed any information in this respect. In this vein, the assessment of the judicial practices will rely on the available information which originates from some empirical research which has been authorized by courts, and from a number of court cases that have become public knowledge.

---

42 Ibid, Art 200.

43 Ibid, Art 199.

44 Ibid, Art 172.

45 *Sadr, S.*, and *Vahdati, S.*, Gender Discrimination in Stoning: http://www. stopstoning.net/spip.php?article20 (accessed 12.06.2016).

46 *Ghassemi, G.*, Criminal Punishment in Islamic Societies, p. 165.

3.1. Consensual heterosexual relationship outside marriage

A consensual heterosexual relationship is criminal in case of sexual intercourse between a man and a woman who are not married to each other. Both the *ḥudūd* and *ta'zīrāt* parts of the IPC contain offences in this respect. The nature and the extent of the punishment varies from fines or lashes to the death penalty by hanging or stoning, depending on the marital status of offender and the circumstances of the crime.

Under the *ḥudūd* part of the code, illicit heterosexual intercourse has been defined as *zinā,* and includes: *zinā* with blood relatives or with a step-mother as incest, both punishable by the death penalty; sexual intercourse outside marriage (fornication) is punishable by 100 lashes,[47] and illegal sexual intercourse of a married person (adultery) is punishable by stoning.[48] However, if both partners are unmarried, the punishment for *zinā* is the death penalty for any non-Muslim man who has sexual intercourse (fornication) with a Muslim woman.[49]

Under the *ta'zīrāt* part of the code, any illicit sexual relationship other than *zinā,* or indecent acts committed by unmarried men and women, is punishable with lashes, the possible number of lashes ranging from one to ninety-nine.[50] However, the relevant article in the *ta'zīrāt* part does not specify the exact meaning of „illicit sexual relationship" or „indecent acts", but just provides two examples of these behaviors, namely kissing and sleeping next to one another. However, these examples are not exclusive and courts have adopted various interpretations in applying this article. In practice any relationship between an unmarried woman and a man which can be considered as an initiation to a sexual relationship, even speaking through telephone or being in a private place without legitimate reason, has been prosecuted under this article.[51] Other examples of the latter's application include: attending mixed gender parties where the Islamic rules on gender segregation were not respected, and other illicit sexual acts that do not meet the evidentiary requirement of *ḥudūd.*[52]

---

47 IPC (1991), Art 63, 82, 88.

48 Ibid, Art 83.

49 Ibid, Art 82.

50 IPC (1996), Art 637.

51 *Ahmadīya, M.* and *Bodāqī , F.*, Khalā'hā-yi qānūnī wa inḥirāfāt-i ijtimā'ī (Legal Gaps and Social Deviation). Muṭāla'āt-i- rahburdī-yi zanān(Women's Strategic Studies), vol. 17, (2009), available at: http://www.ensani.ir/fa/content/89463/default.aspx

52 Ibid.

3.2. Homosexual relationship

Any homosexual relationship is considered as a crime under *ḥudūd*. The homosexual relationships under the criminal code's *ḥudūd* section are defined as: *liwāṭ* (sodomy), *musāḥaqa* (sexual acts between women) *tafkhīẕ* (non-penetrative acts). The IPC defines *liwāṭ* as penetrative sex between two men.[53] *Liwāṭ* is punished much more severely than *musāḥaqa*. According to the IPC of 1991, *liwāṭ* was punished by death, *musāḥaqa* merely by 100 lashes.[54] Moreover, non-penetrative sexual acts between men that still involve sexual organs are defined as *tafkhīẕ* and punished by 100 lashes, that is in the same way as *musāḥaqa*.[55] Furthermore other homosexual acts, in particular „kissing or touching as a result of lust" are punished by thirty-one to seventy-four lashes which are considered a *ta'zīr* crime.

3.3. Rape

Under *ḥudūd* law, having sexual intercourse with a man or women against her/his will and consent is punishable by the death penalty. However, the seriousness of this punishment regularly causes an aversion among criminal court judges, all of whom are men, to convict an accused for rape.[56] Judicial practice refuses to find a lack of consent of the victim in cases where appearance or behavior of the woman was deemed to be provocative.[57] Furthermore, a prior sexual relationship between the victim and the offender, and other actions on the part of the woman that may contradict sexual norms, are taken to indicate consent, thus leading to an acquittal.[58] As a result, the majority of rape allegations are rejected by the courts. For instance, in 2006, while there were 195 rape cases in branch 77 of the Provincial Penal Court of Tehran, only in two cases the accused was convicted of committing rape, with both being related to instances of gang rape that had already received much media attention.[59] It also has to be noted that the IPC does not only refuse to recognize rape within marital relationships, but also does not provide a minimum age of consent. Thus,

---

53 IPC (1991), Arts. 108-134.

54 Ibid, Arts. 110 and 127.

55 Ibid, Art. 122.

56 *Maghzi, A,* Ta'ārīf-i gumshuda dar jurmangārī-yi – jurm-i tajāwuz-i jinsī dar Īrān (Missing Definitions in Criminalization of the Crime of Rape in Iran)' (20 January 2012), available at: https://jahanezan.wordpress.com (accessed 07.05.2016).

57 Ibid.

58 Ibid.

59 *Farajīhā, M. and Anṣārī, H.,* Ḥimāyat-i kaifarī az –bizihdīdagān-i tajāwuz dar ḥuqūq-i Īrān (The Protection of Female Victims of Rape in Iranian Criminal Law). Rifāh-i Ijtimā'ī (Social welfare Journal), Tehran, vol. 40 (1390/2011), pp. 287-314 (307).

in the case of child sexual abuse, the court still has to determine the absence of consent by the victim.[60]

Punishment of rape is further impeded by the fact that victims of rape are exposed to a real risk of themselves being investigated and punished for an illicit sexual relationship under *ḥudūd* law. This is because following Islamic jurisprudence, if one of the parties engaged in an illicit sexual act confesses to the act, even though the other party may deny it, the one who confesses can be convicted of adultery, fornication or *liwāṭ,* and punished accordingly.[61]

3.4. Sexual harassment

There is not yet any provision under the IPC which explicitly criminalizes sexual violence against women. There is only one general provision in the *ta'zīrāt* book of the IPC which can cover some forms of sexual assault against women.[62] According to this article assaulting or disturbing children or women in public places or roads, or insulting them with outrageous language and behavior, is punishable by up to six months imprisonment and up to 74 lashes. However, this provision does not include sexual harassment in the workplace or other private places, and it is rarely enforced.

The child protection law of 2002 constitutes a first step towards the recognition of a need for special protection of children, but still lacks an explicit reference to sexual violence. It prohibits the physical, mental and moral abuse of those under the age of eighteen, though in very general terms. However, certain crimes contained therein, in particular „trading, selling or exploiting children for the commission of criminal acts“[63] and „abuse, exploitation or physical or mental torture of children“[64]allow for the punishment of some forms of sexual abuse of children. Yet the very lenient punishment prescribed for these crimes, carrying only up to one year imprisonment or a fine, does not provide a sufficient deterrent, especially when compared to the punishment applicable to other types of sexual crime.

---

60 *Maghzi, A.,*Ta'ārīf-i -gumshuda, ibid.

61 *Terman, R. and Fijabi,M.*, Stoning Is Not Our Culture: A Comparative Analysis of Human Rights and Religious Discourses in Iran and Nigeria, Report, The Global Campaign to Stop Killing and Stoning Women and Women Living under Muslim Laws: http://www.violenceisnotourculture.org/sites/default/files/Terman_Fijabi.pdf pp. 1-45(9), (accessed 08.05.2016).

62 IPC (1996). Art 619.

63 The Child Protection Law (2002), Art 3.

64 Ibid. Art 4.

As well as the lack of sufficient special regulations for protecting children against sexual violence, children also enjoy little legal protection under the existing sexual offences. For example, while the punishment for adultery under Islamic law is stoning, sexual acts with a pubescent boy (under 15 years of age) when committed by a marital woman only leads to lashes.[65]

3.5. Prostitution and promotion of prostitution

Under the *ta'zīrāt* section of the IPC, „establishing or directing brothels or other corrupt venues" and „facilitating or encouraging people to immorality or prostitution" is punishable by one to ten years imprisonment".[66] The vague wording „corruption" or „encouraging corruption" has led to broad interpretation of this provision by the courts. Even organizing mixed-gender parties without respecting religious rules on gender segregation has led to prosecutions for this offence.[67] In addition, under the *ḥudūd* part of the IPC, bringing together two or more people for the purpose of committing *zinā* or *liwāṭ* is punishable as *qawwād* which is a *ḥudūd* crime.[68]

Under the IPC, prostitution itself is not specifically defined as a crime, because traditional Islamic jurisprudence lacked such a concept. Despite this, prostitution is punishable under various offences, such as the crime of having a sexual relationship outside marriage (under the *ḥudūd* part of the code) and encouraging people to prostitution (as just described as a *ta'zīr* crime).[69] The lack of any definition of the crime of prostitution has led the courts to punish prostitutes in very different ways, depending on the court's approach, punishments ranging from flogging to imprisonment or the death penalty.[70] The death penalty can be applied in case that prostitution is prosecuted as *zinā* (i.e. sex outside marriage) and was either committed for the fourth time or involved a married person (adultery).[71] While the 2013 reformed IPC makes it practically almost impossible to prove adultery, the new offence of „sowing corruption on earth" now gives the courts the power to issue the death penalty for prostitutes or those who are facilitating prostitution.

---

65 IPC (1991), Art 83.

66 IPC (1996), Art 639.

67 *Ahmadīya, M.* and *Bodāqī, F.*, Khalā'hā-yi qānūnī.

68 *Borhani, M.*, Siyāsat-i kaifarī-yi Īrān dar qibāl-i rūspīgarī (Iran's Criminal Policies against Prostitution), Muṭāla'āt-i-rahburdī-yi zanān (Women's Strategic Studies),Tehran, vol. 45(1387/2009), pp. 7-42(34-36), available at: http://www.sid.ir/fa/VEWSSID/J_pdf/48713884501.pdf.

69 Ibid.

70 *Ahmadīya, M.* and *Bodāqī , F.*, Khalā'hā-yi qānūnī

71 Ibid.

3.6. Crimes against public chastity and morality

The crimes against public chastity and morality, formulated in a vague and broad wording, criminalize the acts which are not considered Islamic or are against public morality. In this regard any undesirable acts which are religiously prohibited (*ḥarām*), if committed in a public place are considered a crime which is punishable with up to two years imprisonment.[72] The provision even goes further and extends the crime to public acts that, despite not being *ḥarām*, might nevertheless disturb public chastity.[73] However, the provision doesn't provide any examples for such acts, thus it is up to the judge to decide on the scope of the provision. Many different forms of sexual acts, such as any sexual activity between married people in public or gender cross-dressing (which mostly targets transgender individuals) are prosecuted under this provision. [74]

According to the *ta'zīrāt* book of the IPC non-compliance with the Islamic dress code by women is also punishable with up to two months imprisonment According to the general understanding, women's *ḥijāb* requires the covering of a woman's full body, except face and hands. But the law does not provide clear rules on the exact requirements of the Islamic dress code, despite some legislative attempts to define it. Thus, the criteria for what constitutes proper *ḥijāb* are ultimately left to the authorities.[75]

III. Challenging Islamic sexual offences

In this section after providing an overview over relevant social and political developments in Iran since the 1979 Islamic Revolution, this contribution will present the major elements that incentivized the 2013 reform – international human rights discourse, Islamic reformist discourse, and Iranian civil society activism – and will highlight the main criticism that, within the reformist discourse, was raised against the law on sexuality.

---

72 IPC (1996), Art 638.

73 Ibid.

74 *Amin, S.*, Gender X: A Glance at the Situation of Transgender and Homosexual People in Iran. Bochum 2016, pp. 1-606(311).

75 *Hosseinkhah, M.*, Thirty-Five Years of Forced Hijab: The Widespread and Systematic Violation of Women's Rights in Iran, pp. 1-66(10-14), available at: http://justice4iran.org/wp-content/uploads/2014/03/Hejab-Report-JFI-English.pdf (accessed 04.06.2016).

1. The political history of the 2013 reform

From the introduction of the IPC in 1991, the criminal law, and especially the parts of *ḥudūd* and *qiṣāṣ,* had drawn criticism from legal scholars, human rights and political activists. However, in the early days of the Islamic Republic, these critics were sharply rebuked and even labelled as traitors and apostates.[76] For example, the statements of lawyers, legal professors and judges against *qiṣāṣ,* law in 1982, led to an immediate reaction by some high ranking clerics, who accused the critics of apostasy, and to the removal of those law professors and judges who had signed the declarations. Protests against other gender-related aspects of Islamic law and policy, such as demonstrations against mandatory *ḥijāb*, sit-in protests in the Tehran judiciary against the dismissal of female judges were equally suppressed by the new regime as a counter-revolutionary act.[77]

Serious attempts to reform the Islamic laws related to sexuality and gender were only initiated in the relatively liberal political atmosphere of the 1990s, following gains of reformist candidates in the municipal and parliamentary elections of 1999 and 2000, and the presidency of Mohammad Khatami (1997-2004).[78] In this new political atmosphere, freedom of press and civil society's activities were increasingly tolerated, the Iranian government become also more engaged with international human rights bodies. As a result, some aspects of the IPC could, for the first time, be debated in the press, however, only within the framework of Islam and under the condition of respecting political redlines of the Islamic Republic.[79] At the same time, in social practice, many sexuality-related policies of the Islamic Republic were increasingly ignored by the younger generation, who were increasingly demanding personal freedom. [80]

After several decades of applying the IPC of 1991, the necessity to reform the judicial system had also become undeniable at the judicial level. The high number of prisoners, overly long trials, deficiencies in the definition of crimes

---

76 *Nayyirī, M.*, Qānūn-i qiṣāṣ (The law of qiṣāṣ), available at: http://archive.radiozamaneh.com/society/humanrights/2011/08/25/6480 (accessed 04.06.2016).

77 *Sadr, S.*, Murūr-i si daha-yi mubārazāt-i ḥuqūqī-yi zanān-i Īrān (Overview of three decades of legal struggle of Iranian women), http://nehzatbidaryzanan.com/%D8%B2%D9%86%D8%A7%D9%86-%D9%88-%D9%82%D9%88%D8%A7%D9%86%DB%8C%D9%86.html (accessed 20.06.2016).

78 *Mir-Hosseini, Z.*, The Conservative-Reformist Conflict Over Women's Rights in Iran. International Journal of Politics, Culture, and Society, New York, vol. 16, Issue 1, (Fall 2002), pp. 37-53 (37-39).

79 Ibid.

80 Ibid.

and punishments, and the international and social pressures led Mahmoud Hashemi Shahroudi, who was the head of Iran's judiciary from 1999 to 2009, to initiate a reform process from within the judiciary.[81] Developing proposals for new laws was a key part of this process, and so for the first time since 1979, independent legal researchers and law professors were appointed to draft bills and develop laws based on findings of criminology and comparative criminal law, although within the framework of Islam. Shahroudi also tried to address some of the most sensitive legal issues through the issuing of directives, asking judges for a moratorium on the implementation of stoning, abandoning the death penalty for those under the age of 18, and ceasing the execution of the death penalty in public.[82] However, since these directives had no legally binding force, they were ignored by some judges and therefore, the practice of stoning, executing juveniles and public execution continued.

The period of a relatively liberal discourse came to an end, when Parliament and Presidency were again taken over by hardliners in the 2003 election.[83] Furthermore, the reform attempts in the Judiciary were abandoned and even reversed during the period of Shahroudi's successor Sadegh Larijani, who adopted a highly punitive approach and insisted on the enforcement of Islamic law, especially *ḥudūd* law.[84]

While the reform of the IPC of 2013 was initiated under the relatively reformist political discourse of 1990s, the process of revising the IPC proved to be tedious due to ideological and political differences within the legislative bodies. Between December 2009 and January 2012, the bill was passed several times by Parliament and forwarded to the Guardian Council for approval, but repeatedly sent back by the Council to Parliament for lacking compatibility with the Sharia.[85] When the code was finally approved by Parliament in January 2012 and sent to the President for signature, it was again recalled by the Guardian Council, as the Council considered that the code still included 52 cases of

81 Ruikard-i nuvīn bi zindān (A new approach to prison: reform instead deprivation of liberty)' available at; http://www.dadsetani.ir/Portals/dadsetani.ir/PaperAttch/977.html (accessed 20.06.2016).

82 *Nayyeri, M.H.*, The Question of "Stoning to Death" in the New Penal Code of the Iran. Iran Human Rights Documentation Center (IHRDC)- Available at: http://www.iranhrdc.org/files.php?force&file=pdf_en/LegalCom/The_Question_of_Stoning_to_Death_in_the_New_Penal_Code_of_the_IRI_EN_172447845.pdf (accessed 20.06.2016).

83 *Mir-Hosseini, Z. and Hamzić, V.*, Control and Sexuality, pp. 37-39.

84 Head of Judiciary Challenges Human Rights' available at: https://www.iranhumanrights.org/2013/12/executions-qisas/ (accessed 25.06.2016).

85 *Tavana, M.*, Three Decades of Islamic Criminal Law, p. 29.

incompatibility with Sharia.[86] The legislative history of the 2013 IPC clearly demonstrated the profound clash of the elites of the Islamic Republic over the interpretation and application of Islamic law. While some were in favour of modern interpretations of Islamic law, which would allow them to bring Iranian law in better compliance with Iran's international obligations, others not only preferred to keep the pre-existing criminal code unchanged, but tried to introduce new Islamic offences such as apostasy, witchcraft and claim to prophethood. It also illustrates the structural limitations of the Iranian legislative body in order to meaningfully reform the law as the Guardian council hinders and frustrates meaningful attempts in this regards.

2. Players within the reform process

Various players were involved in challenging different aspects of the criminalization of sexuality. While the international human rights community frequently condemned the enforcement of Islamic sexual offences as a violation of Iran's international human rights obligations, civil society and especially women's rights activists within Iran were successful in raising awareness for the detrimental consequences of the law, especially its effects on women's life. The women's movement's criticism of *ḥudūd* law also found some support from Islamic scholars who were arguing for a reformist interpretation of Islamic law.

After more than a decade of silence following the Islamic Revolution, rights activists re-organized themselves through the establishment of NGOs and independent press organs, especially during the presidency of Mohammad Khatami (1997-2005).[87] However, these campaigns were often confronted by harsh reactions from political hardliners, resulting in prosecution of their activists.[88] As women perceived themselves to be the main target of the criminalization of sexuality, women's rights activists have been at the centre of civic activism for changing the law.[89] Through the establishment of independent journals and newspapers, such as the *Zanān* (Women)journal, both Islamic and secular activists found a platform to cooperate for initiating discourse, raising public awareness about the implications of Islamic laws, such as the *ḥudūd* law, challenging the discriminatory nature of laws and policies, and at the same time, remained within the framework of Islam.[90] Moreover, some human rights activists, through NGOs and Networks, such as the Raahi Institute and the

86 Ibid.

87 *Sadr, S.*, Murūr-i si daha-yi mubārazāt.

88 *Sadr, V. and Vahdati, S.*, Gender Discrimination in Stoning, available at: http://www.topstoning.net/spip.php?article20 (accessed 12.06.2016).

89 *Ibid.*

90 *Sadr, S.*, Murūr-i si daha-yi mubārazāt.

Network of Volunteer Lawyers, specialized on representing victims or suspects of gender-related crimes, and, in particular, defended women threatened by the death penalty, stoning or long-term prison sentences.[91] Women rights activists also launched several public campaigns for women who were sentenced to death, and were often successful in attracting extensive domestic and international attention with regard to the discriminatory character of Islamic sexual offences and the patriarchal nature of Iran's judiciary.[92] One of the most successful initiative was the campaign „Stop Stoning Forever", which was launched in 2006, i.e., by a group of human rights defenders, lawyers and journalists.[93]

Civil society activists also reached out to reformist Islamic scholars, asking them to produce legal opinions regarding the implementation of controversial Islamic laws, in order to demonstrate the availability of alternative Islamic interpretations of Islamic regulations.[94] Similar to other Muslim majority countries, in the last decades Islamic discourse witnessed the appearance of a modernist approach in Islamic scholarship which discards the classical Islamic jurisprudence and considers the Qur'an as contextual and historical text and all legal rules stipulated therein as being in a constant state of change.[95] According to these scholars, the spirit of Islamic law is characterized by a desire to avoid the implementation of harsh *ḥudūd* punishments, especially when they are discriminately enforced.[96] However, this discourse was unable to play any significant role in the policy-making of the Islamic republic as modernist Islamic scholarship which was in the late 1990s suppressed by hard-liner political forces, and some of its prominent representatives were accused of blasphemy, insulting Islamic sanctities, and even of plotting against national security.[97] In this context, the traditional Islamic approach became the only platform that allowed debate over at least some of the critical issues of the 1991 IPC. Within traditional Islamic thought, there are still plenty of – often conflicting – scholarly opinions (*fatāwā*) on a multitude of aspects of Islamic law, such as, the law of evidence or the implementation of *ḥudūd*.

---

91 *Terman,T.* The Stop Stoning Forever Campaign: A Report, Women Living Under Muslim Laws, November, 2007 , pp. 1-26. Available at: http://www.violenceisnotourculture.org/sites/default/files/Terman_stoning.pdf

92 *Sadr, S.,* ibid.

93 Ibid.

94 Ibid.

95 *Alsoufi, R.H. A.*, 'Strategies for the Justifications of Ḥudūd Allah,p. 117.

96 Ibid.

97 *al-Qurtuby, S.,* The Luther of Shi'i Islam. Jurnal Penelitian Sosial Keagamaan, Walisongo Semarang vol. 20, (2012)No 1, pp. 137-164(138-139).

Since the founding of the Islamic Republic, human rights violations in Iran have also continuously been the subject of resolutions and decisions by United Nations bodies. In them, criminalization of consensual heterosexual and homosexual sexual relationships, the use of corporal punishment for sexual crimes, the imposition of the death penalty and the lack of protection of women and children against sexual abuse have been repeatedly criticized[98]. However, despite the undeniable political effect of criticism by international bodies to incentivize reform, due to the Islamic Republic's stance on human rights, in particular its strong claim of cultural relativism, arguments derived from international law played a rather limited role in the reform process. For instance in response to the criminalization of homosexuality in the second Universal Periodic Review of Iran in 2014, an Iranian delegate declared that „the right to choose one's sexual orientation is a relatively recent Western construct, a lifestyle choice promoted by the West and with has very little to do with an Islamic way of life“.[99]

3. Reformist arguments against the criminalization of sexuality

While conservative jurists and hardliners justify the criminalization of sexuality by claiming a need to protect sexual order, personal honour, blood relations, and legitimate paternity, they primarily stressed that, in a Muslim society, God's law must be applied.[100] In contrast, arguments against the IPC of 1991 emphasized the unjust and discriminatory nature of crimes contained therein, which were not only contrary to notions of equality and justice shared by today's Muslim societies, but also pointed at the lacking consensus among Islamic scholars.

The main argument of women's rights activist referred to a discriminatory nature of sexual crimes where women are the main target of criminalizing the sexuality. As Amnesty International reported, out of 15 prisoners sentenced to stoning in Iran in 2008, 10 were women.[101] Moreover, as the head of Iran's

---

98 See; Para 10, Report of the Special Rapporteur on the human rights situation in Iran, UN Doc A/HRC/22/56 (2013), para. 69, the concluding observations of the Human Rights Committee on Iran (CCPR/C/IRN/3) at its 2834th, 2835th and 2836th meetings (CCPR/C/SR/2834, CCPR/C/SR/2835 and CCPR/C/SR/2836), held on 17 and 18 October 2011. At its 2857th and 2858th meetings (CCPR/C/SR/2853 and CCPR/C/SR/2858), held on 2 November 2011), para. 10 and 12, Committee on the Rights of the Child (2005). Concluding observations: The Islamic Republic of Iran: http://www.unhchr.ch/tbs/doc.nsf/%28Symbol%29/CRC.C.15.Add.243.En?Opendocument (accessed 23.06.2016).

99 Human Rights Head Larijani Accuses West of Hypocrisy on Gay Rights'. Available at: https://iranwire.com/en/features/716 (accessed 23.06.2016).

100 *Naubahār, R.*, 'Ahdāf-i- mujāzāthā.

101 Iran: End Executions by Stoning'. Amnesty International, January 2008. Available at:

prison organization declared in 2013, the second category of crimes committed by women were sexual crimes, while sexual crime plays only a minor role with regard to male convictions. [102]

While the definition of most sexual offences appears to be gender neutral, many provisions, result in a discriminatory practice to the detriment of women. Although in some exceptional cases, the law provides for a lesser punishment for women (compared to men) for identical crimes, such as in the case of homosexuality, in most cases the law, as written and as applied, leads to women being more likely to be subjected to harsh punishments. Civil society activists demonstrated that deficiencies in other areas of law, especially in family law and evidentiary law, constituted root causes for specific categories of sexual crime.[103] In particular, adultery and homicide by women are often the result of early age marriage, forced marriage, and domestic violence, demonstrating that Iranian law does not provide sufficient protection of women against such social practices.[104] Men's exclusive right to divorce, and the law on child custody constitute other legal causes, as women are thereby locked into abusive marriages.[105] Iranian law also privileges men with respect to specific sexual rights, such as polygamy and temporary marriage, enabling men to marry up to four wives simultaneously, and to establish a sexual relationship with any other single woman through a temporary marriage (*ṣīġah*).[106] In the case of adultery, this exclusive sexual right of men also gives them more opportunities to escape punishment on evidential grounds.[107] When a husband or a wife commits adultery, their penalty does, in principle, not differ, but since the law allows men to have several wives at a time, when they are charged with extra-marital relations, they will often argue that they were in a temporary marriage, and in this way they can relatively easily avoid the punishment of stoning, while women accused of adultery cannot make such an argument.[108]

---

https://www.amnesty.org/download/Documents/56000/mde130012008en.pdf. (accessed 12.06.2016).

[102] Chi chīzī shāyi'tarīn jurm-i zan-i zindānī ast/ (What Is the Most Common Crime of Female Prisoners?). Available at: http://www.khabaronline.ir/detail/293795/society/social-damage (accessed 23.06.2016).

[103] *Sadr, S.,* and *Vahdati, S.*, Gender Discrimination.

[104] *Mo'azzamī, S.*, Hamsarkushī - (Spouse Killing), Majalla-yi anjumān-i jami'a- shināsī-yi Īrān (*Iranian Sociological Association Journal*), Tehran vol. 3 (1383/2012), pp. 207-232(215).

[105] Ibid.

[106] *Sadr, S.,* and *Vahdati, S.*, Gender Discrimination.

[107] Ibid.

[108] Ibid.

The male domination of the judiciary and the enforcement practice were cited as further reasons as to why women are more likely than men to be convicted of a sexual offence or to be deprived from legal protections.[109] One of the obvious examples of gender bias and a strong patriarchal perspective within the administration of justice can be observed in the way how the judges decide based on the knowledge of judge. The evidential standard of „knowledge of the judge" – which allows the judge to form his conviction on the basis of a general assessment of the evidence before him instead of on the basis of the other stringent evidentiary requirements of *ḥudūd* law – proved to be another crucial deficiency in women-related crimes, such as in cases of prostitutes and adultery, in which the bias and prejudice of the judge do in fact regularly constitute crucial factors for shaping the „knowledge of the judge".[110] Almost all convictions for sexual offences resulting in the death penalty have been based on this weak evidentiary standard.[111]

The lack of fairness in sexual crimes trials was another line of argument that was highlighted by rights campaigners, which were especially critical of the Islamic law of evidence. In particular, they highlighted that the most serious crimes, such as adultery, were often proven by confession – raising questions of possible abuse by investigators.[112] In many cases, convicts claimed that their confession was the result of torture, threats or deception, and a lack of knowledge about the legal consequence of their confession.[113]

In response to the argument which justify the necessity of the application of *ḥudūd* law as God's law, critics pointed out that there are significant disagreements about the type of punishment and the evidentiary rules for sexual crimes.[114] Some Shia scholars even believe that the implementation of *ḥudūd* punishments during the absence of the 12th Imam is *ḥarām*, or religiously forbidden, though this opinion does not enjoy major support.[115] The main arguments are established on the facts that according to the Qur'an, only sexual relationships outside marriage and the false accusation to this effect are explicitly stated as crimes and punishable by flogging.[116] Other sexual crimes

---

[109] Ibid.

[110] Ibid.

[111] Ibid.

[112] *Terman, R.* and *Fijabi, M.*, Stoning, pp. 9-11.

[113] Ibid.

[114] Ibid.

[115] Such as Ayatollah Abu al-Qasim al-Khoei, Ayatollah Ahmad Khansari and Ayatollah Yousef Sanei.

[116] *Ali, K.*, Sexual Ethics and Islam: Feminist Reflections on Qur'an, Hadith, and Jurisprudence. Oxford 2006 (Reprint, Oneworld 2012), pp. 56-57.

and their punishments are therefore solely rooted in the Sunnah (Sunnah is the verbally transmitted record of the teachings, deeds and sayings, silent permissions (or disapprovals) of the Islamic prophet Muhammad, as well as various reports about Muhammad's companions).[117] As a consequence, legal scholars throughout Islamic history have disagreed on the punishment and even the definition of sexual crimes. Some of the most controversial issues among Islamic scholars are the punishment of stoning for adultery, the punishment for homosexuality and the evidentiary requirement for different sexual crime which were debated within the legislative process of the IPC of 2013 and the law adopted some of these opinions to amend the regulation related to the punishment of adultery and homosexuality.

IV. The reform of the Islamic penal code of 2013

In this section, I will identify achievements of the amended IPC of 2013 with regard to the criminalization of sexuality, and try to answer the question whether a meaningful reform in this area of the IPC feasible at all. The first part will assess the state of the criminalization of sexuality under the new code. In view of exploring the scope for furthering reform in the future, the second part will first analyze persisting barriers to reform; subsequently the third part will discuss in which areas of the law and to which extent further reform might be possible while staying within the confines of traditionalist Islamic thought.

1. Assessment of the New Islamic Penal Code of 2013

On June 12, 2013, the reformed IPC came into force. It does not address most of the controversial issue that were presented in the last section, and thus falls short of the majority of demands made in the preceding reform discourse, in particular demands for a repeal of severe punishments such as stoning and other forms of the death penalty and corporal punishment as well as calls for a better protection of women and children against sexual violence. Except for some significant changes regarding the evidentiary requirements and the punishment of adultery, and minor changes regarding rape, sexual abuse of girls and homosexual intercourse, the definition and character of other sexual crimes remained unchanged. Moreover, the introduction of the new offence of „sowing corruption on earth“ empowers the court with drastic authority to enforce the sexual and moral policy of the state.

---

117 Ibid.

1.1. The old law of sexual offences largely preserved

As under the old 1991 IPC, sexual crimes are mostly contained in the *ḥudūd* part of the new code. It continues to include the Islamic offences of *zinā* (illicit consensual heterosexual sexual intercourse), *liwāṭ* (homosexual intercourse between men), *musāḥaqa* (sexual acts between women) and *qadhf (*false accusation *to zinā or liwāṭ)* with fixed punishments and specific evidentiary and other procedural regulations.

In the new IPC, the definition of rape is now extended to sexual intercourse with a woman without her consent while she is unconscious, asleep, or drunk.[118] Moreover *zinā* (illicit consensual sex) resulting of the deception and seduction of a non-pubescent girl is now recognized as rape.[119] While this constitutes an improvement compared to the old law, in particular as it provides better protection of children, it does not go very far. To begin with, Iranian law sets the age of puberty at nine lunar years, thus at a very young age. Moreover, it has to be proven that the girl was actually deceived, thus the law still assumes that children under the age of nine can, in principle, consent to sexual acts. Finally the law covers only girls and not boys.

Another change in the new IPC concerns the financial compensation for women that were victims of rape. According to the old law, compensation was confined to a rape victim's loss of virginity. The *diyat* part of the 2013 code now extends the grounds for compensation to all cases of rape of women.[120] On the other side, the new law does not address the way in which the courts have increasingly limited rape victims' right to claim self-defense. In fact the new code introduced a new rule, providing that self-defense is legitimate only where „the danger and aggression are not results of the person's voluntary action or his/her aggression and another person's defence."[121] The term „voluntary action", unqualified by any substantive criteria, is likely to be used by the courts as a statutory basis to legitimize their existing jurisprudence, according to which self-defense is legitimate only when a woman's preceding behavior complied with the patriarchal behavioral standards of the judiciary.

Some modifications also apply to the punishment of homosexuality. According to the IPC of 1991, the punishment for *liwāṭ* (sodomy) between men was the death penalty for both parties. The new IPC now set out different punishments, depending on the offender's position in the sexual intercourse.

---

118 IPC (2013), Art 224.

119 Ibid, Art 224.

120 Ibid, Art 231.

121 Ibid, Art. 155(3).

From now on, only the passive (i.e. penetrated) partner will be subject to the death penalty, whereas the punishment for the active (penetrating) partner is 100 lashes, unless he is married or acted against the passive partner's will, i.e.raped him.[122] Thus, as to the punishment of *liwāṭ*, the new code follows an approach that not only differs from the old code, but also from the majority opinion of Shia legal experts (*fuqahā*), such as Ayatollah Khomeini, who explicitly supported the execution of both parties involved in sodomy.[123] This change of the law will probably decrease the number of executions in *liwāṭ* cases.

1.2. Limitations on stoning: acceptance of doctrine of maṣlaḥa (necessity) and modification to evidentiary requirements

Adultery is still punished by stoning. However, the 2013 code now allows the court to replace a sentence of stoning by whipping or hanging in cases that the implementation of stoning is „impossible": Such a substitution of stoning must be proposed by the appeal court and approved by the Head of Judiciary.[124] This constitutes a significant change in the law, as it enables the courts of final judgement to avoid the death penalty even if the accused has been found guilty of adultery. Furthermore, the new code states that adultery shall be punished by hanging if the offense is proved by the testimony of four male witnesses.[125] While the law does not define the conditions that render the implementation of stoning „impossible", the reformed law has the potential to significantly reduce the implementation of stoning since almost all stoning cases under the old IPC were founded on the weak evidentiary standard „knowledge of judge", and not on the four-witness rule.[126]

By substantially limiting the knowledge of judge as sufficient proof for adultery, the legislator accepted the minority opinion among Shia scholars against the opposition of the majority, which still considers the „knowledge of judge" standard as sufficient evidence for all types of *ḥudūd* crimes, including adultery.[127] As becomes clear in the discussions in the legislative process, the law's reference to the „impossibility" of an implementation of stoning in fact

---

[122] IPC Art. 234.

[123] Kadīvar, K., Akhfiyat-i mujāzāt-i fā'il az maf'ūl dar liwāṭ (Mitigation of the Punishment of the Active Partner in Homosexual Intercourse). Available at: http://kadivar.com/?p=11118 (accessed 22.06.2016).

[124] IPC (2013), Art 225.

[125] Ibid.

[126] *Baghi, E.*, The Bloodied Stone: Execution by Stoning. Available at: http://www. iranhumanrights.org/2008/08/baghibloodiedstone (accessed 12.08.2016)

[127] Ibid.

constitutes an acknowledgement of the doctrine of *maslaḥa* (necessity), which had, in some cases, been already applied by Ayatollah Khomeini, the founder of the Islamic Republic.[128] According to this doctrine (as was said before), the enforcement of Islamic rules can be abandoned if it harms the national interest or damages the reputation of Islam.[129]

1.3. Reinforcement of the judiciary's arbitrary power: vague statutory language and redefinition of „sowing corruption on the earth“

The principle of legality constitutes one of the core principles of criminal law and also finds recognition in Shia legal sources, such as in the doctrine *qubḥ 'iqāb bilā bayān* („without being informed of the act's criminal nature, punishment is an evil“).[130] Nonetheless, in the IPC, this principle is regularly violated; as was already observed, the code often defines crimes in a very vague and broad language. Moreover, the new IPC of 2013 explicitly states that in cases of *ḥudūd* which are not mentioned in this code, the judge shall deliver his judgment on the basis of authoritative Islamic sources and authentic fatwas. [131]

The possibility of such analogies had been already been mentioned in Article 167 of constitutional law which states that „the judge is bound to endeavour to judge each case on the basis of the codified law. In case of the absence of any such law, he has to deliver his judgment on the basis of authoritative Islamic sources and authentic fatwas ...“. The applicability of this rule in the criminal law was heatedly debated.[132] However, through the new IPC, the legislator brought this debate to an end, as it clearly decided in favour of analogy even in serious criminal cases. This constitutes a highly significant empowerment of judicial power and signifies an important success of conservative elements in the legislative process.

Thus, not only does the new code leave the law's existing ambiguities untouched and now even allows for analogies in *ḥudūd*. The legislator also consciously opted to remain silent on novel questions, leaving it to the judiciary to provide meaning to a variety of new vague and ambiguous provisions. This legislative silence was partly the result of unresolved differences in opinion

---

128 Ibid.

129 Ibid.

130 *Tellenbach, S.*, The Principle of Legality in the Iranian Constitutional and Criminal Law. In: S. A. Arjomand and N. J. Brown, The Rule of Law, Islam and Constitutional Politics in Egypt and Iran, New York 2013, pp. 101-122(112).

131 Penal Code (2013), Art 220.

132 *Tellenbach, S.*, The Principle of Legality, ibid.

between conservative and reformist positions in Parliament and the Guardian Council over many controversial issues, leading Parliament to avoid clear language in order to prevent a veto against relatively progressive provisions by the Guardian Council.[133] In the case of sexual crimes, the most obvious example for this approach can be observed in the aforementioned rules on the punishment of stoning, where the law refers to cases in which the implementation of stoning is deemed to be „impossible“, but does not provide criteria to this effect.

The new code also disturbingly expands the definition of another vaguely worded crime, *ifsād fil-'arḍ* (sowing corruption on earth), which not only provides courts with extensive and flexible power to sentence political dissidents and anti-government critics to death, but can also be used against what, in the eyes of the authorities, contributes to spreading moral and sexual corruption. Although this offence had been in the IPC since 1991, it was, under the title *muḥāraba wa- ifsād fil-'arḍ* (enmity against God and sowing corruption on earth) so far only applied to the use of weapons causing social disorder.[134] Under the new law, the old offence is divided into two crimes, leading to new stand-alone offence under the name „sowing corruption on earth“, defined as committing any crime against internal and international security which would entail the corruption of society.[135] This offence, among many other criminal acts, also makes direct reference to the „establishment of brothels“ and to the „promotion of moral corruption“ which, if it seriously „disturbs the public order and security of the nation“, is punishable by hanging.[136] However, the code does not offer any criteria to determine when and how the listed acts „seriously disturb the public order and security of the nation“, thereby conferring great power to the judiciary, in particular given that this offence is punishable by death.[137] It has to be noted that the courts already issued the death penalty for those involved in prostitution or the operation of brothels by applying the concept of corruption on earth during the first years after the Islamic Revolution. Because before the enactment of the IPC of 1991, Iranian courts were allowed to directly refer to Islamic resources in their judgements.[138] But after the enactment of the IPC of 1991 and given that this code did not contain this offence, the

---

133 *Nayyeri, M. H.,* The Question of "Stoning to Death".

134 IPC (2013), Art. 183.

135 Ibid (2013), Art. 286.

136 Ibid.

137 *Hosseinkhah, M.,*The Execution of Women in Iranian Criminal Law: An Examination of the Impact of Gender on Laws Concerning Capital Punishment in the New Islamic Penal Code. Available at: http://www.iranhrdc.org/english/publications/legal-commentary/1000000102-the-execution-of-women-in-iranian-criminal-law.html (accessed 12.08.2016).

138 Ibid.

death penalty against prostitutes could no longer be based on a charge of corruption on earth.

2. Barriers to the reform of the criminalization of sexuality

Criticism of the criminalization of sexuality in Iran involves questions that go much further than an analysis of specific flaws of criminal policy. Sexual crimes are inseparably linked to the state's very identity and thus legitimacy, and to the political system of the Islamic Republic. A comprehensive repeal of Islamic sexual offences would signify removal of sharia law from the legal system. However, according to Iran's official historic narrative, the Islamic Republic is firmly grounded on the assumption that it was created in the name of Islam. Any significant reversal of laws that were introduced as part of the revolutionary Islamization would constitute an open negation of the ideological rationale of the Islamic Republic, and would therefore undermine its existence. In view of the existence of a variety of approaches to Islamic law, this constraint does not necessarily prevent meaningful structural reform of the issue of sexual crimes. However, any reform must be traced and conceptualized within the framework of Islamic legal though, and must furthermore overcome strong resistance from constitutional intuitions which are designed to preserve the state's adherence to its Islamic identity. These institutions such as the Guardian Council are either unelected institutions or indirectly elected and therefore are immune of being assessed by social opinion.

While the Iranian constitution recognizes the right of the people to directly elect the Parliament and the President, there are many other unelected institutions which have vital impact on political, judicial and social policies. As the head of state and highest ranking political and religious authority, the Supreme Leader of the Republic, according to the constitution, is in charge of „absolute guardianship and leadership of the country" (*wilāyat-i faqīh*).[139] He must be a senior Islamic theologian and is elected and supervised by the Assembly of Experts, which itself consists of Islamic theologians and is directly elected by the people.[140] Many of the key posts are also appointed by the supreme leader, notably the Head of Judiciary who himself has to be a high ranking Islamic scholar.[141] However, another institution, the Guardian Council, beside its authority to review the conformity of Parliamentary bills with the Sharia, is also tasked with the vetting of candidates' eligibility for the election of

[139] The Constitution of the Islamic Republic of Iran, Articles 5, 57,107-112.
[140] Ibid, Art. 107.
[141] Ibid, Art. 110.

Parliament and of the Assembly of Experts.[142] The Guardian Council is composed of twelve members, six of them being Islamic jurists appointed by the Supreme Leader and six laymen nominated by the Head of Judiciary.[143] As becomes clear from the foregoing, the constitutional structures are designed to ensure that religious scholars are in effective control of law-making and the judiciary.

These organs naturally strongly resist any attempts to reform the Islamic criminal law on sexuality.[144] Beside consideration related to the state's Islamic identity, a number of reasons such as interdependence to the patriarchal part of society can explain why, in the eyes of the conservative establishment, change in the area of sexuality appears to be particularly unwelcome. The adherence to Islamic sexual offences seems to be rooted in the fact that the conservative elements within the state get their political legitimacy primarily from the patriarchal sections of society.

In Iran, as in many other Muslim majority countries, „women constantly have been the sign or marker of cultural and political objectives".[145] While emancipation and sexual freedom were symbols of modernization under the Pahlavi regime, the Islamic revolutionaries gained social acceptance partly by arguing that these policies would constitute an attack on Iranian cultural identity and were therefore expressions of imperialism.[146] The Islamic sexual offences complement conservative ideas about family, taken from a patriarchal interpretation of divine texts and Sunnah, according to which „a woman's sexuality, if not her person, becomes a commodity and an object of exchange" and extensive sexual rights are conferred to men.[147] Marriage is based on an exchange of sexual and productive rights of the wife in return for receiving dowry (*mahr*) and maintenance (*nafaqa*) from the husband. Accordingly, the wife can refuse to have sex with her husband only until she receives *mahr*, i.e. the sum of the money that the husband must pay or undertakes to pay to the bride.[148] Moreover, the wife in order to receive *nafaqa*, is supposed to be sexually submissive (*tamkīn*) to her husband.[149] Against the background of such

---

142 Ibid, Art. 4, 72, 99.
143 Ibid, Art. 91.
144 *Mir-Hosseini, Z.* and *Hamzić, V.*, Control and Sexuality, p. 91.
145 *Moghadam, V.*, Patriarchy and the politics of gender in modernising societies: Iran, Pakistan and Afghanistan, International Sociology, Madrid, vol. 7(1992), pp. 35-53(38). p. 38.
146 Ibid.
147 *Mir-Hosseini, Z.* and *Hamzić, V.*, Control and Sexuality, p. 33.
148 Ibid.
149 Ibid.

an understanding of family and the role of women, Islamic sexual offences allow the conservative elements within the state to maintain their support among parts of society, as the continuous far-reaching criminalization of sexuality provides the means to keep women in line with a conservative definition of „correct" behavior which underpins patriarchal family and social structures.[150]

The sensitivity of sexual offences for the religious establishment becomes plainly surfaced in the legislative process leading to the IPC of 2013, while, it also demonstrates the limitations under which Parliament was acting.[151] One of the main concerns of the Guardian Council which led to several back and forth of the bill between parliament and the guardian council was with regard to the punishment of adultery. The first bill that was approved by Parliament had been completely silent on this issue. However, the Guardian Council recalled the bill and directed Parliament that stoning should continue to be explicitly prescribed as punishment.[152]

3. Potential for reforming sexual crime within an Islamic framework

The new IPC of 2013 demonstrated that, within the context of the Islamic Republic, reference to international human rights law cannot serve as the primary basis for reform. However, the existing plurality of opinions among traditionalist Islamic legal scholars regarding the interpretation of Islamic law can have an effect on development of Iranian law, especially on the implementation of *ḥudūd* crimes. On a variety of very controversial legal questions, such as adultery or the death penalty for juveniles, the new code has been strongly influenced by opinions that receive support only from a minority of Shia jurists. But it became equally clear, in particular in the debates on stoning, that a meaningful reform will only result from a challenge to the law by a broad social movement supported by reformist interpretations of Islamic law and external pressure from the international human rights community, and the involvement of ordinary people outside activist circles is required to initiate popular reformist discourse.

For furthering a reformist debate on the criminalization of sexuality, it seems necessary to identify the doctrine and arguments used for reformist objectives in the new IPC that can potentially also apply in other areas of the law. Moreover, it is of crucial importance to look at and learn from the reform experience of other Islamic countries, in particular Pakistan, as this might provide useful

---

[150] Ibid, p. 100.
[151] *Tavana, M.*, Three Decades of Islamic Criminal Law, p. 29.
[152] *Nayyeri, M. H.*, The Question of "Stoning to Death".

strategies and arguments for advancing a reform within Islamic law. Similar to Iran, Islamic criminal law was used as a major instrument to transform Pakistan into an Islamic republic, in particular through the „Hudood ordinance“ of 1979.[153] Due to the serious effects of this law on women, Pakistan's National Assembly in 2006 passed the Protection of Women (Criminal Laws Amendment) Act, which was designed to alleviate the inequities of women under the Hudood Ordinance and, at the same time, purported to conform to Islamic law.[154] It seems that some of the arguments advanced to promote the Pakistani Protection of Women Act could also succeed in the Iranian reformist discourse. In three areas, Iran criminal law appears to have the potential for similar reform, namely the evidential standard for sexual crimes, procedural rules on the use of evidence, and the introduction of new sexual crimes to better protect women and children.

The abolition of the „knowledge of judge“ as an admissible evidential standard for issuing the hanging for adultery is a significant step that can provide the ground for its elimination as admissible evidence for other types of *ḥudūd* crime. „Knowledge of judge“ is nowadays not recognized as valid evidence in most of Sunni schools of Islam. Amongst traditionalist Shia jurists, the admissibility of it is controversial with regard to those *ḥudūd* crimes that do not cause harm to another person.[155] Furthermore, the definition of adultery in traditional Shia jurisprudence should not imply that its evidential requirements should be different from those of other *ḥudūd* crimes. As „knowledge of judge“ represents the most common way to proof sexual crimes under Iranian law, its removal as the valid form of evidence would make a great difference to the practical relevance of *ḥudūd* crimes. Furthermore, it was already said that the current evidentiary rules of *ḥudūd* under Iranian law are problematic in that the complaint of a victim of rape, if it is not backed up by sufficient evidence, can be utilized as a confession of illicit sexual intercourse. In this respect, the Iranian legislator could easily improve the situation by making use of the exculpatory potential of *ḥudūd* law itself. One of the crucial principles within *ḥudūd* law is the doctrine of *shubha* (doubt), which is as such already mentioned in IPC, and which requires an investigation for *ḥudūd* crimes to be dropped if there is a

---

[153] *Imran, R.*, Legal Injustices: The Zina Hudood Ordinance of Pakistan and Its Implications for Women. In: The Journal of International Women's Studies, vol. 7(2005), pp. 78-100(89).

[154] *Lau, M.*, Twenty-Five Years of Hudood Ordinances-A Review. Washington and Lee Law Review Lexington, vol. 64 (2007), pp. 1291-1314(1295).

[155] *Asghari, A and S. Mosavi Rokni, A. S.*, Legal Changes in Personal Knowledge of the Judge with Emphasis on Islamic Punishment Law, International Journal of Social Sciences and Education, Islamabad, vol. 5(2015), pp. 407-416 (409).

slight doubt about the circumstances of the crime.[156] To guarantee this principle, the Protection of Women Act of Pakistan added a special condition to define a confession. According to it, statements that were made in another proceedings, for example a rape complaint, will not be treated as a confession of adultery or other illicit sexual relationships outside marriage.[157] As a consequence, victims of rape in Pakistan are no longer at risk of being prosecuted for illicit sexual acts.[158]

Furthermore, Islamic jurisprudence has a strong emphasis on protecting people's reputation against false accusations of illicit sexual behavior. This is reflected in the criminalization of false accusations under the offence of *qadhf* and the general principle of procedural law that prohibits the investigation of sexual crimes unless very reliable evidence is brought before the court.[159] However, Iranian law lacks clear procedural rules that ensure respect for the latter principles. The Pakistani Protection of Women Act has introduced a new regulation in this regard. To strengthen the offense of *qadhf,* it stated that „once the prosecution of a charge of fornication and adultery has resulted in an acquittal, the trial judge can prosecute and sentence the unsuccessful complainant in the very same proceedings".[160] In addition, the evidence of someone convicted of *qadhf* becomes inadmissible in any future court proceedings.[161] To further safeguard the protection against false accusations, Pakistani law has also raised the evidentiary requirements for allegations of fornication and adultery. In order for any complaint of fornication or adultery to proceed, at least two eye-witnesses (for fornication) and three eye-witnesses (for adultery) must, under oath, testify before the judge before the latter can issue a summons.[162]

As already illustrated in the first chapter, Islamic law, under the name *ta'zīrāt*, allows for the criminalization of a behavior that threatens public order and is not already criminalized under *ḥudūd* or *diyāt*, i.e. is not part of the traditional canon of Islamic offences. This allows the legislator to criminalize certain forms of sexual violence against which *ḥudūd* law does not provide

---

156 *Naubahār,* Ahdāf-i-mujāzāthā, p. 11.

157 Protection of Women of Pakistan (Criminal Laws Amendment) Act, 2006 pmbl. (Pak.). Article 12A.

158 *Lau, M.*, Twenty-Five Years of Hudood, p. 1311.

159 *Naubahār, N.*, Ahdāf-i-mujāzāthā,.p. 14.

160 Protection of Women (Criminal Laws Amendment) Act, 2006 pmbl. (Pak.) (n 204). Offence of qazf (Enforcement of Hadd) Ordinance, Article 6(2) (1979) (amended 2006). (Pak.).

161 Art.7 (2).

162 The Code of Criminal Procedure of Iran. Art 203C(2)(2015).

sufficient protection yet, in particular violence against women, children and other vulnerable persons. In fact, the *ta'zīrāt* part of the IPC is currently under revision and there are attempts by reformist forces, especially in the moderate government of president Rohani, to add new offences to the law that would criminalize some forms of violence against women and children.[163] The approach of the Pakistani Protection of Women Act in this regard has been to restrict the applicability of the Hudood Ordinance to the crimes of *zinā* (illicit consensual sexual act) and *qadhf* (false accusation). Other sexual crimes, in particular rape, have returned to the Pakistani penal code, where they had already been located prior to the enactment of the Hudood Ordinance of 1979.[164] As a result, in Pakistan the law of rape and *ḥudūd* law are strictly separated, which has the crucial effect that the evidentiary rules of *ḥudūd* are not applicable to rape cases. It is precisely these evidentiary rules that, in Iran, so far obstruct an effective protection of women and children against sexual abuse. The solution of the Pakistani reform was based on the argument that „only two offenses, namely *zinā* and *qadhf* are mentioned in the Qur'an", thus it was claimed that the *zinā* Ordinances had exceeded Islamic law.[165] On this basis, Pakistani law was able to overcome some of the deficits of the old law, providing for context sensitive sentencing, going as far as criminalizing marital rape and classifying any sexual intercourse with a girl under the age of sixteen as rape, irrespective of her consent.

While the aforementioned reform strategies could have a significantly limiting impact on the implementation of punishment of consensual sexual acts and provide better protection for women and children, it must be reiterated that a reform of the law on sexuality within the tight framework of traditional Islamic law will not eliminate the latter's structural discrimination and its grave impact on gender relations. It has been rightly claimed that „meaningful consent and mutuality which seem crucial for a just ethics of sexual intimacy are structurally impossible within the constraints of lawful sexuality as defined by the classical Muslim scholars".[166] While the Qur'an and the Sunnah contain some egalitarian elements on the issue of sexuality, one cannot ignore the numerous aspects contained therein that accept sexual relationships only „within hierarchical and gender-differentiated family structures".[167] In the Islamic context, the only

---

[163] Layiha-yi islāḥī-yi qawānīn-i marbūṭ bi khānivada wa-zanān (Bill on amending some laws related to women and families), Available at: http://mehrkhane.com/fa/news/27033/

[164] *Lau, M.*, Twenty-Five Years of Hudood, p. 1308.

[165] Ibid.

[166] *Ali, K.*, Sexual Ethics and Islam Sexual ethics and Islam: Feminist reflections on Qur'an, hadith, and jurisprudence, Oxford 2006, p. 57.

[167] Ibid.

proper way forward ultimately lies in the assertion of modern Islamic thought that adopts a hermeneutic and historical reading of the Qur'an and Sunnah.[168] However, as was already said, the most important obstacle to any reform of Iranian law is the political structure of the Islamic Republic. Consequently, all attempts for a reform of sexual crimes are „part of a larger struggle for gender equality, democracy and rule of law" in Iran.[169]

Conclusion

For now almost four decades, the criminal law, together with family law and rules about women's dress code, has been used to regulate sexuality in line with the Iranian authorities' understanding of Islamic morality.[170] Though precise statistics on the number of prosecutions are not available, empirical research, reports by journalists and human rights organizations show that women are the main target of the Islamic Republic's criminalization of sexuality. At the same time, the criminal justice system not only largely ignores sexual abuse of women and children, but exposes victims of abuse to the risk of being prosecuted for fornication and adultery. Another highly problematic characteristic of sexual offences under Iranian law, in particular under the *ḥudūd* section of the IPC, is the discriminatory nature of prescribed punishments, the latter depending on the gender, religion or the age of a convicted person. Sexual offences thus do not serve as a means to protect individuals from harm, but as a tool of oppression to consolidate the patriarchal structure of the society.

However, the recent reform of IPC of 2013 demonstrated that, while the attempts of rights activists can certainly not lead to a complete repeal of Islamic sexual crimes under Iran's current constitution, progress in this area is well possible. From the perspective of international human rights law, the state of Iranian criminal law might still look dire and most of the 2013 changes appear rather marginal, given the continuing broad criminalization of consensual sexual acts and the existence of cruel punishments. Despite this, one should not underestimate the significance of this reform. For the first time in the history of the Islamic Republic, civil society campaigns, supported by pressure from the international human rights community, were able to place human rights concerns into the heart of public debates about criminal justice, and to challenge hardline political elements. Activists and journalists took the judiciary to task

---

168 Ibid.

169 *Mir-Hosseini*, Z. and *Hamzić*, V.; Control and Sexuality, p. 111.

170 *Mir-Hosseini, Z.*, Criminalizing sexuality, p 4.

and exposed the injustices caused by Islamic criminal law. This opened up a major fault line in society, demonstrating that some aspects of the Islamic Republic's identity are offensive to today's notions of justice and lost their power to convince. Under the influence of this discourse, Islamic reformist scholars started to question the legitimacy of prevailing positions of Islamic jurisprudence and thereby highlighted the diversity of possible interpretations of sacred texts even within an Islamic framework. Given the central role of the Islamic Republic's claim to truth with regard to such interpretations, and indeed its reliance on broad popular acceptance of this claim, the reform discourse about Islamic sexual crimes is likely to have repercussions well beyond this area of the law. There is little doubt that any meaningful amendment, with regard to sexual regulation including sexual crimes, is associated with the change in the legislative and judicial system of the Islamic Republic of Iran. Nevertheless, the recent reform gives hope that under the pressure of public opinion, developed from increased public awareness and continual unfair and unjust application of these laws, the legislative system would be forced to give way to a reformist interpretation of Islam.

Rule of Law or Rule by Law? Iran's Bar Association as a pawn in Islamic-republican contestations

Mirjam Künkler, Uppsala

Introduction

The institution of the bar association and its independence from the judicial branch of power is a key pillar of any rule of law state. Bar associations design and conduct the licensing examinations for future lawyers, and their boards are usually instrumental in screening prospective parliamentary legislation for its compatibility with the constitution and the rule of law. The independence of judges and their professional integrity hinges on training and licensing programs that are shielded from political interference and instrumentalization. Independent bar associations that oversee the training and certification of future lawyers and judges are therefore indispensable to guaranteeing the rule of law. Conversely, where political elites have the power to interfere with the certification of lawyers and inject political considerations into the decision-making process of who can and who cannot join the bar, the legal profession is at risk of becoming subservient to political power and, ultimately, at becoming a tool of authoritarian rule.

The development of the Bar Association of Iran (*Kānūn-i Vūkalā-yi Dādgūstarī*) is intricately bound up with the development of a modern legal system in the course of the 20th century. It is one of the most important achievements of the constitutional revolution in 1906/1907, often credited with signifying and further instilling in 20th century Iran the strong belief in constitutionalism and in fertilizing a rule of law-oriented legal culture. By mid-century, independent bar associations had been established in a number of Iranian cities, although it took until 1953 that the bar was independent from the Ministry of Justice. The 1960s and 1970s saw the heydays of the professionalization of lawyers and judges and the crystallization of public appreciations for an independent judiciary. During the 1979 revolution, lawyers from the bar association made up the backbone of the human rights movement that called for fundamental political reform. Contrary to their campaigns in favor of democratization and the rule of law, the revolution quickly degenerated into a lawless situation, where standards of *habeas corpus* were abrogated. In the aftermath of the systemic transformation of the legal system that followed the establishment of the Islamic Republic, the bar association was effectively neutralized in the 1980s, but rose from the ashes during the post-Iran/Iraq war re-construction period under President Rafsanjani (1989-1997) when it attempted to re-assert itself as the primary institution for the licensing of lawyers. Expectedly, this attempt met with fierce resistance from among officials inside the judiciary who had built up alternative training and recruitment programs for future lawyers and judges. Nevertheless, they were not able to replace the bar association entirely and to date no head of the judiciary has succeeded in closing it down once and for all. Ever since the early 2000s, the bar association has been a pawn in the internal contestations between those forces aiming to strengthen the independence of the judiciary, and those insisting that the Islamic character of the regime demands the judiciary's subservience to the executive.

This article offers an overview of the history of the bar association in modern Iran, with particular focus on its regulation by the state following the 1979 revolution. Although the bar association is one of the most important non-state institutions capable of strengthening the rule of law, it has received only scant academic attention so far, with no single non-Persian article or book chapter dedicated to it to date.[1] The article will first offer a brief history of the establishment of the modern judiciary in the first part of the 20th century and the development of the bar association as part of it. It will then turn to an overview of the justice system and the Islamization process that the judiciary underwent as a result of the 1979 revolution, and examine how the consolidating revolutionary regime dealt with the bar association as the most important body that could present a counter-weight to a politically controlled judiciary. It will be suggested that over time the judiciary has succeeded in creating a parallel institution that fulfils the functions of the bar association, and allows it to control the training and certification of lawyers. This process is representative of two larger trends in the institutional development of the Islamic Republic: a) the subordination of law and the legal profession to political considerations, and b) the creation of institutions parallel to those beyond the regime's purview in order to tighten spaces over which it could otherwise not exert full control.

Methodologically, the research for this chapter is based on textual analysis of decrees, ordinances, bills, laws and regulations, and documentation of judicial appointment decisions. It also incorporates some ethnographic work consisting of interviews with judges in a high court. A third type of source consists of

---

1 For a recent overview in Persian, see *Najafi, A.*, Jaygāh-i kānūn-i vūkalā-yi dādgūstarī va vakīl dar jāmi'a-yi ḥuqūqī va-qānūn-i ā'īn-i dādrasī-yi kayfarī-yi Irān. In: Ghulāmī, Ḥ. (ed.) 'Ulūm-i jināyī-yi taṭbīqī dar partū-yi hamkārīhā-yi bain al-milalī. Majmū'a-yi maqālāt-i nikūdāsht-i duktur-i Sīlviyā-yi Tillinbākh. Tehran, 2017, 458-478.

domestic and international news coverage and reports by human rights organizations.

Popular Sovereignty and Clerical Veto Actors

The Islamic Republic presents a unique hybrid of a republican regime that on the one hand seeks to maximize participation and – with recourse to revolutionary rhetoric – legitimacy, but which on the other hand concentrates political power in the office of the revolutionary Leader (*Rahbar*) with virtually no checks and balances vis-à-vis other branches of power and nearly full executive control over the judicial and security system. A key institution of legislation and judicial review is the Guardian Council (*shūrā-yi nigahbān)*, which is made up of six jurists trained in Shiʿite law (*mujtahid*s) and six secular-trained jurists.[2] The entire council screens draft legislation for its consistency with the constitution. Only the six *mujtahid*s probe the congruence of draft legislation with (their interpretation of) Shiʿite Jaʿfari law. As the revolutionary Leader appoints half of the Guardian Council and as he also appoints the head of judiciary who in turn proposes the other half of the Guardian Council, the Leader's votum is decisive in the make-up of this central institution. If the Guardian Council decides that draft legislation violates constitutional or Shiʿite law, it can veto it and send it back to the parliament (*Majlis*) for revision. The parliament then has the choice of either revising the draft legislation in line with the Guardian Council's demands, or to vote with a two-thirds majority in favor of forwarding it on to the „Council for the Discernment of the Expediency of the System" (*Majma'-i Tashkhīṣ-i Maṣlaḥat-i Niẓām*), hereafter Expediency Council.

The Expediency Council, which is entirely appointed by the Leader and on which the jurists of the Guardian Council also sit ex officio, may then decide to pass the bill with the changes recommended by the Guardian Council or pass its own version, which may substantively deviate from the original.[3] Due to these inbuilt mechanisms of potential clerical veto, a parliament committed to a

---

2 For an overview, see *Saffari, S.* „The Legitimation of the Clergy's Right to Rule in the Iranian Constitution of 1979." In: British Journal of Middle Eastern Studies Vol. 20 (1993), No 1, 64-82, and analyses by the bar association itself: *Mihrpūr, H*, 'Aṣl-i chahārum-i qānūn-i asāsī va-qalamrū-yi shumūl-i ān' 146-147 Majalla-yi Kānūn-i Vukalā', (1989), 15-31, 17.

3 For the internal bylaws of the council, see the bylaws and translation available on the Iran Data Portal: http://irandataportal.syr.edu/internal-bylaw-of-the-expediency-council-the-council-for-expediency-of-the-system-majma-e-tashkhis-e-maslehat-e-nezam

reform agenda may not get very far, unless the Leader has appointed into the Guardian Council and the Council of Expediency individuals committed to the same agenda.

Instituted as a body to advise the *Rahbar*, the Expediency Council also passes its own budget, despite the fact that budgetary power is constitutionally assigned to the parliament. The Council can thereby endow certain institutions with independent or additional funding. These include the court system that lies outside the official judiciary, such as the military courts, the press courts and the Special Courts of the Clergy.[4]

The *Rahbar* also is commander in chief of the regular army and the revolutionary guards. He entertains personal representatives in all ministries, and appoints the chairmen of the country's *bunyāds*, major economic institutions that often consist of conglomerates of economically powerful parastatal enterprises.[5] He has personal representatives in all embassies and consulates around the world, as well as in all major cities of Shiʿite learning in the region, where his office funds several religious seminaries and thousands of their students.[6]

The judiciary is under the supervision of the Leader who in accordance with article 158 of the constitution, revised in 1989, appoints the head of judiciary for five-year terms. The office of the head of judiciary is responsible for the appointment, dismissal, suspension and promotion of all judges and often makes requests for certain cases to be tried in specific courts. While it is independent from the other branches of power, i.e. the parliament and the presidency, it is not independent from the *Rahbar*.

---

4 *Künkler, M.* „The Special Court of the Clergy (Dādgāh-i Vīzhah-ʾi Rūḥānīyat) and the Repression of Dissident Clergy in Iran. In: Arjomand, S. and Brown, N. (eds.) The Rule of Law, Islam, and Constitutional Politics in Egypt and Iran, SUNY Press, 2012, 57-100.

5 See the three part Reuters series:
Assets of the Ayatollah. Land Grab: http://www.reuters.com/investigates/iran/#article/part1;
National Champion: http://www.reuters.com/investigates/iran/#article/part2;
Rough Justice: http://www.reuters.com/investigates/iran/#article/part3.

6 See *Gleave, R.* (ed.). Knowledge and Authority in Shi'i Islam: Volume 1: Clerics and the Hawza System in the Middle East (British Institute of Persian Studies), IB Tauris, forthcoming 2018; also *Lob, E.* An Institutional History Of The Iranian Construction Jihad: From Inception To Institutionalization (1979-2011), Ph.D. Dissertation in Near Eastern Studies, defended at Princeton University in 2013, in which he documents how the Islamic Republic is also sponsoring *hawza* and *hawza* students in Lebanon, among other places.

Thus, on the one hand, the process of legislation is highly dependent on individuals who are directly or indirectly appointed by the revolutionary Leader. On the other hand, the Islamic Republic features regular and usually quite competitive elections for the parliament and the presidency, and since 1999 also the municipal councils. The highest political office, the *Rahbar's*, is itself the product of an election, i.e. that of the Assembly of Experts, a clerical council of now 88 members (previously 86), which is directly elected by the people for eight-year terms and could theoretically depose the Revolutionary Leader if it found him to have violated the law or to be otherwise unfit to rule (this, however, has never happened). Moreover, the elected institutions are not powerless. The parliament's most important mandate is its budgetary power, while the president's primary purview is in designing economic policy. Foreign and security policy, by contrast, is the mandate of the National Security Council and not that of an elected body. Given the long-standing sanctions against Iran, and also given that economic policy is highly dependent on security policy, the president's powers are de facto limited even in the realm of economic policy. Further, given that all major reforms in favor of privatization must pass not only parliament but also the clerical councils, the president is unable to fundamentally work towards economic reform unless this is also backed by the Guardian and Expediency Councils. Finally, electoral competitions is limited by virtue of the fact that the Guardian Council has the power to screen and disqualify all candidates intending to run for political office beforehand, a mandate the Council has interpreted in maximalist ways and has made use of extensively since 1992.

The institutional design of the polity encourages political contestation and, to a limited degree, open political discourse *qua* a constitution that guarantees a range of civil liberties on a level unparalleled by Iran's neighbours. For instance, the principle of the presumption of innocence is specified in Article 37, and Article 169 stipulates the non-retroactivity of new laws. Article 32 recognizes the right of arrested individuals to know the reason of their detention within 24 hours, and Article 34 their right to call on justice. According to Article 35, the accused have a right to legal representation in court. Article 36 lays out that only competent courts have the right to pass sentences. Articles 165 and 166 assert that courts are open to the public and that verdicts can be passed only after the examination of evidence.[7] The severe limitations of the justice system

7 See the 1979 constitution (as amended in 1989) on the Constitute Project website: https://www.constituteproject.org/constitution/Iran_1989?lang=en. For an excellent overview of the process of constitution-making and key ideas in the drafting process, see *Schirazi, A.* The Constitution of Iran: Politics and the State in the Islamic Republic. London: I.B. Tauris Publishers, 1997.

notwithstanding, the 1979 constitution does recognize several key rights that might facilitate a rule of law state, if they were immutable.[8] With its space for contestation in elections, relatively pluralist media, and a functioning legislature, Iran exhibits notable pockets of contestation that make it difficult to classify it as a closed authoritarian regime.

As will be shown, the institution of the bar association with independent recruitment of future lawyers and judges could be a primary tool in holding potential abuses of power at bay, but the association's struggle to re-assert its place after 1979 has continuously been met with strong resistance among judiciary officials.

History of the Modern Judiciary and the Bar Association

The Bar Association was established as a consequence of the Constitutional Revolution 1906/1907 and apart from the constitution itself and the parliament, was one of the revolution's long-term institutional achievements. The revolution ushered in a period of state formation with the gradual build-up of a state-run legal system, slowly taking the administration of justice out of the hands of the *'ulamā'* (Islamic scholars).[9] New civil courts were established, although in the absence of any codified law, the courts continued to follow *sharī'a* and those that were recruited as judges had still overwhelmingly been trained in the religious schools (*madrasa*). The court decisions on similar cases could vary widely from place to place and as no formal appeals procedure existed, claimants would often turn to religious authorities outside the court room to resolve their cases, thereby undermining the legitimacy of the new state-run system.

In 1911, a major justice reform was enacted through the passing of the Provisional Code of Judicial Organization (*Qānūn-i muvaqqatī-i tashkīlāt-i 'adlīya*) and the Provisional Code of Civil Procedure *(Qānūn-i muvaqqatī-yi uṣūl-i muḥākamāt-i ḥuqūqi*). The latter stipulated that lawyers licensed by the

8 Among the most detailed analyses in Persian is *Hāshimī, M, Ḥuqūq-i asāsī-yi jumhūrī-yi islāmī-yi Īrān*, 2 vols. (Qom, Mujtama'-i Āmuzish-i 'Ālī), 1996/1375.

9 For overviews, see *Mohammadi, M.* Judicial Reform and Reorganization in 20th Century Iran: State-Building, Modernization and Islamicization. New York: Routledge, 2008; and *Enayat, H.* Law, State, and Society in Modern Iran: Constitutionalism, Autocracy, and Legal Reform 1906-1941, Palgrave, 2013.

Ministry of Justice be present during court proceedings.[10] It was thus a first step towards the state-run certification of lawyers (and future judges), although the dearth of applicants for certification meant that this guideline was de facto seldom followed.

The 1911 codes were passed as temporary laws (*muvaqqatī*) in order to circumvent a discussion with the Islamic scholars in parliament about the laws' compatibility with *sharī'a*. It was hoped that the laws and regulations were more likely to meet approval for their permanent adoption after they had been shown to withstand the test of time, had been put into practice and in some cases had been improved upon through legal reform.

In the same year, 1911, the first civil code was promulgated, again on a temporary basis. It had been written by Adolphe Perny, who functioned as the French legal advisor from 1911 to 1926. Perny had also been instrumental in the opening for the *Madrasa-yi ḥuqūq* (judicial school) in 1920 that was staffed mainly by French judicial personnel and whose primary function was to train future lawyers and judges.[11]

The coup d'état of February 1921 that marked the end of the Qajar dynasty also put a preliminary end to this recent build-up of a mostly secular, state-administered judiciary. In many regions of the country the entire judicial personnel was dismissed after the coup, and in some the old religious courts were re-established.[12] When Reza Pahlavi assumed the throne in 1925, one of his chief objectives was to present to Western powers new permanent codes in order to put an end to Western capitulations, which reserved Western countries the right to try their citizens for crimes committed in Iran in their own rather than Iranian courts. These capitulations had been justified with reference to the absence of permanent codes and the general weakness of the justice system, effectively immunizing foreign citizens from criminal prosecution in Iran.

---

10 *Matīn Daftarī, A.* Ā'īn-i dādrasī-yi madanī va bāzargānī, 2 vols., Tehran, 2002. [1945]. Here 1945, 263f.

11 *Gulshā'iyān, 'A.* Guzashtahā va andishahā-yi zandagī yā khāṭirāt-i man, 2 vols., Tehran, 1998, Vol. 1, 52-54. The law school was later expanded and renamed the Faculty of Law, Political Science, and Economics (*Dānishkada-yi ḥoqūq al 'ulūm-i siyāsī va iqtiṣādī*). On the school, see *Kasravi, A.* Zandagānī-yi man yā dah sāl dar 'adliya, Tehran, 1944, esp. 146-48.

12 In Kerman, „in August [1921] the old corrupt department [i.e. pre-reform] was opened again with its original staff" (See GIAR (Government of India, „Administration Report of the Persian Gulf Political Residency for the Year …") in *The Persian Gulf Administration Reports: 1873-1947*, 10 vols., n.p., Archive Editions, 1986, vols. 8 and 9, here for the Year 1921, p. 23.

Between 1925 and 1928, several permanent laws were passed, among them a new commercial code (*qānūn-i tijārat*) in February 1926 and a new criminal code later that year, also penned by Perny, based on the French code.[13] The Code of Civil Procedure (*qānūn-i āʾīn-i dādrasī-yi madanī)* and the first book of a new civil code *(qānūn-i madanī*) were passed in 1928. The latter consisted of the codification of *sharī'a* following the format of the French Code Civil (the Napoleonic code). The new Judicial Organization Act (*qānūn-i tashkīlāt-i 'adlīya*) of 1928 provided that in order to practice, lawyers had to have either a law degree, a certificate from the Ministry of Justice, or previous experience as a judge. A disciplinary court for judges was established, which would impose stricter disciplinary regulations.

The law of 1911 had established that professional lawyers (*vakīl-i rasmī*) had to be Iranian, at least thirty years of age, of good conduct, and not in the employ of the government. To be certified, they had to pass a special examination in the Ministry of Justice. While the 1911 law still allowed „occasional" (as opposed to professional lawyers) to serve in court from time to time, the new Judicial Organization Act allowed only professional lawyers to represent clients in a court of law. A law of 1930 once again reversed this due to a shortage of lawyers and stipulated that district or sub-provincial courts could authorize certain competent persons to act as lawyers, but only in the court that had given such permission. A 1936 law then created a three-tiered (*pāya*) system, whereby first-grade lawyers could appear in any court, second-grade lawyers in provincial, sub-provincial, and district courts, and those of the third grade only in sub-provincial and district courts. Each tier had standardized examinations, and official dress became obligatory at court appearances.

As per the law of 1911, appointment to the Supreme Court, the court of appeal, and as chiefs of the courts of first instance occurred by imperial decree at the proposition of the minister of justice. The religious judge (*ḥākim-i sharʿ*), appointed by the Shah, had to agree to the appointment of the public prosecutors of the Supreme Court and the court of appeal. All candidates had to be Iranian citizens and Muslim, and at least twenty-five years of age for the lowest ranks and forty years of age for the highest ranks. Candidates were generally *madrasa*-trained or, after the opening of the law school, increasingly law school graduates. After a 1936 law that further reformed the organization of the judiciary, those who were *madrasa*-trained could rise only to a certain level

[13] *Marin, S.*, „La réception mitigée des codifications napoléoniennes en Iran (1911-1935)", Droit et cultures [online], 48 | 2004-2, accessed 21 August 2017. URL: http://droitcultures.revues.org/1723. and *Daftary, A*. Geschichte und System des iranischen Strafrechts, Bonn 1935.

(grade six out of eleven) while the upper echelons were attainable only by the law school graduates. A 1955 law then stipulated that only law school graduates were eligible for any judgeship.[14]

A first professional association of lawyers (*Kānūn-i Vūkalā-yi Dādgūstarī*) was founded in 1930. One of its founders remarked during the opening: „There is no doubt that court proceedings cannot rest on the dossier alone, the judge cannot rule on the dossier by itself. Other elements exist, and of these the most important is defense lawyers who should not allow a judge to deviate from the law in the proceedings or in his judgment. Throughout the civilized world those acquainted with legal affairs know that without the provision of good lawyers justice is impossible."[15]

Initially functioning as an organization under the auspices of the judiciary, the bar association was formally recognized as the sole institution certifying future lawyers in 1937, although it was still not entirely independent from the Ministry of Justice at this point. During the brief period of parliamentary democracy (1941-1953) after Shah Reza Pahlavi was deposed by the Allied Powers, a law was passed under prime minister Mossadeqh in 1953 that secured the independence of the Bar Association from the state, the Independence of the Bar Act (*Lāyiha-yi qānūnī-yi istiqlāl-i kānūn-i vūkalā-yi dādgūstarī).*

From 1954 on, when the law came into effect, lawyers were no longer licensed subject to Ministry approval nor any other state institution. They were certified in the now independent bar association and only the disciplinary court of the bar could try lawyers for professional transgressions and offenses.

The bar, now an autonomous authority vested with an independent legal identity, consisted of four sub-entities: a Board of Directors, a disciplinary investigation bureau, a disciplinary tribunal, and a legal aid section.[16] Its main tasks included to grant (and extend) licenses to qualified persons to practice law; to administer the Bar examinations; to discipline lawyers in breach of professional ethics; to provide legal aid to represent those who are financially unable to hire a lawyer of their choice; and to assist the Ministry of Justice in the preparation of legal rules and regulations.

---

14 *Matīn Daftarī, A., fn. 8*, pp. 33, 103-8.

15 Ibid.

16 The Board of Directors, consisting of 12 full-time and six substitute members, and whose task was to manage the bar and oversee the conduct of its various responsibilities, was elected in free elections by lawyers for a two-year term.

Despite all other interferences of the state into societal matters and the authoritarian character of Mohammad Reza Pahlavi's regime, it did respect the autonomy of the Bar Association, and the latter remained independent until its purging during the 1979 revolution. At the height of its activities in the late 1970s, the Bar was composed of around 7000 members. As Said Arjomand has pointed out, the bar association and legal scholars and professionals associated with it constituted the backbone of the liberal-nationalist opposition during the 1960s and 1970s.[17] As „guardians of the fundamental laws", lawyers had been instrumental in denouncing the violations of the constitution by the Pahlavi regime. The 1977 creation of the Association of Iranian Jurists (*Jāmi'at-i Ḥuqūq-danān*) and the Iranian Committee for the Defense of Freedom and Human Rights (*Jāmi'at-Irānī-yi Difā' az Ḥuqūq-i Bashar*), headed by Mehdi Bazargan, set up to monitor prison conditions and publicize abuses of the intelligence services (SAVAK), constituted a decisive movement towards a liberal extra-parliamentary opposition. When in the summer of 1977, the bar association demanded the abolition of all extra-constitutional tribunals including military courts, the episode seriously damaged the legitimacy of the Pahlavi regime.[18]

Islamization of the Justice System after 1979

In the aftermath of the revolution, the Iranian justice system underwent a far-reaching Islamization process. As the Islamic Republican Party sought to Islamize the legal system and redraw the country's codes in accordance with (some interpretation of) Ja'fari jurisprudence in the 1980s and 1990s, it also needed to replace secular trained lawyers and judges with those trained in the „new law" – a law consisting, in theory, of positivized Shi'ite law, and pre-revolutionary codes that had been transformed to bring them in line with Ja'fari jurisprudence. The new and transformed laws required a new class of lawyers and reformed curricula in the country's schools of law, a process complicated by the fact that the Islamization of the legal system was not completed until the

---

17 Said Amir Arjomand, *The Turban for the Crown, The Islamic Revolution in Iran*, Oxford University Press, 1988, 109.

18 „The Iranian Bar Association headed by Hasan Nazih and Hedayatollah Matin-Daftari (a grandson of Mosaddeq) was particularly audible in its call for free elections and the release of political prisoners." *Green, J. D.* Pseudoparticipation and countermobilization: roots of the Iranian revolution. In: Iranian Studies, 13 (1980),1-4, 31-53, 13.

mid-1990s and that even the most important codes, such as the penal law, have since undergone repeated changes and reforms.[19]

Judges appointed prior to the revolution continued to enforce the pre-revolution laws and regulations until on August 22, 1982 Ayatollah Khomeini ordered all such laws null and void, and threatened criminal prosecution to those who continued to enforce pre-revolutionary legislation. He further decreed that in those areas not yet covered by post-revolutionary legislation, judges should render decisions based on their own knowledge of Islamic law (in line with Art. 167 of the 1979 constitution) and extant fatwas. As new legislation only very gradually filled the space voided by the August 1982 decree, individual judges were granted wide discretionary powers.[20]

After the marginalization of prime minister Bazargan's liberal-nationalist faction as the internal power struggles of the revolution unfolded, the Bar Association was purged in June 1980.[21] The revolutionary prosecutor (*dādsitān-i inqilāb*) and the chief religious judge (*ḥakīm-i shar'*), both appointed by Khomeini, successively drew up lists of lawyers to be expelled from the bar,[22] and their names were published in the official newspapers *Kayhān* and *Ittilā'āt.*[23] Shortly after the purge, lawyers were barred from defending those accused in the Revolutionary Courts, the main courts at the time.[24] The offices of the Bar, located in the Ministry of Justice, were occupied in May 1981, and its archives, documents, and funds seized.[25] Eight months later, those sitting on the Board of Directors were arrested, unless they had gone into hiding or exile beforehand. In 1984, the association was deprived of the right to hold its own elections and was put under the supervision of an appointed official (a *sarparast*, „supervisor") from the judiciary. The exclusion of lawyers from the revolutionary courts meant that many closed their offices and re-trained or went into exile. In addition, a number of lawyers had been Jews and Bahais who already left Iran in the early years of the revolution due to the discriminations against them on religious grounds.

---

19 *Tellenbach, S.* Zum Strafgesetzbuch der Islamischen Republik Iran von 2013, Zeitschrift für die gesamte Strafrechtswissenschaft, 126, 775-801 (2014).

20 *Āqilī, B.* Dāvar wa 'adliya, Tehran 1990.

21 1980 Law by the Revolutionary Council on Purging the Bar Association.

22 A first purge banned 57 lawyers, a second 32 and the third 52.

23 *Kayhān* 6/20/1983 and 8/30/1983.

24 Thereby directly contravening Art 164 of the constitution which states „A judge cannot be removed, whether temporarily or permanently, from the post he occupies except by trial and proof of his guilt, or in consequence of a violation entailing his dismissal."

25 *Lahidji, A*, La justice Islamique, Khavaran editions, Vincennes, 2000.

Enface the dearth of lawyers and judges familiar with the new legal environment, the judiciary often awarded judgeships *ad hoc* to leading revolutionaries without closely probing their jurisprudential credentials. An Islamized justice system, it was assumed, would function best with *mujtahids* in the seats of judges, but little attention was paid initially as to whether a *mujtahid* had actually specialized in *fiqh* during his training, or had instead focused on theology (*kalām*), ethics (*akhlāq*), mysticism (*taṣawwūf*), or some other branch of Islamic knowledge. Numerous courts therefore came to be presided over by individuals who had spent years in the religious seminaries, but had little idea of the legal profession, let alone of the positive law according to which they were expected to adjudicate. Incidentally, until today, no regulation requires a „*ḥujjat al-islām*" (mid-ranking Shiʿite cleric, literally „proof of Islam") to have specialized in *fiqh* in order to qualify for a judgeship.[26]

In order to justify legal reform after laws had been „Islamized" and to allow for greater responsiveness of Islamic law in rapidly changing times, Khomeini introduced towards the end of the Iran-Iraq war in 1988 the principle of *maṣlaḥat*, „expediency." In essence, the introduction of *maṣlaḥat* suggested that contextual considerations could overrule strict adherence to Jaʿfari jurisprudence. The principle found its institutional home in the newly established Expediency Council (1988-) which could now overrule the clerical Guardian Council. It was therefore no longer guaranteed that legislation would be strictly in line with Islamic jurisprudence. From now on, the decision of a potentially non-clerical Expediency Council could outweigh that of the clerical Guardian Council. Sami Zubaida aptly commented on the introduction of *maṣlaḥat* with the remark that twelve centuries of legal and jurisprudential thinking could not achieve what eight years of Islamic governance had done to Shiʿite jurisprudence: the Shiʿite adoption of a principle at the heart of Sunni jurisprudence in order to justify deviation from the tradition.[27]

With the increasing normalization of politics after the Iran-Iraq war (1980-1988) had ended and as a period of reconstruction began, the leadership signalled greater adherence to the constitution and the rule of law from now on. In a letter to the parliament, Khomeini asked for the extra-judicial court systems (the revolutionary courts and the special courts of clergy) to be integrated into

---

26 *Lawyers Committee for Human Rights*, The Justice System of the Islamic Republic of Iran, May 1993, 43-44.

27 *Zubaida, S.* Law and Power in the Islamic World. London: I.B. Tauris, 2003, 210ff. See also *Amanat, A. and Griffel F.* (eds.) Shari'a: Islamic Law in the Contemporary Context. Stanford: Stanford University Press, 2009, especially the chapters by Amanat, Arjomand and Opwis.

the judiciary or else be abolished. Lawyers and litigants started to demand the re-establishment of the bar association. A 1990 draft bill by parliament re-affirmed: „The parties of a lawsuit have the right to appoint an attorney at law, and all the courts.... are obliged to receive the attorney at law...“[28] The final version that passed the Expediency Council, however, replaced „attorney at law“ (*vakīl-i dādgūstarī*) simply by „attorney“ (*vakīl*), thus opening up the possibility for anyone who had not passed the bar to be accepted in court.[29] The resultant article of the „Law of Appointment of Attorney by Parties to a Lawsuit“ read: „The parties of a law suit have the right to appoint any attorney and all the prosecution offices and courts including the civil, penal, revolutionary, military, and the special courts for the clergy are obliged to receive the attorney in all stages of interrogation and court process.“ This interpretation violates Art. 35 of the constitution on the rights of the accused to legal counsel, nor is it in line with Article 9 of the UN Basic Principles on the Role of Lawyers which requires that „Governments, professional associations of lawyers... shall ensure that lawyers have appropriate education and training and be made aware of the ideals and ethical duties of lawyers and of human rights... recognized by national and international law.“

After a visit by the UN Representative for Human Rights in 1991, new assurances were made that the Bar would be revived and elections held for it in October 1991. However, one day before the scheduled election, a new law was passed whose first article read: „In order to reform the Bar Association of the Islamic Republic of Iran, a Revitalization Board of the Bar Associations, comprising of six attorneys at law and three practicing judges, chosen by the Head of the Judiciary, is appointed for a one year period to implement and enforce this act.“ As a result of this 1991 Law of Correction of the Bar Association, a further 133 attorneys were purged from the bar and the elections were indefinitely postponed.[30]

As the 1990 bill solidified the possibility for those who had not passed the bar to serve as recognized legal counsel, more and more graduates of the religious seminaries moved into the legal profession.[31] Still by the mid-1990s,

---

28 Report on the human rights situation in the Islamic Republic of Iran by the Special Representative of the Commission on Human Rights, Feb 12, 1990, (UN Doc. No E/CN.4/1990/24), at para.213

29 *Majmū'a-yi muosavvabāt-e Majma'-i Tashkhīs-e Maṣlaḥat-i Niẓām az tārīkh-i 1369.*

30 Final report on the situation of human rights in the Islamic Republic of Iran by the Special Representative of the Commission on Human Rights, Mr. Reynaldo Galindo Pohl, para 130, E/CN.4/1993/41, January 28, 1993.

31 *Kashāni. M..* Barrasī-yi qānūn-e nahva-yi isṣaḥ-i kānūnhā-yi vūkalā-yi dādgūstarī. Tehran 1992.

only about 2,500 trained judges were available for over 10,000 positions, and the newly recognized study programs of law produced only 600 graduates a year.[32] The status of *ḥujjat al-islām* now became useful for all sorts of jobs and few were more lucrative than those in the court system. Incidentally, the demand for *mujtahids* to serve in positions of the state bureaucracy in the aftermath of the revolution contributed its share to the inflation of clerical titles the regime has witnessed since.

In 1994, a new judicial reform was drawn up (the 4 June 1994/15 Tīr 1373 Law of General and Revolutionary Courts) under the Head of Judiciary Mohammad Yazdi (1989-1999) that combined the civil, criminal and family courts in so-called „general courts".[33] With devastating consequences for *habeas corpus*, the role of investigator, prosecutor and judge were merged in one.

When Ayatollah Sayyed Mahmud Hashemi-Shahrudi took over the judiciary in 1999, he declared the judiciary to be a wreck („*virāna*").[34] With the support of the Expediency Council, he reintroduced in 2002 the division of courts into criminal (*kayfarī*), family and personal status (*madanī*), civil and commercial (*ḥuqūqī*) courts, and reinstated an appellate system.[35] He also passed separate laws of procedure (*dādrasī*) for each, and reintroduced in most but not all courts, the differentiation of the offices of judge and prosecutor.[36]

In order to deal with problems and questions arising from the new Islamic penal code, Shahrudi instituted regular sessions of expert judges in towns and provincial capitals to answer questions and requests for guidance by the courts under jurisdiction. He also strengthened the Legal Office (*idāra-yi ḥuqūqī*) of the Judiciary and instituted a Research Center in Jurisprudence (*markaz-i*

---

32 According to the Iranian representative appearing before the 46th Session of the U.N. Human Rights Committee in New York, April 7, 1993. in April 1993 there were 2,661 registered lawyers in Iran, including 185 women.

33 See http://www.wipo.int/wipolex/en/text.jsp?file_id=324557.

34 *Ittilā'āt*, 11/23/1999.

35 *Ittilā'āt*, 7/10/2000.

36 *Manshūr-i tawṣi'a*, 3: 52. In theory, the office of the public prosecutor was re-established in Oct. 2002 for general and revolutionary courts (in the Amendment to The Law of Formation of General and Revolutionary Courts (1994), dated 28 Mehr 1381), but in practice it was not in place everywhere as late as 2008. Further, it is not entirely clear which courts are covered by the 2002 reform. According to Article 3 of the 2002 reform (for the 2002 law, see: http://mellat.majlis.ir/archive/1382/MOSAVABAT/MOSAVABAT1.HTM#48), there should be an office of prosecution (*dādsarā*) in every urban jurisdiction now. But according to the Official Gazette (*Ruznāma-yī Rasmī*) # 16823 on 7/9 (Ādhar)/1381 (Nov. 2002), the prosecution has only been reestablished for the lower criminal courts.

taḥqiqāt-i fiqh) that would answer enquiries from the courts and provincial branches of the Ministry of Justice, and keep a registrar of the most important *fatwās* of those *marja's* (sources of emulation, the highest religious authorities in Shi'i Islam) that are officially recognized by the regime. A given judge might then compare the *fatwas* of the highest Shi'ite authorities in the country and if no positive law existed to be applied on a given case, invoke one of the *marāji's fatwās*.

Revival in 1997 and threatened closure thereafter

It was not until the early years of the Khatami administration (1997-2005), that the bar experienced a revival. Under the influence of the reform movement, bar associations were (re)established in all major jurisdictions across the country.[37] The Iran Bar Associations Union in Tehran was given the right to (re-)establish subcommittees, such as a Legal Aid Committee and a Human Rights Commission, and to position delegates in the Ministry of Justice and in the foreign ministry.[38] In 1997, during the visit of the United Nations Human Rights' envoy, promises were made that the bar would be re-authorized to hold elections for its board – something it had not been permitted to do for nearly two decades. In tandem with that promise, however, the conservative-dominated parliament passed a law in the same year allowing the judiciary to vet candidates running for the Bar's board of directors.[39] While it was internationally signalled

---

37 The Ardabil Bar Association, serving Ardabil province; the East Azarbayejan Bar Association in Tabriz (one of the oldest in the country), the Fars Bar Association in Shiraz, also one of the oldest, covering attorneys in Fars, Booshehr, Kohgiloyeh and Boyerahmad provinces; the Gilan Bar Association located in Rasht, the Golestan Bar Association for Golestan province; the Hamedan Bar Association, the Isfahan Bar Association for Isfahan and Markazi provinces; the Kermanshah & Ilam Bar Association, for Kermanshah and Ilam provinces, the Khoozestan & Lorestan Bar Association, located in Ahwaz; the Khorasan Bar Association, Mashhad, for Khorasan province; the Kordestan Bar Association, Sanandaj; the Mazandaran Bar Association, Sari; the Qazvin Bar Association; the Qom Bar Association; the West Azarbayejan Bar Association; the Central Bar Association in Tehran covering the attorneys in Tehran. The Iran Bar Associations Union based in Tehran was established to coordinate between the 22 region-based Iranian Bar Associations. See for example: www.iranbar.org (Persian), www.iranbar.org/pltren.php (English), www.iranbar.org/pltrfr.php (French), www.centralbar.ir, www.azarbar.org, www.khoozestanbar.org.

38 *Mūsāvī-Bujnurdī, S. M.* Naqsh-i Zamān va Makān dar taghyīr aḥkām. Majalla-yi Kānūn-i Vūkalā-yi Dādgūstarī. No 10 (1376/1996/97).

39 The Act on How to Be Admitted to the Bar Association (*Qānūn-i nahw-i akhz-i parvāniya-yi vikālat)* 1376[1997] also stipulated the admissions requirements: candidates

that the bar would be revived and its autonomy re-instated, internally the electoral rules for the bar's board were changed in a manner that the judiciary could now cherry-pick its candidates. Specifically, candidates had to be confirmed by the Supreme Disciplinary Court for Judges and satisfy, among other requirements, „commitment to the revolution“ and prove they had not ever been members of or „cooperated with“ organizations deemed politically oppositional. As Mohammad H Nayyeri correctly notes, „it would be true to say that until 1997 the independence of the Bar Associations was denied in practice, while in 1997 it was attacked in law.“[40]

An interview with one of the members of the Bar Association's Human Rights Commission reveals the internal tensions the bar faced at that time, where the work of relatively independent commissions often failed to receive approval from its own board whose candidates had been vetted by the judiciary:

> „[During the violent repression of student protests in the summer of 1999] we informed the International League of Human Rights of the abuses and violent acts of the [Revolutionary Guards]. When demonstrators were shot in different cities, we recorded the complaints of the families and wrote reports to the UN. We demanded the release of political prisoners and the freedom of expression. Our present activities are very limited. Even if internal elections took place for the first time after the revolution in 1997, we are under close scrutiny, given the pre-selection of our candidates. A candidate who would write against the *qisas* [retributive justice] or the *lex talionis* will never be admitted by the judiciary apparatus. […] We receive many complaints and we cannot cope. For instance, we have received many testimonies of members of the Bahai community whose graveyards have been sacked and their graves turned upside down. We denounced these acts of violence. But the Bar's [board of directors] refused to sign our protest letter. Actually, it does not sign half of the letters of its own Human Rights Commission. When the members wrote an official request demanding an inquiry about the conditions of Zahra Kazemi's murderer

---

would need to have Iranian citizenship; be at least 25 years of age; be a regular resident of the location for which the license is applied for; have a clear record and a reputation for honesty and integrity; have completed legal studies in one of the Iranian or foreign recognized universities; have rendered legal services for at least for 18 months under the supervision of a professional lawyer approved for such purpose by the Bar; have successfully passed the Bar examinations.

40 *Nayyeri, M.H.* Iranian Bar Associations. Struggle for Independence, New Haven: Iran Human Rights Documentation Center, 2012: http://www.iranhrdc.org/english/english/publications/legal-commentary/1000000211-iranian-bar-associations-struggle-for-independence.html?p=12 (accessed 31 August 2017).

[an Iranian-Canadian who while visiting Iran was arrested for political activism and died under torture in Evin prison in spring 2003], this letter did not receive the signature of the Bar's representatives".[41]

In the subsequent years, the judiciary repeatedly intervened in the internal affairs of the bar. Abdul Fattah Sultani, lawyer of the dissident journalist Akbar Ganji and of the family of journalist Zahra Kazemi, was excluded from the board despite his election to it in February 2005.

Apart from Human Rights advocacy, the bar also fulfilled an important cultural role when it emerged as a defender of cultural and historical heritage during the first Khatami administration (1997-2001). When construction permits were issued for towers in Isfahan that would have imperilled the historical site of the Safavid *Naqsh-e Jahān,* the city's central square of exceptional beauty, and a UNESCO World Heritage Site, the Bar Association issued several letters of protest. In another instance, when media in February 2004 uncovered the extent of human trafficking rings between Iran, the United Arab Emirates and other countries bordering the Persian Gulf, the Bar issued an official letter to the Minister of Interior and demanded the inception of a commission of inquiry on human trafficking in the region. The regime denied the phenomenon all together.

As was the case with most civil society organizations and media in the early years of the Khatami presidency, the Association's revival was short-lived. When the third five-year plan for economic and social development (2000-2005) was passed by the outgoing conservative parliament in 2000, the judiciary attained the power to make its own selection and to confer, per Article 187 of the law[42], the title of lawyer and jurist to applicants who are not admitted to the Bar.[43] This was to be done through the creation of a new institution, the Center for the Affairs of Advisors, Judges, and Experts of the judiciary (*markaz-i umūr-i mushāvirān, vukalā va kārshināsān-i quwwa-yi qazā'īya).* The step to institutionalize an additional accreditation process for lawyers through the judiciary was legitimized with reference to high levels of unemployment. In other words, in order to fight unemployment, the regime claimed, it would certify more lawyers through a less transparent certification process rather than

41 Interview with Dr. I., May 2005, cited in *Farkhondeh, S.* Rule of law, authoritarianism and theocracy in Iran: the role of secular specialists of law. Paper presented at Sciences Po, Paris, November 2006.

42 2000 Law of the Third Economic, Social and Cultural Development Plan.

43 At this point the membership of the Bar had re-grown to about 6000 attorneys at law as well as over 2500 trainees.

expanding upon and improving on the training possibilities for future lawyers. De facto, the new accreditation process was instituted for graduates of the religious seminaries and students of the social sciences who did not have sufficient legal training to pass the bar, as well as for law graduates who had failed to pass it.[44]

A key function which the bar had fulfilled for nearly thirty years between 1953 and 1979, i.e. to exclusively certify lawyers through a comprehensive and demanding examination, had thus been stripped from it. Its role in guarding over the professionalism of the judicial complex was thereby officially neutralized.

The new parallel accreditation process was also less challenging in terms of the training required. Unlike those seeking accreditation through the bar, applicants to the judiciary do not need to have a BA degree in Law, do not need to take an entrance exam, and in contrast to the bar's 18 month-training, their training lasts for only six months. Moreover, their license to practice as a lawyer needs to be renewed with the judiciary on an annual basis, which de facto ensures that such applicants do not take on politically delicate cases for fear of not getting their license renewed in the following year.[45]

Since the 2000 law then, defendants have the choice of either accepting a lawyer who has been certified through the judiciary and will likely lack the capacity to be an impartial and professional adjudicator, or, perhaps worse, defend themselves.

While the bar through its disciplinary board used to be able to take disciplinary actions against lawyers who had compromised the integrity of the profession, this function is now undertaken in the Judges Disciplinary Court run by the judiciary. The latter is known to discipline judges who are not in line with the politics of the Leader's office. For instance, a judge of Iran's Supreme Court was called before the Judges Disciplinary Court for having advocated the eradication of the extra-constitutional and extra-judicial courts of the clergy.[46]

After Mahmoud Ahmadinejad assumed the presidency in 2005, the Iranian state showed remarkable efficacy in rolling back the political and civil liberties

---

44 In order to be accredited, applicants would undergo a six-month training program designed by the judiciary, then pass an exam and take an oath. The judiciary then assigns those who are accredited as lawyers to a specific city, where they have to establish their law firms or join an extant one. Accredited lawyers may file claims and defend cases in any court throughout the country.

45 *Nayyeri, M.H.* Iranian Bar Associations, accessed 31 August 2017.

46 Personal interview, 2009.

societal actors had succeeded – with varying success – in carving out from the state's legal and judicial apparatus in the previous years. Especially in the aftermath of the June 2009 presidential elections and the subsequent anti-governmental demonstrations that were brutally repressed, the government further limited the space of civil and political engagement. Societal organizations were forced to accept governmental appointees on their boards, which discredited their legitimacy in the eyes of the public and compromised their political autonomy. The (limited) ties that civil society organizations were able to build during the first and second Khatami presidencies (1997-2001 and 2001-2005) with foreign and international organizations were effectively outlawed, with the result that domestic organizations lost important sources of funding and were often compelled to accept para-statal subsidies, or to cease operating officially all together.

While Mahmud Hashemi-Shahrudi, who headed the judiciary from 1999-2009 made some improvements to the efficacy of the judiciary by reconstituting the office of the prosecutor in many courts and by partly re-establishing the appeals procedure, his position vis-à-vis the Bar Association was ruinous. Although the 2000 Law that had established the parallel accreditation process in Art. 187 expired in 2005 with the end of the five year-plan, the new institutional structures for certifying lawyers inside the judiciary were retained – illegally as the Bar Association argues. When the Association issued a critical assessment on the eve of Shahrudi's second term in the spring of 2009, he responded with a draft Amendment to the Executive Regulations of the Law of the Bar Association on 17 June 2009 (that is, five days after the consequential presidential elections) that would have effectively dissolved the association by stripping it of any rights, functions and responsibilities.[47] The proposed amendment would now *de facto* eradicate the external certification process (through the bar association) by moving the mandate to certify lawyers and apprentice-lawyers to a new „selection committee" appointed entirely by the judiciary. The amendment would also give the Ministry of Intelligence the right to surveil defense lawyers of political activists and to pull their credentials if deemed „necessary".[48] The draft amendment also comprised a catalogue of „professional ethics" that compromised the defense counsel in criminal cases by suggesting, per Article 44, that lawyers would abet a sin if they endorsed the plea of a client they knew to be false.

---

47 *E'temād*, #1993, 5 July 2009/14 Tir 1388.

48 Compare the open letter by Mostafa Mohaqqeq Damad, an ayatollah and well-known scholar of Islamic law, to Hashemi Shahroudi, published in *Ettelā'āt* newspaper on August 2, 2009, „محقق داماد خطاب به شاهرودی: کاش در حوزه مانده بودید - آفتاب". *Aftab News*. Retrieved 7 December 2016.

In 2011, in an astounding act of defying the judiciary, 153 members of the parliament introduced a new bill according to which the merger envisioned by the 2009 draft would bring the judiciary's accreditation process under the control of the Bar Association (rather than the other way around). Expectably, the bill did not see the light of day and the judiciary instead introduced its own bill for a merger under reverse conditions. As of 2017, after rejection by the plenary in November 2016, the bill was returned to the Legal and Judicial Commission of the Parliament for modification.[49] According to the most recent update (of July 2017), no modifications have been undertaken.[50]

Conclusions

Despite the fact that the 1979 constitution grants all political rights and civil liberties political scientists consider fundamental for electorally competitive politics, civil liberties are frequently and systematically curtailed in the Islamic Republic. After the reform era of 1997-2001, civil liberties and the rule of law have been systematically undermined by the mass closures of critical newspapers and magazines; the ban on particular political parties and the persecution of its members; the rejection by non-elected clerical councils of a third of legislative proposals of the elected parliament; and the widespread disqualifications of political candidates wishing to run in elections. The bar association experienced a brief revival in the 1990s, when it was permitted to (re)open branches across the country and when its rights for internal autonomy were reinstated by permitting it to hold elections once again and to resume its work in various internal committees. However, as soon as a date for internal elections were announced in 1997, the judiciary asserted its right to screen candidates, thereby compromising the association's autonomy and curtailing its legal aid and human rights work. The bar association was further compromised when in 2000, at the height of the reform era, a parallel accreditation process for lawyers was created inside the judiciary, allowing those not trained in the professional law schools and those who have failed the bar to seek certification through this alternative channel. Importantly, it allows the judiciary to cherry-pick its own candidates for a pool from which it can recruit future high court judges. The regulation of the recruitment of lawyers and judges, and the status of the bar association in the post-revolutionary period exhibit two larger trends in regime-societal contestations: the regime's attempt at controlling electoral outcomes, and the creation of institutions paralleling those that hardliners do not

[49] http://www.isna.ir/news/95082417104/

[50] https://www.irinn.ir/fa/news/510111/

control with the aim of replacing the latter by the former in the long run. We witness the first dynamic when conservatives in 1997 started to exert the same control mechanism on the bar association which are exerted on popular elections in the country: electoral candidates can be disqualified if found to lack „revolutionary credentials." Elections thus become a farce where only the *khodi* (insiders) and those from whom no political disturbances are feared are permitted to throw their hat into the game. The second dynamic manifests itself when the judiciary established its parallel accreditation process for legal advisors and henceforth attempted to blur public distinctions between lawyers accredited independently by the bar versus those that are trained and accredited with lower professional standards inside the judiciary. Instead of being eliminated altogether, the bar association is being marginalized, with the goal of making it superfluous over time.

But this parallelism also bears opportunities for contestation. One version of the new Bill of Attorneyship foresees that the judiciary's accreditation process is integrated into the Bar Association and the latter regains its monopoly over recruiting and certifying future lawyers and judges. Another version provides for the absorption (and ultimate dissolution) of the bar association in the judiciary. With the bill pending in committee, the jury is out over which will prevail.

Autor*innen des Bandes

Hanstein, Thoralf, Dr.
Orientabteilung der Staatsbibliothek zu Berlin,
Thoralf.Hanstein@sbb.spk-berlin.de

Künkler, Mirjam, Prof. Dr.
Swedish Collegium for Advanced Study, Uppsala
mirjam.kuenkler@swedishcollegium.se

Maghzi Najafabadi, Afrooz, LL.M.
Max-Planck-Institut für ausländisches und internationales Strafrecht, Freiburg
afroozmaghzi@gmail.com

Mahmoudi Janaki, Firouz, Prof. Dr.
Universität Teheran
firouzmahmoudi@ut.ac.ir

Naarmann, Benedikt, Dr., LL.M. (HKU)
Referent Internationale Beziehungen (Naher und Mittlerer Osten, Süd- und Südostasien) im Bundesministerium für Ernährung und Landwirtschaft, Berlin
benedikt.naarmann@gmx.de

Peters, Rudolph, Prof. em. Dr.
Universität Amsterdam
r.peters@uva.nl

Tabatabaei, Seyed Emadeddin LL.M.
Max-Planck-Institut für ausländisches und internationales Strafrecht, Freiburg
tabatabaee_emad@yahoo.com

Tellenbach, Silvia, Dr. Dr. h.c.
Max-Planck-Institut für ausländisches und internationales Strafrecht, Freiburg
s.tellenbach@mpicc.de

LEIPZIGER BEITRÄGE ZUR ORIENTFORSCHUNG

Herausgegeben von Hans-Georg Ebert
Begründet von Günter Barthel

Die Reihe *Leipziger Beiträge zur Orientforschung* widmet sich Themen und Problemfeldern der islamischen Welt in Vergangenheit und Gegenwart. Dabei werden unterschiedliche Disziplinen, Regionen und Methoden erfasst. Das Spektrum reicht von rechtlichen, historischen, religiösen, kulturellen, sprachlichen, politischen und sozial-ökonomischen Fragestellungen bis hin zu vergleichenden "area studies". Innerhalb der Reihe erscheinen die in Zusammenarbeit mit der "Gesellschaft für Arabisches und Islamisches Recht e.V." herausgegebenen Tagungsbände. Die einzelnen Veröffentlichungen sollen das interkulturelle Verständnis fördern, neue Forschungsansätze aufzeigen und Ergebnisse wissenschaftlicher Untersuchungen präsentieren.

Band 1 Lutz Knörnschild: Zur Geschichte der Nilwassernutzung in der ägyptischen Landwirtschaft von den Anfängen bis zur Gegenwart. 1993.

Band 2 Henner Fürtig / Rolf Müller-Syring (Hrsg.): Ursachen gewaltförmiger Konflikte in der Golfregion. Internationale und zwischenstaatliche Faktoren. 1993.

Band 3 Ingelore Goldmann (Hrsg.): Beiträge zur Fachdidaktik Arabisch. Didaktische und methodische Probleme des modernen Arabischunterrrichts. 1993.

Band 4 Roland Kühnel: Die sprachliche Situation an Hochschulen des Maghreb und die offizielle Sprachpolitik – Eine soziolinguistische Untersuchung. 1995.

Band 5 Henk Knaupe / Ulrich G. Wurzel: Aufbruch in der Wüste. Die Neuen Städte in Ägypten. 1995.

Band 6 Wolfgang Reuschel: Aspekt und Tempus in der Sprache des Korans. 1996.

Band 7 Hans-Georg Ebert: Das Personalstatut arabischer Länder. Problemfelder, Methoden, Perspektiven. Ein Beitrag zum Diskurs über Theorie und Praxis des Islamischen Rechts. 1996.

Band 8 Uwe Pfullmann: Politische Strategien Ibn Sa^{c}ūds beim Aufbau des dritten saudischen Staates. Eine historische Studie unter besonderer Berücksichtigung deutschen Archivmaterials. 1996.

Band 9 Hans-Georg Ebert (Hrsg.): Beiträge zum Islamischen Recht. 2000.

Band 10 Anja Wünsch: Innenansichten ökonomischer Restrukturierung. Wirkungen und Wirksamkeit der Strukturanpassung in Jordanien, 1989-1999. 2001.

Band 11 Thoralf Hanstein: Islamisches Recht und Nationales Recht. Teil 1 und 2. Eine Untersuchung zum Einfluß des Islamischen Rechts auf die Entwicklung des modernen Familienrechts am Beispiel Indonesiens. 2002.

Band 12 Hans-Georg Ebert / Thoralf Hanstein (Hrsg.): Beiträge zum Islamischen Recht II. 2003.

Band 13 Hans-Georg Ebert / Thoralf Hanstein (Hrsg.): Beiträge zum Islamischen Recht III. 2003.

Band 14 Hans-Georg Ebert: Das Erbrecht arabischer Länder. 2004.

Band 15 Silvia Tellenbach / Thoralf Hanstein (Hrsg.): Beiträge zum Islamischen Recht IV. 2004.

Band 16 Almut Hinz: Die Sanktionen gegen Libyen. Sanktionen im modernen Völkerrecht und in der Staatenpraxis sowie ihre Anwendung am Beispiel Libyen. 2005.

Band 17 Hüseyin Demir: Die osmanischen Medresen. Das Bildungswesen und seine historischen Wurzeln im Osmanischen Reich von 1331–1600. 2005.

Band 18 Sebastian Maisel: Das Gewohnheitsrecht der Beduinen. Der Stellenwert von Urf in den Rechtsvorstellungen tribaler Gruppen im Norden der Arabischen Halbinsel. 2006.

Band 19 Irene Schneider / Thoralf Hanstein (Hrsg.): Beiträge zum Islamischen Recht V. 2006.

Band 20 Anja Wehler-Schöck: Ehrenmorde in Jordanien. Ursachen und mögliche Gegenstrategien. 2007.

Band 21 Hans-Georg Ebert / Thoralf Hanstein (Hrsg.): Beiträge zum Islamischen Recht VI.

Band 22 Naseef Naeem: Die neue bundesstaatliche Ordnung des Irak. Eine rechtsvergleichende Untersuchung. 2008.

Band 23 Hans-Georg Ebert: Die Qadrî-Pâshâ-Kodifikation. Islamisches Personalstatut der hanafitischen Rechtsschule. 2010.

Band 24 Hans-Georg Ebert/Assem Hefny: *Der Islam und die Grundlagen der Herrschaft*. Übersetzung und Kommentar des Werkes von Alî Abd ar-Râziq. 2010.

Band 25 Nedim Zahirović: Murteza Pascha von Ofen zwischen Panegyrik und Historie. Eine literarisch-historische Analyse eines osmanischen Wesirspiegels von Nergisi (El-vaṣfü l-kāmil fī-aḥvāli l-vezīri l-'ādil). 2010.

Band 26 Hatem Elliesie (Hrsg./ed.): Beiträge zum Islamischen Recht VII. Islam und Menschenrechte / Islam and Human Rights / الإسلام وحقوق الإنسان. 2010.

Band 27 Ibrahim Salama: Muslimische Gemeinschaften in Deutschland. Recht und Rechtswissenschaft im Integrationsprozess. 2010.

Band 28 Sabaheta Gačanin: The Persian Divan by Ahmad Khatem Aqovalizade. 2011.

Band 29 Martin Heckel (Hrsg.): Rechtstransfer. Beiträge zum islamischen Recht VIII. 2011.

Band 30 Hans-Georg Ebert/Thoralf Hanstein (Hrsg.): Heinrich Leberecht Fleischer – Leben und Wirkung. Ein Leipziger Orientalist des 19. Jahrhunderts mit internationaler Ausstrahlung. 2013.

Band 31 Hans-Georg Ebert/Assem Hefny: Islamisches Zivilrecht der hanafitischen Lehre. Die zivilrechtliche Kodifikation des Qadrî Pâshâ. 2013.

Band 32 Bruno Menhofer/Dirk Otto (Hrsg.): Recht nach dem Arabischen Frühling. Beiträge zum islamischen Recht IX. 2014.

Band 33 Hans-Georg Ebert (Hrsg.): Beiträge zum Islamischen Recht X. Zu Ehren von Hilmar Krüger. 2015.

Band 34 Irene Schneider/Thoralf Hanstein (Hrsg.): Beiträge zum Islamischen Recht XI. 2016.

Band 35 Hans-Georg Ebert: Die Religiöse Stiftung im Islam (waqf) nach hanafitischer Lehre. Die stiftungsrechtliche Kodifikation von Qadrî Pâshâ. 2018.

Band 36 Silvia Tellenbach/Thoralf Hanstein (Hrsg.): Beiträge zum Islamischen Recht XII. 2018.

www.peterlang.com

www.ingramcontent.com/pod-product-compliance
Ingram Content Group UK Ltd.
Pitfield, Milton Keynes, MK11 3LW, UK
UKHW021855290926
8980IPUK00005B/853

9 783631 743850